THE
SHADOW
KING

THE SHADOW KING

THE BIZARRE AFTERLIFE OF KING TUT'S MUMMY

JO MARCHANT

DA CAPO PRESS
A Member of the Perseus Books Group

Designed by Pauline Brown

Library of Congress Cataloging-in-Publication Data

Marchant, Jo.

The shadow king : the bizarre afterlife of king Tut's mummy / Jo Marchant.

  p. cm.

Includes bibliographical references and index.

ISBN 978-0-306-82133-2 (hardcover : alk. paper) — ISBN 978-0-306-82134-9 (e-book) 1. Tutankhamen, King of Egypt. 2. Tutankhamen, King of Egypt—Death and burial. 3. Mummies—Conservation and restoration—Egypt. 4. Egypt—History—Eighteenth dynasty, ca. 1570–1320 B.C. 5. Forensic sciences. I. Title.

DT87.5.M34 2013

932.014092—dc23

2012041912

Published by Da Capo Press
A Member of the Perseus Books Group
www.dacapopress.com

Da Capo Press books are available at special discounts for bulk purchases in the U.S. by corporations, institutions, and other organizations. For more information, please contact the Special Markets Department at the Perseus Books Group, 2300 Chestnut Street, Suite 200, Philadelphia, PA 19103, or call (800) 810-4145, ext. 5000, or e-mail special.markets@perseusbooks.com.

10 9 8 7 6 5 4 3 2 1

To Dora and David Wood

CONTENTS

vii

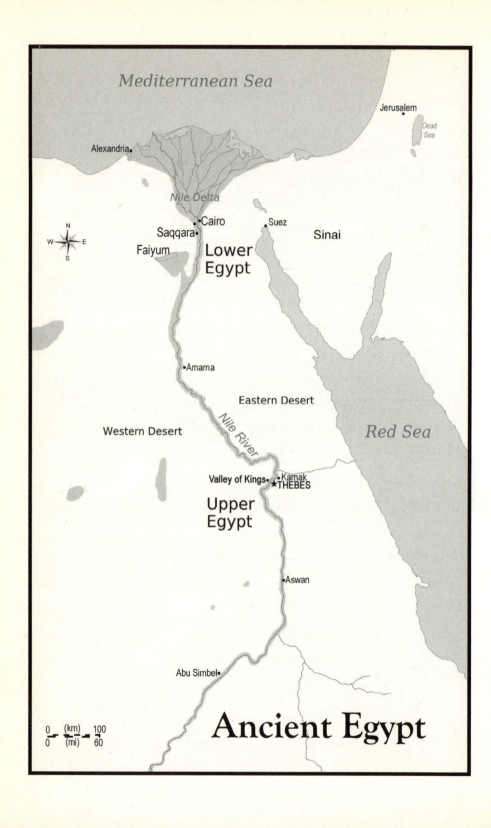

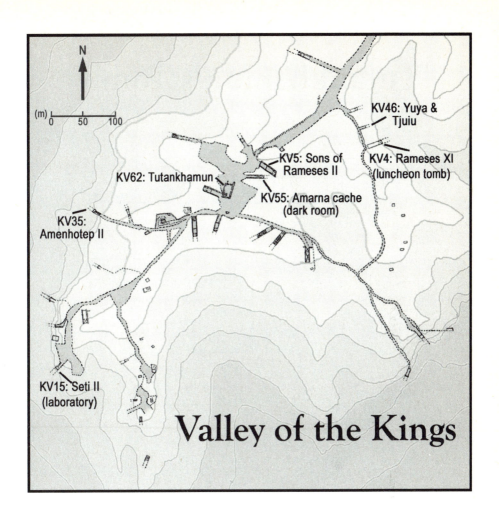

Valley of the Kings

Tutankhamun's Tomb

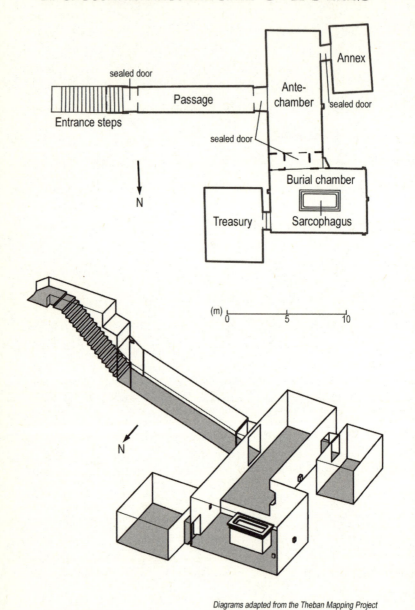

sealed door

Passage

Entrance steps

Ante-chamber

Annex

sealed door

sealed door

N

Burial chamber

Treasury

Sarcophagus

(m) 0   5   10

N

Diagrams adapted from the Theban Mapping Project

TUTANKHAMUN FAMILY TREE

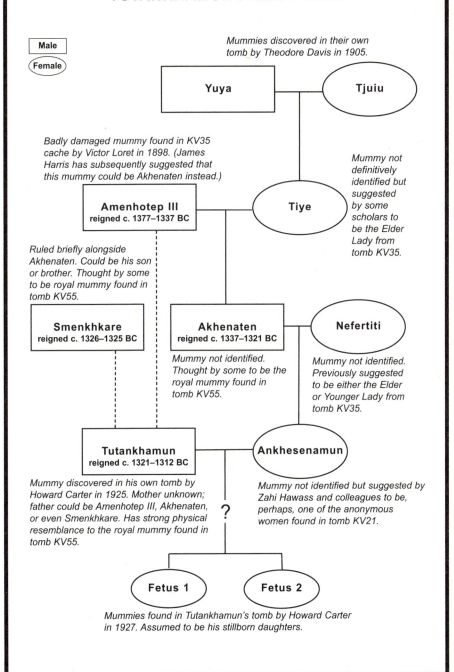

Male

Female

Mummies discovered in their own tomb by Theodore Davis in 1905.

Yuya

Tjuiu

Badly damaged mummy found in KV35 cache by Victor Loret in 1898. (James Harris has subsequently suggested that this mummy could be Akhenaten instead.)

Mummy not definitively identified but suggested by some scholars to be the Elder Lady from tomb KV35.

Amenhotep III
reigned c. 1377–1337 BC

Tiye

Ruled briefly alongside Akhenaten. Could be his son or brother. Thought by some to be royal mummy found in tomb KV55.

Smenkhkare
reigned c. 1326–1325 BC

Akhenaten
reigned c. 1337–1321 BC

Nefertiti

Mummy not identified. Thought by some to be the royal mummy found in tomb KV55.

Mummy not identified. Previously suggested to be either the Elder or Younger Lady from tomb KV35.

Tutankhamun
reigned c. 1321–1312 BC

Ankhesenamun

Mummy discovered in his own tomb by Howard Carter in 1925. Mother unknown; father could be Amenhotep III, Akhenaten, or even Smenkhkare. Has strong physical resemblance to the royal mummy found in tomb KV55.

Mummy not identified but suggested by Zahi Hawass and colleagues to be, perhaps, one of the anonymous women found in tomb KV21.

?

Fetus 1

Fetus 2

Mummies found in Tutankhamun's tomb by Howard Carter in 1927. Assumed to be his stillborn daughters.

AN
ARCHAEOLOGICAL
ADVENTURE

═══

SOMETIMES THE MOST MUNDANE-SEEMING TASK can set you on a journey that you didn't expect. In the summer of 2010, flicking through the latest issue of the *Journal of the American Medical Association* (*JAMA*), I found something that did just that. Squeezed between papers on routine medical topics from diabetes to Down syndrome were five short letters about the mummy of the Egyptian pharaoh Tutankhamun. They were barely noticed by the rest of the world. But they started me on an adventure that led from forgotten archives in rainy London to the heat of the Egyptian desert, and ultimately to this book.

Like so many others, I've always been fascinated by ancient Egypt: the wonders of an advanced civilization, the romance of the pyramids, the pharaohs' fierce determination to live forever, and of course those perfectly preserved mummies that bring us face to face with the distant past. Tutankhamun—a young king found intact in his tomb surrounded by the greatest ever haul of ancient treasure—is the most powerful draw of all.

Scientific studies of the king's mummy have kept him in the news, providing a string of intimate insights into his life and the cause of his untimely death. Ninety years after the discovery of his tomb, King Tut is more famous than ever. The star of countless books, feature films, and documentaries, his golden mask is instantly recognizable and his tomb is visited by millions.

In February 2010, *JAMA* published the most dramatic study yet. As part of the King Tutankhamun Family Project, led by Egypt's top antiquities official, Zahi Hawass, researchers carried out sophisticated scans and DNA tests of Tutankhamun and other royal mummies from his time—the rich and powerful Eighteenth Dynasty, which ruled more than three thousand years ago.

It was a groundbreaking study, full of new information about the pharaohs. Among other things, the scientists quashed decades of speculation about the identity of Tutankhamun's father. They also reversed the view of Tutankhamun as an active king, as suggested by chariots, weapons, and sporting equipment found in his tomb, and recast him as an inbred genetic weakling. His parents were apparently brother and sister, and he had a range of inherited deformities, including cleft palate and clubfoot.

The same day the paper was published, the Discovery Channel broadcast the story of the research in a glossy documentary called *King Tut Unwrapped*. The findings, which Hawass described as "the last word" on Tutankhamun—made news headlines around the world. At last we knew the truth about a life lived 3,300 years before.

Then I saw the letters. Written in the calm, cutting language that is scientists' code for utter disdain, they took the *JAMA* study apart. Experts from different fields and from prestigious institutions around the world criticized nearly every aspect of the research, from Tutankhamun's family relationships to the analysis of the bones in his feet. In particular, geneticists at one of the world's foremost ancient DNA labs in Copenhagen complained that from everything we know about Egyptian mummies, it is highly unlikely that any ancient DNA survives inside them. The latest results, they feared, were caused by contamination of the mummy samples with modern DNA.

The letters got little or no press coverage. But I was intrigued. Was the study by Hawass's international team really so full of holes? Could the entire family tree be based on a mistake? And if these scientists were right, what do we really know about Tutankhamun?

To find out, I called the authors of the *JAMA* study and of the letters, as well as a range of other experts. I found that when it comes to Tutankhamun's mummy, very little is as it seems. One letter plunged me straight into a bizarre and bitter argument that has long split the field of ancient

DNA. Another revealed an ongoing debate over whether Tutankhamun had female breasts. A third introduced me to the mystery of an anonymous mummy found dripping with gold, which over the years has been identified as everyone from Tiye, one of Egypt's most powerful queens, to the biblical prophet Moses.

In every case, the science was clouded in argument and uncertainty. But none of this was making it through into the bestselling books and documentaries about King Tut. I looked back at previous studies and found that this disparity between reporting and reality is nothing new. It seems that Egyptology, as sold to the public, is sometimes not so far from show business.

Over the years, we have been presented with a range of different stories about this frail mummy. There's Tut the murder victim. The inbred cripple. The sickly youth who succumbed to malaria. The active king who died at war, or in a chariot accident. The hunter who was mauled by a hippo. Not to mention the black-magic artist who laid a deadly trap for those who would invade his tomb more than three thousand years later.

Worryingly often, science studies are reconstructed and packaged for the cameras—with researchers routinely acting out their roles after the event—while contested or ambiguous results are shaped into dramatic new discoveries. But what's really going on behind the scenes? To find out, I decided to set out on an archaeological investigation of my own.

I have a PhD in genetics, combined with over a decade's experience as a journalist. I used both sets of skills to trace the secret history of Tutankhamun—not the ancient pharaoh, but the modern mummy.

Investigating the mummy's story, and talking to the scientists involved about their experiences, made me realize how much more there is to their work than the glib headlines we see on television. Deciphering the clues left in a three-thousand-year-old mummy has pushed these researchers to their limits. From the 1920s until today, they have stretched the technology available to them and struggled with hellish conditions, media pressures, and political unrest. They have been brought to Tutankhamun's mummy by interests in everything from deadly fungi to dinosaur DNA, and their results have been used to probe questions from the origins of civilization to the truth of the Bible. Never far away is the allure of treasure—the ancient, buried kind, and the sort that goes straight into the bank.

From the mummy's brutal first autopsy in 1925 to the multimillion-dollar profits and political turbulence surrounding today's high-tech studies, the fate of Tutankhamun has been entwined with the development of

Egyptology as a field, and of Egypt as a nation. What started as a classic archaeological treasure hunt—perhaps the most famous ever—has become a tale of cutting-edge science debates and modern-day politics, from the war on terrorism to the Egyptian revolution.

Within this story, I found plenty of mysteries to delve into. What is a piece of Tutankhamun doing in a drawer at the University of Liverpool? Why did fears for national security cause the Egyptian authorities to cancel a plan to DNA test his mummy? Who are the two mummified fetuses, embalmed with great care, found stuffed into an ill-fitting wooden box in Tutankhamun's tomb? Why is everyone so interested in the pharaoh's penis? And above all, can peeling away the layers of myth and misconception that surround the mummy bring us any closer to understanding the ancient king himself?

The Shadow King is the result of my two-year adventure on the trail of Tutankhamun's mummy. I've done my best to bring the people and situations I encountered—from the distant past to the present day—to life. I've given sources and references for as much as I can without making the text unreadable. But even where there's no citation, every word and phrase is based on extensive research—including interviews, academic papers, unpublished manuscripts, videos, diaries, private correspondence, contemporary newspaper accounts and visits to the relevant locations.

Tutankhamun isn't on his own, however. He has a whole family of royal relatives, whose mummies are on display in the Egyptian Museum in Cairo. Their stories are enmeshed with his. They have been subjected to the same scientific tests, and have triggered almost as much speculation. They too were discovered in the most dramatic of circumstances, and they too are now household names to millions—starring characters in the soap operas of modern Egyptology documentaries.

I cannot tell Tutankhamun's story without telling theirs too. So we start this adventure not in 1922 with the discovery of Tutankhamun's tomb, but in the hot Egyptian summer of 1881, just before one of the most bizarre and unexpected archaeological finds of all time.

CHAPTER ONE

TUNNEL
OF LEGENDS

===

É MILE BRUGSCH WAS OUT OF BREATH, and nervous. The slight German curator was used to tending antiquities in Egypt's first national
museum, a chaotic and desperately crowded establishment in the bustling
Cairo port of Bulaq. Now he was scrambling up a remote desert path in the
foothills of Thebes with little idea of his destination and a shoulder sore
from the weight of a loaded rifle.

Along with two trusted colleagues from Cairo, Brugsch was following
a dark, wiry figure in a white galabiya robe, who led them wordlessly along
the valley floor. His name was Mohammed Abd el-Rassul. He had brought
with him a group of local workmen, and Brugsch eyed them anxiously as
he walked, aware that they had every reason to kill him and his friends if
given the chance.

Centuries after Egypt's rulers built their huge pyramids at Giza, near
Cairo, the seat of power moved south to Thebes. Some of the richest and
most mighty kings in Egypt's history built a series of impressive temples,
palaces, and tombs by the river here. The east bank of the Nile was for the
living, hosting among other things the densely populated city of Thebes
itself and a sprawling temple complex a couple of miles away at Karnak.
The west bank—where Abd el-Rassul led the curator on that stifling July

day—was for the dead, with a string of memorial temples and desert cliffs dotted with tombs.

Brugsch's guide headed uphill toward Deir el-Bahri, a natural amphitheater in the rock that's bounded by steep cliffs. The air was oven hot and the soft sand underfoot made for a tiring, monotonous walk. As the group reached the foot of the cliffs, the path turned sharp right and they saw a small nook, shaped like a chimney, almost hidden in the rock face. At its base was a deep shaft, around ten feet across, with jagged, roughly cut sides that were covered in treacherous-looking rocks and boulders.

"There," said Abd el-Rassul, as Brugsch stepped forward to peer down the hole. The secrets it held were about to change the field of Egyptology forever.

AFTER THE DECLINE of the great civilizations of the ancient world—including the Egyptians, Greeks, and Romans—this area's prestigious past was forgotten. Thebes was a fabulous legend, described in classical accounts from the Bible to Homer, but no one knew where it actually was. The site became home to a little village called Luxor, whose inhabitants had no interest in the ancient stone ruins that surrounded them, save for use as building materials.

A French Jesuit priest called Father Claude Sicard was the first to realize Luxor's glorious claim to fame when he visited at the beginning of the 1700s, and scholars sent by Napoleon at the end of that century later described and publicized the ancient wonders there. After that, Luxor started to attract a growing stream of explorers, adventurers, merchants, and scholars from Europe, who wrote about their experiences to the excitement of audiences back home.

By the 1880s, Luxor was growing fast from rural backwater to fashionable tourist destination—the tour operator Thomas Cook even led steamboat trips down the Nile—and archaeology was booming, with a new discovery practically every day. Awesome statues and columns at Karnak and Luxor temples were being excavated from the piles of rubbish that had hidden them for centuries. On the west bank, a series of tombs had been found, yielding items from amulets and jewelry to tools, furniture, and papyri. And mummies. Quite apart from the impressive structures and antiquities being discovered, what distinguished Egypt from other regions with a past was that its ancient inhabitants were still around.

The Egyptians had gone to great lengths to ensure that their bodies didn't decompose after death—removing the organs and drying out the flesh before embalming with preservative oils and resins and wrapping in bandages. It captured the imagination, coming face to face with these individuals— male, female, fat, thin, young, old—who all shared one thing: their absolute determination to live forever.

As in other areas of Egypt, there were a lot of them. Further north in Saqqara, near Cairo, vast underground chambers containing thousands of bodies had already been unearthed. In Thebes itself, excavators were finding everything from elegantly painted tombs containing one or two individuals to "mummy pits"—tunnels running into the hillside that were stuffed full of bodies. An Italian explorer and ex-strongman called Giovanni Belzoni, excavating in 1817 for the British consul Henry Salt, described being almost suffocated by them when he ventured down one particular passage: "It was choked with mummies, and I could not pass without putting my face in contact with that of some decayed Egyptian. . . . I could not avoid being covered with bones, legs, arms, and heads rolling from above."[1]

Soon, no self-respecting tourist could go home without their own Egyptian mummy, or part of one, and these trophies were carried triumphantly to the libraries and salons of Europe. Not that they all made it. In 1874, one pair of well-to-do ladies, the Misses Brocklehurst, reportedly bought from a local dealer a papyrus and mummy, in a bidding war against a well-known English writer called Amelia Edwards.* According to Edwards, the women brought the prized items aboard their houseboat on the Nile, but "unable to endure the perfume of the ancient Egyptian they drowned the dear departed at the end of the week."[2]

One of the most exciting archaeological developments was an ongoing string of discoveries in Biban el-Moluk—now known as the Valley of the Kings†—a remote, barren spot tucked away behind the cliffs of Deir el-Bahri. Here, travelers and archaeologists were uncovering the resting places of the pharaohs themselves. Stunning paintings and reliefs on the walls were

---

* Edwards wrote extensively about her travels in Egypt, and also founded the Egypt Exploration Fund (now the Egypt Exploration Society) in 1882.
† The literal translation of Biban el-Moluk is actually "Gates of the Kings."

initially indecipherable, but the decoding of hieroglyphs in the 1820s soon allowed scholars to identify the monarchs who had built these tombs and to read about their lives and beliefs.

The pharaohs buried here had abandoned the ostentatious pyramid tombs of their predecessors. They had seen how one by one, despite security devices such as false doors and blind tunnels, each was inevitably robbed for the treasures inside—a king needed an awful lot of stuff to get by in the afterlife. Instead, these pharaohs opted for quiet, hidden burials in this remote valley that they hoped would be better protected from looters. Thutmose I, the third king of the Eighteenth Dynasty,* seems to have been the first to break with tradition and build a secret tomb in the valley. His architect, Ineni, wrote proudly on the wall of his funeral chapel that he alone oversaw the excavation of the tomb, "no one seeing, no one hearing."[3] In doing so, he began a tradition that continued for five hundred years.

Ultimately, however, this cunning plan was in vain. The big disappointment for archaeologists was that every single royal tomb found in the valley had been robbed bare. Some had lain open for centuries, ancient tourist attractions that were scrawled with Greek and Latin graffiti before being gradually forgotten about. Others had been buried by rocks and rubble since ancient Egyptian times, but even they were already looted in antiquity.

Of the original riches buried with the pharaohs, only a few scraps were left—a damaged stone sarcophagus perhaps, or pieces of pottery and wooden figures. The finest tomb discovered was a series of chambers dug by a Nineteenth-Dynasty ruler called Seti I, entered for the first time in three thousand years by Belzoni in 1817. The walls were covered with brightly colored paintings, while the floor was littered with statues and pieces of broken burial equipment. Belzoni found hundreds of glazed blue figures of the king, the carcass of a bull, and a gorgeous alabaster coffin, which he shipped to London. But even here, the hoped-for treasures were long since gone.

There were no royal mummies in these tombs either—none of the kings and queens were still to be found in their original resting places. It was as-

---

* Historians divide events in ancient Egypt into three main spans of time, the Old Kingdom, Middle Kingdom, and New Kingdom, separated by intermediate periods when order collapsed. (There was also an Early Dynastic Period before, and a Third Intermediate Period and a Late Period after.) Within all that, there were thirty-one dynasties of pharaohs. The New Kingdom—the period when these rulers were based in Thebes—encompasses Dynasties Eighteen to Twenty (roughly 1550–1070 BC).

sumed they had long ago been destroyed. Egyptologists like the expansive and easygoing Frenchman Gaston Maspero, head of the Bulaq museum, began to doubt that an undisturbed royal burial would ever be found.

Then in the 1870s, that changed. A series of intriguing antiquities began to appear on the international market. Hundreds of scarabs, statues, and scrolls of papyri from the burials of Twenty-First-Dynasty kings and queens were popping up as far afield as Suez and Syria. To Maspero, the only explanation was that looters had discovered an unspoiled royal tomb or tombs and were gradually pilfering and selling the contents.

For decades, Egypt had been a kind of lucky dip, a free-for-all treasure-hunters' paradise where you couldn't turn around for stumbling over priceless antiquities and there was nothing to stop you from taking home as much as you could carry. Adventurers descended, shipping everything from delicate jewelry to entire monuments home with them to the west. Some of this was done by private individuals, but much was carried out on behalf of governments such as those of Britain and France. The heritage of an entire country was slowly but surely being drained.

In 1858, the French Egyptologist Auguste Mariette had set up Egypt's antiquities service in an attempt to stamp out the illegal antiquities trade and stem the flow of artifacts abroad. In the spring of 1881, Maspero was appointed his successor, which meant that if ancient royal treasures were being looted and sold, it was his job to stop it. Along with Brugsch, his deputy, Maspero sailed the antiquities service steamboat down the Nile to Luxor, desperate to track down the looters and uncover the lost tomb before its priceless contents were completely gone.

It wasn't hard to discover that the main seller of antiquities in the area was a certain Ahmed Abd el-Rassul. He was one of several brothers who lived in Gurna, a village on a hill that forms the south side of Deir el-Bahri. The villagers had intimate knowledge of the tombs in the area—in fact the houses of Gurna were built onto ancient nobles' tombs, ingeniously using their outer chambers as extra rooms. Many of the inhabitants made a living from selling antiquities they unearthed, but the Abd el-Rassul family, who lived in a particularly extravagant white-painted house, were widely known to be at the center of this illicit trade.

Maspero interrogated Ahmed on board his steamboat but the Egyptian revealed nothing, so Maspero had him and his brother Hussein arrested and taken to the capital of the province, Kena, to be questioned with rather less compunction by the governor, Daoud Pasha. Despite techniques that ranged from offering bribes to beating the soles of their feet (a torture technique known as bastinado), the brothers staunchly denied all knowledge of looting or tombs. After two months of this, they were provisionally released, and a disappointed Maspero left Luxor, vowing to renew his search the next winter.

A few weeks later, however, on June 25, a third Abd el-Rassul brother, Mohammed, handed himself in to the Pasha. In return for a £500 reward, he promised to reveal the location of the long lost tomb.

By this time, Maspero was on his way to France for the summer, so Brugsch was sent back to Luxor in his place to meet Mohammed and track down the precious find. On July 6, Brugsch followed Abd el-Rassul and his workmen up the sandy path. He had high hopes that he was about to see a royal tomb complete with at least some of its treasures—though probably just one belonging to an obscure king or queen of the weak Twenty-First Dynasty, as this was the period of the antiquities that the Abd el-Rassuls had been selling.

Then again . . . Above Brugsch's head, up past the top of the cliffs, were the tiny silhouettes of soaring vultures. The Abd el-Rassul family would be desperate to prevent such a valuable source of income falling into the hands of the authorities. Maybe Mohammed's story was nothing but an elaborate—and deadly—trap.

***

TODAY, IT'S EASY ENOUGH to climb onto the cliff top above Deir el-Bahri. From the eastern edge of the Valley of the Kings, you scramble up a stony slope to the top of the ridge, now lined with satellite dishes rather than loitering vultures. Then, walk over the top and hold your breath as the entire sweep of the Nile valley opens out before you. It's one of the best vantage points around (save for a hot air balloon) to see how this dramatic landscape is laid out.

In the distance, the blue ribbon of the Nile runs south to north, parallel to the horizon as you look east. It's bordered on each side by a bright green strip a mile or two wide—fields of wheat, sugar cane, and berseem fed by fertile black silt from the river and tended by the local villagers. Then the green turns abruptly to the amber of the desert sand, which rises to the cliffs on which you're standing.

For the ancient Egyptians, this border between green and amber, fields and desert, marked the boundary between the worlds of the living and the dead. Look along this line and you can see the remains of the pharaohs' memorial temples dotted along it—from the once-glittering* achievement of Amenhotep III, now marked chiefly by two giant statues (known as the Colossi of Memnon) rising tall from the fields, to the ruined columns of the Ramesseum, built by Rameses II. Here the two worlds met—where the people would visit and pay respect to the eternal spirits of their dead kings.

Back the way you've just come, the Valley of the Kings nestles behind the ridge, overlooked by El-Qurn, a naturally pyramid-shaped peak with its sloping shoulders spread protectively over the valley. This is where the pharaohs thought they would be safe for eternity. Beyond it, the desert stretches, harsh and featureless, all the way to the sea.

The cliffs beneath you are dotted with less grandiose noblemen's tombs—visible from the plain below as rows of small, dark holes, like windows peeping out of the rock. And down to your right, a collection of square mud-brick houses painted orange, yellow, and blue is perched on the hillside: all that's now left of the village of Gurna. Thousands of people used to live here, but most of the houses were recently bulldozed by the Egyptian government as part of an effort to turn the entire area into the equivalent of an open-air museum. The residents, who now mostly make their living as taxi drivers and tour guides, were relocated to a new village at the base of the hills.

As you stand looking over the valley, you can turn left and walk along the top of the ridge for a few minutes, then gradually pick your way down toward the Temple of Hatshepsut, a grand columned structure built right into the base of the cliffs. Or you can turn right and almost immediately scramble down through a cleft in the rock, on a near-vertical cliff path—a treacherous short-cut traditionally used by Gurna's villagers.† The bottom of the path deposits you very close to the shaft where Mohammed Abd el-Rassul once led the nervous curator and his friends.

The details of Brugsch's experiences were recorded in just three places—two academic reports (in French) published by Maspero in 1881[4] and 1889,[5]

---

* Amenhotep III's inscriptions record that the floors of the temple were plated with silver, and the doorways with electrum (an alloy of silver and gold).
† This route is also known as Agatha Christie's Path, as it featured in one of her murder mystery stories.

and an 1887 magazine article in which Brugsch described what happened to the U.S. photographer Edward Wilson.[6]

———

TO FIND OUT what he had to say, I visit the British Library in London, a modern-day treasure-hunters' delight, where tapping a few computer keys is all it takes to unearth the most obscure, forgotten gems.

Maspero's reports are tied up with string, with battered corners and yellowed, brittle pages. They're also huge, landing with a satisfying thud on my desk. I untie the string and start to read the century-old words, scanning for the key passages—"Le premier objet qui frappa les yeux de M. Émile Brugsch . . ."*—and the story comes to life once more.

Brugsch had to admit that the ancient Egyptians chose their hiding place well. They had dug their shaft at the base of a hollow chimney that ran up through the cliff, and was invisible from most lines of sight. One place you can see it from, however, is that steep cliff path.

Abd el-Rassul's men had been carrying with them a sturdy palm log. They now tied a rope to it, heaved it across the top of the hole, and used the rope to haul up the most dangerously balanced rocks from its walls and floor. Then, led by Abd el-Rassul, Brugsch lowered himself into the shaft— a neat figure in a dark suit and fez, swaying precariously from side to side as he descended.

At the bottom was a tiny doorway that led to a low corridor, less than three feet high. Brugsch had to drop to his knees to get through and in the darkness almost bumped into a huge wooden coffin, shaped like a mummy and decorated in yellow paint, that half-filled the corridor just beyond the entrance. It was inscribed with the name of a priest: *Nebseny*. Behind it were three more coffins. Brugsch crawled past them all with a candle in one hand, gingerly placing his knees and remaining hand on a floor that was scattered with small statuettes, vases, and jars.

After about twenty feet, the corridor turned sharp right and continued north into the heart of the mountain. A princess's crumpled funeral tent was carelessly thrown into the corner. This passage was higher so Brugsch could stand, but the floor was still strewn with antiquities that glittered in

---

* "The first object that caught Mr. Émile Brugsch's eye . . ."

the candlelight. About seventy feet farther on, he found a side chamber, nearly twenty feet square. Piles of huge coffins were stacked upright against its walls, some of them more than twice his height.

Brugsch raised his candle over the coffins to read some of the inscriptions inked onto their lids, and was stunned. The looted antiquities that had appeared for sale belonged to the family of high priests who ruled Thebes during the Twenty-First Dynasty. But here, all in one place, were the most famous rulers of the great Eighteenth and Nineteenth Dynasties, who ruled when ancient Egypt's power was at its height, with an empire that stretched north as far as Syria and south into Sudan. Scholars had read about these pharaohs in the hieroglyphs carved in stone all over the country: on statues, temples, palaces, and of course the empty royal tombs.

There was Ahmose I—first pharaoh of the Eighteenth Dynasty, who famously founded the New Kingdom when he liberated Egypt from an Asiatic people called the Hyksos. He was joined by Amenhotep I and Thutmose I, II, and III—several of whom had reputations as great warriors—and one of the best-known Egyptian queens, Ahmose-Nefertari. Most impressive of all, here lay Rameses II—in Brugsch's time (when Tutankhamun was barely heard of) the most famous pharaoh of all. Nicknamed Rameses the Great, he was a mighty conqueror king, often compared with Napoleon, and many scholars then thought he was the biblical ruler responsible for enslaving the Israelites. It was widely believed that without Rameses II, there would never have been a Moses.

Stunned at coming face to face with such an illustrious assembly, Brugsch felt as if he was dreaming. He later described the experience of being surrounded by ancient royals to Wilson: "Their gold coffins and their polished surfaces so plainly reflected my own excited visage that it seemed as though I was looking into the faces of my own ancestors. The gilt face on the coffin of the amiable Queen Nefertari seemed to smile upon me like an old acquaintance."

After reading the names, Brugsch withdrew from the chamber, aware that if he stumbled or fainted in such a tinder-dry environment, his candle could easily spark a fire. As he continued, the corridor became gradually wider and taller, until a hundred feet or so further on, it opened into a large, final chamber.

This room was again filled with coffins, but this time they were from the expected Twenty-First Dynasty. Here lay the family of Pinedjem—high priests who ruled the southern part of Egypt on behalf of the official pharaohs who were based in the north. Overall, Brugsch found nearly forty mummies of kings, queens, princes, and priests, and even more enormous coffins.

After nearly two hours in the tomb, Brugsch emerged back into the valley. It was almost sunset, and not far off he could hear the howl of hyenas. He had stumbled across one of the greatest archaeological finds of the century, and its safety now depended on him. Previously the Abd el-Rassul brothers had kept their knowledge of the tomb closely guarded. Now, thanks to the presence of the workmen, its secret was out. He had to get the coffins out of the shaft and to safety before the villagers of Gurna, who now knew that a great treasure was being taken from them, came to claim it for themselves.

Brugsch went back across the river to Luxor and spent nearly the whole night hiring men to help remove the precious relics from their hiding place. Already rumors were starting to spread among the locals—stories of coffins filled with diamonds, rubies, and gold. By the next morning, he had a team of three hundred workers assembled at the shaft. One by one, they wrapped each coffin in matting, sewed it in white sailcloth, and hoisted it up using the rope tied to the palm log.

Then the precious packages had to be carried through the fields to the river. It was an eight-hour trudge across the plain, often with twelve or sixteen men to a coffin, carrying the dead kings past the ruins of the ancient temples that they themselves had built. As Brugsch watched the strange procession, he felt closer than usual to the stories he had read in the Bible: "As the Red Sea opened and allowed Israel to pass across dry-shod, so opened the silence of the Theban plain, allowed the strange funeral procession to pass—and then all was hushed again."[7]

The royal haul was then ferried across the river to Luxor and loaded onto the antiquities service steamer. It had taken six days in all to empty the tomb—later dubbed the Deir el-Bahri cache. A unique ancient treasure had been rescued, but at the same time, an invaluable source of knowledge was lost forever. Brugsch was so keen to get the mummies to safety that even though he was a skilled photographer, he didn't take a single picture of the coffins in their resting place, or make a single drawing of how they were arranged—much to the frustration and disappointment of generations of archaeologists since.

When Brugsch and his colleagues set off on the steamer back to the museum in Cairo, they found that news of their cargo had traveled down the Nile ahead of them. At each town they passed, crowds gathered at the quays, gesticulating wildly. Men fired their guns. Disheveled women ran after the boat, tearing their hair and wailing. The pharaohs were being treated to traditional mourning rites that had barely changed since ancient times.

According to one version of the story, when the steamer finally arrived in Cairo, the government customs officer had no suitable category on his lists for imports of royal mummies.[8] Eventually he chose *farseekh*—dried fish.

CHAPTER TWO

CLUES BY
CANDLELIGHT

═══

O NCE INSTALLED IN THE BULAQ MUSEUM, it wasn't long before some of the mummies started to smell. Conditions in Cairo were much more humid than in the dry Theban desert, and the ancient corpses started to rot. Brugsch unwrapped a couple of them but it didn't go too well. One of the first, in 1885, was the mummy of Queen Ahmose-Nefertari, a balding old woman with worn teeth and a wig made of plaits of human hair tied to strings. Her body had barely been exposed to the air when it began to ooze a stinking black pus, and she had to be buried until the stench wore off.

Unraveling another mummy promised to reveal the body of the great warrior Thutmose III, known mainly for a dizzying series of military conquests, as well as his efforts to erase the name of his stepmother, the female pharaoh Hatshepsut (whom we'll learn more about later), from history. Yet beneath the bandages, Brugsch found that the head and all four limbs had been broken from the battered torso, the body apparently smashed by ancient looters before being gathered together and roughly rewrapped in the general shape of a man.

Meanwhile, Maspero studied the mummies' coffins and wrappings, in an effort to understand what all these famous kings and queens were doing bundled into a remote cliff tomb that dated from hundreds of years after they had actually ruled.

The bodies of Pinedjem and his family seemed to be intact—as originally interred—or at least they had been until the Abd el-Rassuls started pilfering their burial goods. But the great kings in the side chamber, as Thutmose III showed, were not in their original state. By deciphering inscriptions written on the mummies' wrappings, together with what was known of the history of the time, Maspero was able to piece together what had happened. The sequence of events he suggested is still largely accepted—with a few tweaks—by scholars today.

Under the Nineteenth Dynasty, ancient Egypt was at the peak of its power. But a series of weak kings in the Twentieth Dynasty left Thebes in the midst of civil war. As order crumbled, the memorial temples and tombs—including those of the Valley of the Kings—were robbed and vandalized. By this time, Egypt's pharaohs had moved to the north of the country, in Memphis, and a family of high priests effectively ruled the south. The New Kingdom had come to an end.

These high priests of the Twenty-First Dynasty gradually brought Thebes back under control, but security in the Valley of the Kings remained lax, and they were unable to stop the royal tombs from being repeatedly looted. The Valley had been home to a thriving community of priests, guards, and workmen—the sacred resting place of Egypt's rulers for five hundred years. But all that was now over, and with the valley left empty, thieves moved in. Repeated reburial commissions were set up to inspect and restore the ravaged tombs, rewrapping the royal mummies and sometimes moving them between tombs in an attempt to keep them safe. But the thefts continued, and the dead pharaohs were progressively stripped of their riches.

Eventually, around 975 BC, high priest Pinedjem II decided to remove the royal mummies from the Valley altogether. He collected them and stripped them of their remaining gold—a welcome addition to the declining state coffers—so they would no longer be a target for thieves. The bodies were (more or less) carefully rewrapped, and placed in plain wooden coffins.

It seems they were taken to the now-lost tomb of a long-dead queen called Inhapy, where they rested until 930 BC, when King Shoshenq I, of a new Twenty-Second Dynasty, moved them yet again, to Deir el-Bahri and the remote tomb that Pinedjem II had constructed for himself and his family. It was intended to be the pharaohs' final journey and it very nearly was. After depositing their royal charges in the tomb's outer corridors, Shoshenq's reburial party sealed the door and climbed back up the shaft, the last people to know of its existence for nearly three thousand years, until the arrival of the Abd el-Rassuls.

═══

IT WAS TIME, decided Maspero, to treat his royal mummies with a little more respect. He organized a series of grand unwrapping ceremonies, starting on June 1, 1886. The guests included the Khedive Tewfik, Egypt's nominal head of state (the British were really in charge since storming Alexandria in 1882, though they left the antiquities service to the French), and other illustrious figures including the consul-general of Russia and Queen Victoria's commissioner, Henry Drummond Wolf.

Proceedings began at ten minutes to ten in the morning with the illustrious Rameses II, identified by an inscription on his coffin written by Pinedjem II's priests. The mummy was laid on a wooden trestle table in front of the crowd of spectators—the men in turbans or tarbooshes, the women in corsets and floral hats. It took Maspero and Brugsch just fifteen minutes to strip the king's body bare, leaving the bandages in an exploded mess around them on the floor.

Underneath it all, they found a scrawny, old man, as to be expected after nearly seventy years of rule, still strikingly lifelike though, with a strong jaw, hook nose, and particularly satisfied expression. Perhaps that was to be expected too for a man who had eight wives and a harem of beautiful women. Maspero was relieved and pleased not to let his guests down. "The face of the mummy gives a fair idea of the face of the living king," he wrote afterward.[1] But like the previous unwrappings, the event doesn't seem to have achieved much of scientific value. In Maspero's time, archaeology was still more of a treasure hunt than a science.

Instead, the conclusions reached were highly subjective by today's standards, with the king being judged rather like a student in school. One writer described Rameses II's "somewhat unintelligent expression, slightly brutish perhaps, but haughty and firm of purpose," adding that "his conduct at [the battle of] Khadesh* suggests a good trooper, but a dull general, and his mummy does nothing to cause a revision of the judgement."[2]

---

* A confrontation between the Egyptian Empire, under Rameses II, and the Hittites, which took place around 1275 BC. It was probably the largest chariot battle ever fought.

Buoyed by this success, Maspero immediately brought out another, unidentified mummy. Once he had cut through an outer shroud of orange linen, inscriptions on the wrappings beneath revealed it was none other than Rameses III, considered the last New Kingdom ruler to wield any substantial authority over Egypt. The excited spectators abandoned their chairs and crowded round the investigators' table. After numerous layers of canvas and linen, which Maspero and Brugsch cut through with scissors, they finally revealed the king's head.

But it was a disappointment. Though the mummy was in good condition, the pharaoh's face was completely covered with a mass of black resin. It was enough for the Khedive, who seems to have been unimpressed by meeting his illustrious predecessors. At twenty past eleven, he walked out.

Unwrapping of other inhabitants of the cache soon followed, and revealed various pieces of information. Seqenenre Tao (Ahmose I's father, and the penultimate king of the Seventeenth Dynasty), was found to have been killed by a succession of dreadful wounds to the head, perhaps inflicted in battle by Egypt's dreaded enemies, the Hyksos. Seti I turned out to have been great-looking, with a face that apparently amazed the investigators with its beauty.* One king not subjected to the procedure was Amenhotep I. His wrappings were in near-perfect condition, still adorned with blue flowers and even the fragile body of an ancient wasp. Maspero couldn't bear to ruin the mummy, so he left it wrapped.

Overall, it was an amazing haul—talk about bringing history to life. These kings and queens, with fame that was almost legendary, had ruled the most powerful country on earth more than three thousand years before. Now, instead of being distant historical figures, they were real people, with bodies, faces, personalities, and weaknesses. In all of history, there had never been anything like it; no wonder Maspero, like Brugsch before him, sometimes had trouble believing it was real. "I am still wondering if I'm not really dreaming," he said, "when I see and touch what were the bodies of so many characters of whom we thought we would never know more than their names."[3]

---

* He still looks pretty good today, on show in the Egyptian Museum in Cairo, with jet black skin, great bone structure, and a strong, open face. Although perhaps he's not to everyone's taste. "He's handsome!" exclaimed a middle-aged Australian woman standing next to me when I visited, as we both considered his mummy. "But his nose is a bit small."

═══

I went forward with my candle and, horrible sight, a
body lay there upon the boat, all black and hideous its
grimacing face turning towards me and looking at me, its
long brown hair in sparse bunches around its head.

—VICTOR LORET, 1898[4]

IT WAS OVER A DECADE before any more royal mummies were unearthed. But when they were, the find was just as dramatic. By this time, the antiquities service had a new director, another Frenchman (it was the 1950s before the service was headed by an Egyptian) called Victor Loret, who cut a distinguished figure with wire-rimmed glasses and a pointed goatee. During his three-year tenure, he discovered a total of sixteen tombs, but is remembered for one of them in particular.

Work in the Valley of the Kings had been continuing, though no more pharaohs' tombs had been found since Belzoni's discoveries in 1817. In February 1898, Loret discovered the tomb of Thutmose III, the original resting place of the battered mummy unwrapped by Brugsch. The tombs in the Valley were given numbers, starting with KV1,* according to the order of their discovery, and this one became KV34. Like all the previous finds, it had been heavily robbed in antiquity. All that remained were a few odds and ends—boxes of veal and beef, plants, alabaster jars, and some model boats.

That March, when Loret came across the doorway of the Valley's thirty-fifth tomb, he didn't expect anything different. His workmen cleared away the stones that covered KV35 until there was a hole big enough for Loret and his foreman to clamber into a steeply descending corridor. After coming to a deep well, which they had to cross with a ladder, they ended up in a large chamber supported by two square pillars.

The floor was covered with smashed up funerary equipment and broken pieces of wood. The tomb had clearly been robbed in antiquity, but didn't

---

* KV stands for Kings' Valley.

seem to have been entered since then. Then, deep inside the chamber, Loret saw by candlelight what must rank as one of the most scary-looking boats in history. The wooden vessel was topped by a hideous corpse, lying on its back with its head turned toward the entrance, teeth bared as if in a gruesome warning. It turned out to be a mummy, robbed while the oils and resins poured on it were still fresh, then thrown across the room, where it had stuck to the top of the boat.

Undeterred, Loret picked his way through a series of further stairs and chambers, stepping carefully over the rubbish—pottery, glass, ancient garlands, splintered wood—that covered the floor. Eventually he came to a crypt, centered on a hefty stone sarcophagus. It held a coffin with the royal titles of an Eighteenth-Dynasty king: Amenhotep II. The body was still inside.

That wasn't all. In a side chamber, Loret found three near-naked mummies—two women and a boy. Rigid as wood, they were lying in a neat row on the floor, their feet pointing toward the door. Another side chamber was piled high with nine coffins, all coated with a thick layer of dust. Loret leaned over the nearest and blew on it to reveal the name. It was another king: Rameses IV. He went from coffin to coffin and found royal titles, called cartouches, on eight of them, including Siptah, Seti II, and Thutmose IV. All were well-known rulers from the Eighteenth, Nineteenth, and Twentieth Dynasties. He had stumbled across another royal cache, just like the one at Deir el-Bahri.

Inscriptions on their wrappings subsequently told a similar story. These pharaohs, including Amenhotep II in his sarcophagus, had been stripped and rewrapped during the Twenty-First Dynasty and hidden in the tomb for safety. When Pinedjem II emptied the Valley of its royal occupants, he had left this group behind. Put together with the Deir el-Bahri mummies, they formed almost a full house of New Kingdom kings.

Loret cleared the tomb but was ordered by Sir William Garstin, the minister for public works, to leave the mummies where they were found. Garstin feared that moving them might stoke the already prevalent belief among locals that foreigners were robbing Egypt's royal tombs. Most Egyptians felt that once buried, kings should not be disturbed, so the tomb was barred and bolted, and the mummies left in peace.

IN 1900, THE BRITISH CONSUL-GENERAL, Lord Cromer, effectively Egypt's ruler, removed Loret as head of the antiquities service and reinstated Maspero, who put a rising young archaeologist in charge of the monuments of Upper Egypt. His name was Howard Carter.

Carter had come to Egypt when he was seventeen to help record the extensive artwork being uncovered in tombs and temples at various sites. But he soon showed great promise as an archaeologist in his own right, learning rigorous methods from Flinders Petrie—who pretty much invented the idea of archaeology as a science, and is today perhaps the only Egyptologist who can rival Carter's fame.

In his new post at Thebes, Carter supervised much clearing and restoration work, installed iron doors and electric lights in many tombs in the Valley of the Kings, and made several important finds, including the Eighteenth-Dynasty tombs of Hatshepsut and Thutmose IV.

Meanwhile, Maspero removed the cached kings and queens from tomb KV35 and took them to the Egyptian Museum in Cairo,[*] arguing that they were at risk from looters, and that as they had been moved in antiquity anyway, there was no reason to leave them undisturbed. He left Amenhotep II in his tomb, along with the boat body and the three stripped mummies— he assumed they were all lesser figures who had formed part of the king's original burial, as family members or perhaps even human sacrifices. I expect the Frenchman would be rather surprised to hear that a century later, those lowly mummies from the side-room floor, especially the two women, are among the most talked about individuals in the whole royal mummy saga— TV stars with famous faces and glamorous suggested identities that range from famed beauty Nefertiti to the female pharaoh Hatshepsut.

Leaving anything in the tomb at all turned out to be a bad idea. A few months later, Carter, while working at a temple south of Thebes, was summoned to the Valley of the Kings by telegram. KV35 had been broken into. The boat was stolen, its mummy smashed, and the king stripped of his fine bandages and broken open in a fruitless search for jewelry.

Carter was incensed. He set about tracking the culprits with all the cunning and determination of Sherlock Holmes (he later noted that if he hadn't

---

[*] In 1890, the museum had moved from Bulaq to a site in Giza, a palace donated by the Khedive, after the original building—which was far too small anyway—was permanently damaged by floods. But this still wasn't big enough for all of the antiquities being unearthed in Egypt, and in 1902, the museum moved again to its present location, a huge, neo-Classical building next to Tahrir Square.

become an archaeologist, he might have made a competent detective[5]). He took plaster casts of footprints by the tomb door, identified the instrument used to break open the lock, and traced both to none other than the Abd el-Rassuls. When searched, their white house was found to be full of stolen artifacts from other tombs. Mohammed Abd el-Rassul was put on trial, but the court wasn't persuaded by Carter's evidence, and the accused went free.

In 1904, Maspero transferred Carter into the job of chief inspector of the antiquities of Lower Egypt, a prestigious posting that included responsibility for the Great Pyramids, near Cairo. He didn't last long. A few weeks later, a party of drunken French tourists tried to force their way onto a site and attacked one of the Egyptian guards. Carter told his men to defend themselves, and the situation descended into a rowdy fight with sticks and chairs, with men on both sides left beaten and unconscious.

It caused a minor diplomatic storm that Carter should have encouraged mere Egyptians to strike Frenchmen, regardless of the provocation. Maspero and then the mighty Cromer asked him to apologize, but to Carter—principled, stubborn, with a general distrust of authority—the idea was unthinkable. He refused, and was later transferred to the remote northern town of Tanta.

Carter hated it there and, despite Maspero's efforts to convince him otherwise, he resigned—the end of a promising career with the service. He eventually moved back to Luxor, where he scraped a living as an artist, as well as by selling an antiquity or two.

He dreamed of excavating in the Valley of the Kings, convinced there was still an intact—un-looted—royal tomb hidden there, and that he could track it down where everyone else had failed. But he could only stand by and watch as others made a series of impressive finds. The antiquities service was increasingly strapped for cash, so Maspero started working with rich amateurs who funded excavations in return for a share of the antiquities they unearthed. The process was organized by concession, meaning that only one person could dig in each area at a time. Once you had the concession for a particular area, it was yours until you decided to give it up.

The man who won the coveted concession for the Valley of the Kings was Theodore M. Davis, a retired lawyer from New York. He was short, aggressive, very rich, and had no patience for any kind of scientific procedure—the polar opposite of a careful archaeologist like Carter. He was in this game for the treasure.

In February 1905, he found it: the most intact tomb yet in the Valley. It belonged to an elderly couple called Yuya and Tjuiu. They weren't royal (the Valley of the Kings hosted the tombs of various high-status nobles and courtiers as well as the pharaohs themselves), but their daughter Tiye had been a queen—wife of the powerful Eighteenth-Dynasty King Amenhotep III. The tomb had suffered some thefts in antiquity but hadn't been touched since, and was still packed full. Davis entered with the elderly Maspero and a British archaeologist called Arthur Weigall, who had taken over Carter's old job as inspector general at Thebes.

"The chamber was dark as dark could be and extremely hot," wrote Davis afterward. "We held up our candles but they gave so little light and so dazzled our eyes that we could see nothing except the glint of gold."[6]

Once their eyes adjusted, they saw that although the tomb was small and undecorated, its contents were gorgeous, including two gold-covered carved armchairs complete with cushions, two beds fitted with springy string mattresses, a wicker trunk, some lovely alabaster vases, and a chariot. Weigall later compared the stuffy, stiff feeling of the tomb to that of a town house closed for the summer. And lying peacefully in their coffins were the occupants—the wonderfully preserved, smiling mummies of Yuya and Tjuiu themselves.

In January 1907, Davis found another tomb close to Yuya and Tjuiu's that had been sealed since ancient Egyptian times. But this one—KV55— was a chaotic and confusing sight. Piles of stone chippings almost filled the entrance passage. Inside, water dripping from the ceiling had seriously damaged the contents, which seemed to be a random and scattered collection of burial goods, including dismantled parts of a gilded wooden shrine plus smaller items such as jars, mud bricks, and beads.

In the center of the tomb, a gold-covered coffin lay on the floor where the wooden bier beneath it had rotted and collapsed. Its lid had come off in the fall, revealing a royal mummy covered with gold jewelry, including a vulture-shaped collar that had been crudely bent around its head as a crown. Someone had disturbed this burial in antiquity, but it didn't look like thieves.

In a perfect demonstration of what not to do when you find a royal mummy, Davis, along with Maspero and an artist called Lindon Smith, who it seems just happened to be around, stripped the body. Together, they pulled away sheets of gold from on top of the mummy, and peeled gold foil bracelets from its arms. The mummy initially looked intact, until Davis very effectively determined otherwise: "Rather suspecting injury from the evident dampness, I gently touched one of the front teeth (3,000 years old), and alas! it fell into dust, thereby showing that the mummy could not be well preserved. We then cleared the entire mummy. . . ."[7]

By the time the three were done, the mummy was reduced to a bare skeleton, which you can see today in the Egyptian Museum: looking strangely like it's in bed, with its large, dark-stained skull resting on a comfy-looking brown shroud and a smart, cream sheet tucked under its chin. We'll never know what the mummy looked like originally, as no one thought to draw or photograph it before Davis and the others pulled it apart. But an account written by one eyewitness[*] describes its "dried-up face, sunken cheeks and thin leathery-looking lips."[8]

There was confusion too over the identity of this royal figure. The name on the coffin had been hacked away, and its golden face violently ripped off, leaving bare wood beneath—someone had obviously been very keen to obliterate this person's identity.

Davis located a holidaying American obstetrician and a local doctor and brought them to examine the bones. According to him, they duly pronounced the mummy female. The gold shrine had been made for Queen Tiye (Yuya and Tjuiu's daughter), and Davis, who apparently had a penchant for ancient Egyptian queens, remained convinced until he died that he had found her tomb.

But as well as Tiye's shrine, there were objects in the tomb inscribed with several other royal names. There were "magic bricks" inscribed with the name of her son, King Akhenaten, for example, and canopic jars (used for holding a mummy's internal organs) that are now tentatively ascribed to various royal women. The gold sheets from the coffin were reportedly also inscribed with the titles of Akhenaten, although the investigators never drew or photographed them, and the gold was stolen from the Cairo museum before it could be properly cataloged.

And when an Australian anatomist called Grafton Elliot Smith examined the bones in Cairo several months later, he was surprised to find that they were actually those of a man, leading most scholars to conclude that the body wasn't Tiye at all, but Akhenaten.

---

* The illustrator and travel writer Walter Tyndale.

The mysterious burial focused archaeologists' attention on a poorly understood period at the end of the Eighteenth Dynasty. After thousands of years of stable religion and unchanging tradition, Egypt was stronger than ever under Amenhotep III and Queen Tiye. Amenhotep III's military conquests brought unprecedented riches into the royal court, and he embarked on a huge building program, including grand additions to Karnak and Luxor Temples, his silver-plated memorial temple, and a palace with a gigantic artificial lake. Then it all came to a dramatic end. The couple's son, Amenhotep IV, threw out Egypt's traditional religion, which worshipped the chief god of Amun-Ra*—and all the machinery of priests and temples that went with it.

He started to worship a single, more abstract god, the Aten or sun disc, and appointed himself as the Egyptian people's sole point of contact with it. He changed his name to Akhenaten, meaning "living spirit of the Aten," abandoned Thebes, and built a brand new capital city from scratch, in a remote desert spot 250 miles up the Nile.

The site is now called Tell el-Amarna (or Amarna for short), and Carter knew it well as in 1892 he had spent his first season in Egypt there, working alongside Petrie. Akhenaten seems to have largely withdrawn from military endeavors and in inscriptions found at Amarna, he vowed never to leave the city as long as he lived; his now-empty tomb had indeed been found there too. He reigned with his principal wife Nefertiti—famed for her great beauty ever since a bust of her looking gorgeous was discovered in Amarna by a German team in 1912.

Then, just seventeen years after it all began, Akhenaten's new world crumbled. The beautiful Nefertiti mysteriously disappeared from the historical record, and not long afterward, Akhenaten died. He was succeeded—directly, or after a short intervening reign—by his son-in-law, Tutankhamun, in whose name every change that Akhenaten had put in place was systematically reversed: the old gods were reinstated and the capital was moved back to Thebes. Tutankhamun appeared to have died without any heirs and just a few years later, the Eighteenth Dynasty was over and a new line of kings, descended from a general called Rameses, had taken the throne.

---

* The sun god, Ra, who became merged during the New Kingdom with the patron deity of Thebes, Amun.

Akhenaten's brief revolt seemed dramatic, bizarre, unbelievable. Ancient Egypt was pretty much the most stable culture in history. Every few centuries, wars or natural disasters would cause things to fall apart a bit. But the civilization picked itself up and became powerful again with pretty much the same political structure and belief system as before. The artwork, too, barely changed over the centuries. All of the pharaohs were shown as youthful, strong rulers, the idealized symbol of a god ruling on earth. Some kings lived longer than others; some had more military successes to boast about. Their faces differed just enough to be recognizable. But glimpses of the people behind the propaganda are rare. In the records they left behind, each king was basically the same ruler, reincarnated, again and again and again.

Then Akhenaten broke the mold, throwing out those thousands of years of tradition to do his own thing. Instead of going to war, he wrote a poetic "Great Hymn to the Aten" that has been compared to the Bible's Psalm 104. The art changed too. From a very prescribed, formal style, the depictions being found at Amarna were much more naturalistic. You see the king being intimate with Nefertiti in family scenes, for example, and bouncing his little daughters on his knee.

Then there are his statues. Instead of the usual cookie-cutter image of a young, strong king, the way that Akhenaten represented himself is weird and uncomfortable, if not downright alien. His muscular chest and shoulders mix with burstingly female curves: full breasts, a saggy tummy, and wide hips, and no sign of male genitalia. Yet he makes Egypt's other kings look fluffy and adorable, almost comical. A long, thin head with high cheekbones and slanted almond-shaped eyes give him a sinister look, like a "humanoid praying mantis" as one scholar put it,[9] or the villain in some crazy kids' cartoon. Staring into the half-closed eyes of one of Akhenaten's statues gives the eerie feeling of being sized up by a superior intelligence.

No wonder Egyptologists—actually not just Egyptologists, Akhenaten has been written about by everyone from psychiatrists to politicians, and starred in countless novels, films, and even an opera—have been fascinated by him ever since. He has variously been described as a madman, a poet, a pathological study, and a prophet—no less than the inventor of monotheism.

In 1907, very little was known about the whole story beyond what was being discovered at the deserted city of Amarna, because subsequent rulers had tried to remove every trace of Akhenaten and his "heresy" from the record, scratching out the names of him and his family from paintings and statues wherever they were found. Now in tomb KV55, a jumble of objects belonging to figures whom archaeologists assumed had been buried at Amarna was found right in the middle of Thebes.

What were they doing in the Valley of the Kings? Several seals of Tutankhamun were found in the tomb, so it seemed most likely that Tutankhamun, after moving back to Thebes, had removed goods from the burials of several of his relatives in Amarna and reburied them in the Valley for safety, presumably because they could no longer be kept secure at the deserted site.

The idea that Tutankhamun also reburied there Akhenaten himself caused great excitement among archaeologists. It meant that they no longer had to rely just on inscriptions and statues to understand this unique revolutionary. They potentially had the body of the man himself. In decades to come, this mysterious mummy, so harshly treated by Davis, would become central to efforts to solve just what made this king so different. But there were niggling doubts. When Elliot Smith examined the bones, he concluded that they belonged to a young man, perhaps in his mid-twenties when he died, whereas Akhenaten was assumed to be significantly older. He ruled for seventeen years, and as he introduced such dramatic changes was presumably a grown man when he took the throne. He was also known to have several daughters, at least one of whom married during his lifetime.

Throughout all this excitement, Carter looked on. These two tombs discovered by Davis—Yuya and Tjuiu's and the Amarna cache—both undisturbed since the Eighteenth Dynasty, were close together in the center of the valley and had been hidden from looters long before the Twenty-First-Dynasty reburial efforts by rubble deposited in ancient floods. So perhaps they weren't all that the floods had covered over. Davis was focusing his search for more tombs in the Valley along the edges of cliffs and the sides of gullies. But Carter reckoned that here, in the valley floor beneath the flood debris, would be the best place to find another intact tomb from the same time period. And he knew just whom he wanted to look for—one of the only Eighteenth-Dynasty kings for whom neither a mummy, nor an empty tomb, had been found.

THE YOUNG, reckless Fifth Earl of Carnarvon didn't do anything by halves. But then, as one of the richest men in England, he didn't have to. Thanks partly to marrying the illegitimate daughter of (allegedly) the stupendously wealthy banker Alfred de Rothschild, Lord Carnarvon owned so much land he couldn't even count it all. He made the most of his circumstances, owning a string of racehorses, sailing around the world, and racing down country roads in one of the first automobiles to be registered in England after it became legal to drive without someone carrying a red flag down the road in front of you.[10]

"Porchy,"* as he was generally known, survived all kinds of far-flung adventures from tropical storms to elephant attacks, but it was two cattle-drawn carts that nearly killed him. Driving at high speed through German countryside in 1901, he didn't see the carts, which were stopped in a blind dip in the road, until it was too late. He swerved to avoid them, went off the road, and landed in the mud with his car on top of him.

From that day onward, Carnarvon's health was shattered and it seemed his days of adventure were over. His lungs were particularly weak, so rather than risk catching bronchitis in chilly England he started wintering in Egypt, and became captivated by archaeology. He threw himself into this new pursuit just as he had his previous sports, and decided that buying up antiquities wasn't enough. He wanted to dig for them.

In 1906, Maspero awarded Carnarvon a concession, and Weigall, who disapproved of amateurs being let loose in the area, gave him a dud site in some "rubbish mounds"[11] on top of the hill of Gurna. Sure enough, his first season brought him nothing more than a mummified cat. His second season wasn't much better, but Carnarvon wasn't deterred. For his third season, Maspero suggested that he work with Carter.

The pair were given a more promising site in front of Hatshepsut's temple at Deir el-Bahri, where Carter brought professionalism to the enterprise. Despite their very different backgrounds, they became firm friends. When back in England, Carter often visited Carnarvon at Highclere, the lord's grand estate in Berkshire (now used as the location of the hit British TV series *Downton Abbey*).

Between them, they discovered a haul of reasonably important tombs, including that of Queen Ahmose-Nefertari, and Carter painted Carnarvon's

---

* Before inheriting the title of Lord Carnarvon from his father in 1890, he was Lord Porchester.

baronial crest above the door of each one. When Carnarvon came to visit the dig, he stayed at the plush Winter Palace hotel across the river in Luxor, while Carter built a house for himself, nicknamed "Castle Carter,"[12] a twenty-minute donkey ride from the Valley of the Kings.

Which of course is where he still desperately wanted to excavate. But Davis refused to let his concession go, despite diminishing returns in his excavations, until shortly before his death in 1915. By this time, he was convinced there was nothing left to be found, writing: "I fear the Valley of the Kings is now exhausted."[13]

Carter and Carnarvon seized their chance, though their peers thought they were wasting their time. Even Maspero, as he signed the concession over to them, said bluntly that he didn't think the site would repay further investigation. But Carter had carefully studied the scars left in the valley by previous excavators. He was certain there were areas that hadn't yet been searched—particularly in the central floor of the valley, near the un-looted Amarna cache.

Several of Davis's finds strengthened Carter's conviction that this area would yield the tomb of Tutankhamun. First, several items bearing Tutankhamun's name, including a blue pot, stashed carefully under a rock, and some fragments of gold foil. Second, the seals in the Amarna cache. If Tutankhamun had buried his predecessor here, he might therefore choose a similar location for his own tomb. A third clue was a mysterious pit that Davis had found in 1907.

It contained a collection of large, earthen pots, inscribed with Tutankhamun's name. They were full of debris—broken pottery, small bags of powder, dried wreaths of leaves and flowers. Davis wasn't impressed by the lack of valuables and had no use for the pots or their contents, aside from tearing the flower necklaces as a party piece for guests to show how strong they were. He donated them to the Metropolitan Museum of Art in New York. Carter didn't yet understand the significance of the pit either, but he saw it as one more sign that Tutankhamun was buried close by.

Before the pair could start digging, world war broke out, and all excavations ceased. Carnarvon, too ill to fight, turned Highclere into a military hospital. Carter worked as a courier for the foreign office in the Middle East, but in an episode reminiscent of the Saqqara affair, he was soon dismissed for a "trivial yet distinct" breach of discipline,[14] and returned to Thebes where he carried out some small-scale fieldwork.

During the later years of the war, archaeological activity slowly restarted, and Carter drew up a search plan. He would focus on a triangle between three tombs in the central floor of the valley. Close to the Amarna cache, this was the area he thought had been covered by flood debris in ancient times. By December 1917, Carter and Carnarvon were finally ready to start their search for Tutankhamun.

CHAPTER THREE

OPERA OF A
VANISHED CIVILIZATION

═══

FROM THE CIRCULAR MAIN HALL of the Sackler Library in Oxford, UK, a short corridor leads to a staircase that takes you down below street level. Through a door marked *Archive*, office ceiling tiles and fluorescent lights stare down onto cheap blue carpet and a row of plain gray rolling stacks. It doesn't seem the most fertile ground for archaeological discovery. But the hum of the air conditioner lets slip that this modest room is hiding something special. The temperature is held at 65° F, several degrees cooler than the sunny July day outside, while a humidifier keeps the moisture level tightly controlled.

This is the archive of the Griffith Institute—arguably the best Egyptology library in the world. And this is as close as it's possible to get today to Howard Carter and his discovery of the tomb of Tutankhamun, resting place of the world's most famous mummy. The story of this incredible find has been recounted so many times it becomes more like a myth with every retelling; some of the details wear ever deeper, like ruts, while others have faded from memory. But the notebooks and diaries held in these dull-looking gray stacks contain the thoughts and experiences that Carter wrote down at the time. To learn about the discovery of Tutankhamun and his tomb, this seems as good a place as any to start.

I visit the archive accompanied by its soft-spoken keeper, Jaromir Malek,[*] and his assistant, Elizabeth Fleming. On the wall hangs another clue that this uninspiring room is something more than cheap office space— a somber portrait of Carter, with small but piercing black eyes gazing irritably down. To be honest, he looks a bit middle management, with the slight awkwardness of a low-grade accountant or banker. But this man had vision, and a sense of beauty. To prove it, Fleming brings out perhaps the archive's most aesthetically pleasing items—a collection of graceful watercolors, painted by Carter himself.

Artistic ability was what took Carter to Egypt in the first place. He was born in Norfolk, youngest of eight surviving children, and his father painted animal portraits—mainly dogs and horses—for rich local clients. Carter accompanied his father to one such engagement where he was introduced to an Egyptologist called Percy Newberry, who arranged for him to go to Egypt, aged seventeen, to copy tomb paintings.

He continued to paint in later life, even when working as an archaeologist. In the watercolors Fleming shows me, Carter has copied ancient Egyptian depictions of various animals and birds, then painted alongside their modern-day equivalents—inhabitants of the desert around him from the scimitar-horned oryx and Nubian ibex to the Egyptian vulture, falcon, and red-backed shrike. The pictures are elegant and effortless, with the attention to detail of someone who is both knowledgeable and passionate about his subject.

Indeed, Carter seems to have spent a lot of time contemplating the wildlife he encountered in the Valley of the Kings. You get the impression that sometimes he was keener on the vultures and jackals around him than the people. Perhaps it was a rare source of pleasure during his early years of excavations in the Valley, which from his notebooks sound like a pretty horrendous endeavor.

In the first season, the winter of 1917–1918 (archaeologists generally prefer to work in Thebes in the winter, to avoid the searing temperatures of summer), Carter started to investigate his chosen triangle. It wasn't a large area but this was still a monumental task. In those days, the Valley looked like a huge quarry, covered with piles of stones and chippings up to thirty feet high that had been left by previous excavators. Carter had no

---

* Malek has since retired.

choice but to clear these waste dumps—tens of thousands of tons of them—before he could embark on his own hunt, digging through the unexcavated layer of flood debris all the way down to bedrock.

To remove the rubbish, he borrowed a railway track from the antiquities service, with tipping trucks that were pushed along the rails by manpower. His team of local workmen and boys filled their baskets with picks and hoes, then emptied them into the trucks, thousands of times a day.

Toward the end of this first season, right in front of the tomb of the Nineteenth-Dynasty ruler Rameses VI, Carter uncovered a group of workmen's huts, also from the Nineteenth Dynasty. They were undisturbed, suggesting that no one had penetrated the layer of flood debris beneath them since at least that time. What's more, they were only forty feet from where the unplundered Amarna cache had been found.

If there was an intact Eighteenth-Dynasty tomb in the area, beneath those ancient huts seemed a pretty good place to look. Yet Carter didn't. Instead, he set his workers digging elsewhere. Carter always said it was because to excavate there would have cut off visitor access to Rameses VI's tomb, one of the most popular in the Valley, so he wanted to wait for a quieter time before exploring the area.[1] But he found the huts at the end of World War I, a slack period with few visitors—presumably the perfect time to carry out such work.

An alternative explanation is that Carter knew how exciting the site was, so wanted to save it for a time when Carnarvon's enthusiasm for funding the work was flagging. Finding Tutankhamun's tomb was important to Carter, but so was the less glamorous task of methodically checking every undug part of the Valley before his patron found something else to do.[2]

He started looking elsewhere—for five depressing seasons. In month after month of back-breaking work, Carter's men literally moved mountains, clearing hundreds of square feet of the valley right down to bedrock. The waste layers were so closely fused with the natural soil, he had to keep a close watch for charcoal and fish bones to tell whether they were digging through untouched layers of earth or artificial layers dumped by previous excavators.

During that time, he found hardly anything for Carnarvon—just a few ritual deposits marking the foundations of previously discovered tombs, and a cache of thirteen alabaster vases, which Carnarvon's daughter Evelyn Herbert (who always accompanied her father on his trips to Egypt) insisted on digging out of the ground with her bare hands.

It was a lonely time for Carter. But he loved the remote, solitary valley, with its rugged, savage rocks, which he once said, in certain conditions of mind, "were not unproductive of delight."[3] He found it especially impressive when riding home alone late at night, the noise of his donkey's footsteps interrupted only by the gloomy booming of a desert eagle owl or the occasional howl of a jackal.

By 1922, Carnarvon had serious doubts about continuing the work. He was tired of digging with so little reward, not to mention being the butt of other Egyptologists' jokes. As a racing man, he was happy to gamble, but only if the odds were in his favor. That summer, he invited Carter to Highclere, intending to bring the partnership to an end. But Carter didn't give up that easily. He told Carnarvon about the prime site he had been saving beneath the workmen's huts, and even offered to pay for the work himself, as long as Carnarvon allowed Carter to keep excavating under his name.

Carter may also have mentioned a new clue that Tutankhamun really was buried in the Valley. It had just come from Herbert Winlock, an Egyptologist at the Metropolitan Museum of Art in New York, who was studying the debris-filled jars, inscribed with Tutankhamun's name, that Davis found in 1907 then gave away. After similar finds were made for other kings, Winlock finally realized what they were—the materials used in Tutankhamun's embalming. The ancient Egyptians didn't throw away anything that touched the king's body as it was being prepared for burial; instead they carefully gathered all the rubbish up and buried it close to the relevant tomb.

Some of the jars contained the powdered salts used to dry out the body, and rags the embalmers cleaned up with afterward. Some limestone slabs that Winlock left at Davis's house must have been the stones that the body was laid on while it was being mummified. Other pots contained broken pottery, animal bones, and the flower necklaces that Davis was so fond of ripping up—these were the remains of the banquet held at Tutankhamun's funeral, including floral garlands worn by the guests. It was the surest sign yet that this king's tomb had to be nearby.

Carnarvon relented, and in October 1922, Carter returned to the Valley for one last season.

═══

AT THE GRIFFITH INSTITUTE, Fleming brings out the notebooks describing Carter's subsequent discovery. There's a small Letts diary, cream with a red spine, as well as a larger ring binder—Carter's excavation journal. Together with his popular books about Tutankhamun, they give—in most cases—a pretty good sense of what he was up to in those historic days and weeks.

Carter started excavations on November 1, 1922, exactly where he had left off back in 1918, by those workmen's huts in front of Rameses VI's tomb. He spent the next couple of days uncovering more huts, noting their details, then removing them, to clear away the three feet or so of stony soil that lay between them and bedrock.

On Saturday November 4, Carter arrived at the dig site at about ten in the morning, to find his usually rowdy team of workmen strangely quiet. At first he feared there had been an accident, but his foreman, Reis Ahmed Gerigar, told him the good news—a step had been discovered, cut into bedrock, under almost the first hut the men had cleared.

As the men dug further over the rest of that day and the next, a steep, sunken staircase started to emerge, cut into the rock about twelve feet below the entrance of Rameses VI's tomb. Carter tried to suppress his excitement. This was exactly how he would expect to find a hidden tomb. But he had been humiliated once before by jumping to conclusions. In 1898, Carter had stumbled on what he thought might be an intact royal tomb, just in front of Hatshepsut's temple at Deir el-Bahri. Two years later, after months of burrowing, he proudly invited Lord Cromer to witness the final discovery. But the last chamber contained only some wooden boats and a few pots. "There was *nothing*," Carter wrote. "I was filled with dismay."[4] Perhaps a similar fate awaited him with this latest find.

Toward sunset on Sunday, the men exposed the upper part of a plastered doorway, and Carter breathed a small sigh of relief. The seals on the door were intact, and showed the jackal god Anubis (associated with mummification and the afterlife) over nine bound captives—the official seal of the Royal Necropolis. There was no visible sign of exactly who was buried inside, but the style was Eighteenth Dynasty. The entrance seemed small for a pharaoh's tomb, but the royal seal indicated that the occupant must be someone important.

Carter made a small hole in the upper right corner of the door and shone in an electric torch. The passage beyond was completely filled with stones and rubble, more evidence that the last people to enter had been priests, not thieves. "It was a thrilling moment for an excavator," he wrote in his journal on November 5, 1922, "quite alone save his native staff of workmen, to suddenly find himself, after so many years of toilsome work, on the verge of what looked like a magnificent discovery—an untouched tomb."

Carter reluctantly closed the hole he had made. It was dark by now, so he rode his donkey home by moonlight. The next morning, he cabled Carnarvon at Highclere: "At last have made wonderful discovery in Valley; a magnificent tomb with seals intact, recovered same for your arrival, congratulations."

The next day, the men worked feverishly, covering up the door and steps, then rolling boulders over the entrance. The tomb had vanished, and more than once Carter found himself wondering if the entire thing was even real. He spent the next couple of weeks making preparations for opening the tomb, and hiring staff including his old friend Arthur Callender, a retired railway engineer who was to be his right-hand man in the work ahead. Carnarvon and his daughter arrived in Luxor on November 22, and Callender was put in charge of reopening the tomb.

He got to the doorway on November 24, at the bottom of sixteen steps in all. Now the lower part of the door was uncovered for the first time, revealing just what Carter had been hoping for—seal impressions with the cartouche of Tutankhamun. But there was bad news too. On closer inspection, the door seemed to have been opened, and resealed, twice, suggesting that the tomb had after all been entered in ancient times.

The workmen pulled down the rough stones of the door, and emptied the corridor beyond of its rubble. It was mostly filled with white stone chips, but in the upper left corner, where the door had been resealed, there was a stripe of dark flint. Robbers must have tunneled through the chippings, and their hole later refilled with a different kind of stone.

By the afternoon of Sunday November 26, after clearing a steep passage about thirty feet long, the workmen came across a second sealed door. Again, Carter made a tiny hole in the top corner to see what was beyond. The layout so far was just the same as the Amarna cache, so Carter feared this wasn't a proper tomb after all, but another cache. He poked an iron testing rod into the darkness and found empty space, then lit a candle to check for foul gases. Reassured that the air wasn't poisonous, Carter widened the hole and looked in, while Carnarvon, Evelyn, Callender, and the foremen waited anxiously behind him.

Carter's candlelight crept uninvited into the darkness beyond. Inside the tomb, time creaked into motion. Blurred shapes were forced into focus.

Objects lumbered into being. After thousands of years of enduring silence, the tomb had visitors.

═══

FROM READING CARTER'S DIARIES, "He was obviously a man of few words," comments Malek, keeper of the Griffith Institute's archive. "He was very prosaic, very down to earth." A typical diary entry reads simply, "Two donkeys," a reference to that day's transport to and from the tomb. "But when you read Carter's description of when they first opened the tomb, he suddenly becomes a poet."

With white-gloved hands, Malek's assistant Fleming pulls Carter's yellowed journal from a cardboard case and lays it gently on a cushion on the table in front of us. She finds the famous page—squared paper filled with neat, black ink—and starts to read Carter's stiff but evocative words: "It was sometime before one could see, the hot air escaping caused the candle to flicker, but as soon as one's eyes became accustomed to the glimmer of light the interior of the chamber gradually loomed before one, with its strange and wonderful medley of extraordinary and beautiful objects heaped upon one another."

At first, Carter thought he was looking at wall paintings; then he realized he was seeing actual three-dimensional things. He was quiet, taking in the confusing, flickering sight until Carnarvon couldn't bear it any longer: "Can you see anything?"

"Yes, it is wonderful," was all Carter was able to reply.* He made the hole in the door big enough so that the others could see in, and they shone an electric torch into the dark space. What they saw probably still stands as the most amazing archaeological discovery of all time.

Looming out of the darkness were two ebony-black statues of a king, with gold staffs, kilts, and sandals; gilded couches with the heads of strange beasts; exquisitely painted ornamental caskets; flowers; alabaster vases;

---

* As with many details of this story, different sources give varying accounts. In his excavation journal held at the Griffith Institute, Carter says he answered, "Yes, it is wonderful." An account written by Carnarvon gives the rather less catchy "There are some marvellous objects here."[5] But the most memorable (and most quoted) version is the one Carter came up with later (probably due to editing by his coauthor Arthur Mace) in his popular account of the discovery, published in 1923, in which he simply says: "Yes, wonderful things."[6]

strange black shrines adorned with a gilded monster snake; ordinary-looking white chests; finely carved chairs; a golden throne; a heap of curious white egg-shaped boxes; stools of all shapes and designs; and a scramble of overturned chariot parts glinting with gold, peering from among which was a manikin. In short, it was utter confusion, with a mindboggling assortment of objects piled all on top of one another. The first impression, said Carter, was not so much that of an orderly royal tomb, but "the property-room of an opera of a vanished civilisation."

The little group closed the hole, locked the wooden grill that had been placed over the doorway, and rode their donkeys home in silence. Carter barely slept that night, with two questions that he turned over and over: Was the jumble of objects he had discovered merely a cache, or was it really Tutankhamun's tomb? And if so, what were the chances of finding the king's mummy intact?

The next day, Callender rigged electric lighting in the tomb, and the four explorers entered the chamber for the first time.* It was much easier to see with the electric lamps, but the effect was still utterly confusing. The room was fairly small, roughly twenty-six feet by thirteen feet, but a bewildering mass of objects was heaped everywhere in disarray. It was hard to move around, and impossible to take everything in.

Opposite the entrance, a strange gilded couch was propped against the wall, and beneath it, there was an opening in the rock wall—another sealed doorway, though this too had been broken open. Carter and Carnarvon crawled under the couch and peeped through. They saw another room, smaller than the one they were in and on a lower level (Carter subsequently named it the annex, and the room in which they were standing the antechamber). The state of this room was even worse. Stones from the forced wall lay on top of crushed objects, and there was a mass of beds, chairs, boxes, vases, statuettes—all overturned, with boxes opened and their contents scattered all over the floor. Looking at the chaos, Carter realized for the first time what a daunting task clearing this tomb was going to be.

---

* Although this is what Carter says in his journal, it has been claimed, for example in Thomas Hoving's 1978 book *Tutankhamun: The Untold Story*,[7] that Carter and his three British companions actually first entered the tomb the night before. This is tough to prove but it doesn't seem that unlikely, especially as Carter and his friends almost certainly did enter the burial chamber ahead of its official opening (see page 34), though they probably didn't get that far on this first night.

There was no trace of any mummies in either chamber. And then, on the right as the party came in, they saw a sealed doorway, flanked by two statues of the king—their gorgeous gold-lined eyes keeping patient watch for intruders. That was when Carter realized that his dream had come true. What they had seen so far were just the outer rooms. This was Tutankhamun's tomb after all, and behind that wall was his burial chamber. But, ominously, the doorway had a small hole at the bottom, which had been plastered over and resealed.

News of the discovery started to spread, as did a variety of tall stories. One version popular among the locals was that three airplanes had landed in the Valley and taken off to an unknown destination with loads of treasure.[8] Partly to try to stem these rumors, Carter held an official opening of the antechamber a few days later, on November 29. It was attended by various Egyptian and foreign notables, and a reporter from *The Times*, who sent a special report to his London paper by telegram from Luxor.

By the next day, the discovery was worldwide news. *The Times* raved about the tomb's contents: a child's stool, quaint bronze musical instruments, a dummy for wigs and robes, and food including trussed duck and haunches of venison.[9] One of the boxes appeared to contain rolls of papyri—which caused great excitement as any written records found had the potential to revolutionize understanding of this intriguing period in history.

Meanwhile, Egyptologists and journalists alike were falling over themselves to amass what little information was known about Tutankhamun, and newspaper articles about the Amarna period became required reading at breakfast tables across the educated world. Soon it was common knowledge that the heretic king Akhenaten and his queen Nefertiti had six daughters. One of them married a man called Smenkhkare, who ruled briefly (as Akhenaten's coruler and perhaps alone after Akhenaten died) just before Tutankhamun's accession. A younger daughter married Tutankhamun, originally called Tutankhaten, when both were children. Before long, Tutankhaten was on the throne, had changed his name, and returned to Thebes.

The main source of information about Tutankhamun was a sandstone slab found at Karnak temple, on which he boasts about restoring Egypt to its former glory: "I found the temples fallen into ruin, with their holy places overgrown with weeds. I reconstructed their sanctuaries, re-endowed the temples and made the gifts of all precious things. I cast statues of the gods in gold and electrum and decorated them with lapis lazuli and all fine stones."[10]

Carter went to Cairo for supplies. He ordered a steel gate for the tomb's doorway, and bought provisions including more than a mile of wadding and as much again of surgical bandages, as well as photographic material, chemicals, packing boxes, and a motorcar. He also amassed a small team of helpers including two draftsmen, a government chemist and conservator called Alfred Lucas, plus photographer Harry Burton and archaeologist Arthur Mace, both on loan from the Metropolitan Museum in New York.

On December 27, they were ready to start removing objects from the antechamber. Unlike previous tomb clearances, where everything was stripped out in hours or days with few or no records taken, Carter's approach was a model of patient, meticulous archaeology. Before moving anything, he put numbered cards next to each object, which Burton photographed in situ, lighting his pictures with two portable three thousand–candlepower lamps. The draftsmen followed with a scale plan, drawing on every object in its position in the tomb. Only then were the artifacts—starting with a painted casket—carried out on padded wooden stretchers.

The Valley of the Kings became like a little village, with Carter and his team using a variety of nearby tombs for different purposes. Burton set up a darkroom in KV55, the tomb that had held the Amarna cache. He hung a pair of heavy black curtains over the entrance, and posted a boy outside with his watch, to call out the minutes so he'd know when to take out each plate[*] and put it in the fixing bath.

KV4, originally built for Rameses XI, was already established as a "luncheon tomb"—the sloping floor leveled with earth so that the wine wouldn't slide off the table. And most importantly, the tomb of Seti II, tucked beneath overhanging cliffs in a remote corner of the valley, became Lucas's storeroom and laboratory. The secluded spot could be protected from visitors, and was sheltered and cool (relatively—the temperature inside was still a steady 80° F). The space was a long, narrow passage—three hundred feet long by just twelve feet wide. The farther recesses—past where the electric lights could reach—were used for storage, while the upper part was used for restoration work. Here, Lucas set up wooden trestle tables as well as benches and shelves filled with bottles of his favorite conservation materials, including acetone, paraffin, celluloid solution, and beeswax. You could smell the chemicals while you were still walking up the path to the lab.

---

[*] Photography has changed a bit since the 1920s. Burton took his pictures directly onto glass plate negatives, rather than film.

Trying to stabilize and conserve the objects from Tutankhamun's tomb was horrendously difficult as they were fragile and liable to fall apart when moved. Sandals of patterned beadwork crumbled to the touch, leaving just a handful of loose beads. Funerary bouquets needed three or four sprayings of celluloid solution before they could be moved. It took Mace three weeks to empty a single casket of the king's clothing—one robe alone sported over three thousand gold sequins and twelve thousand blue beads, all in danger of falling off.

Work inside the tomb was just as tricky. Because the objects were in such a tangled mess, it was hard to remove one thing without disturbing everything else. Carter described it as like "a gigantic game of spillikins," for which he had to devise an elaborate system of props and supports.[11]

As he cleared the antechamber, it became clear that much of its messy state was the result of ancient robbers, who it seemed had indeed broken into the tomb. Helping him to interpret the clues they left behind was Lucas, who happened to be an expert in forensics and crime scene investigations. In one trial, Lucas had identified the poison on the tip of an arrow used in a murder. Another time, he calculated the trajectory of a bullet that a British soldier had accidentally fired from a train, killing a passenger in an adjacent compartment. The bullet deflected off ironwork in a station back through the window of the train—Lucas calculated where the bullet must have struck and identified the mark.[12]

The multiple seals on the tomb doors showed that this crime scene had been broken into twice, both within just a few years of Tutankhamun's burial. The thieves were clearly in a rush, and only able to take small, portable objects. They upturned boxes and tipped their contents over the floor, looking for small gold items. The antechamber had later been hastily tidied, with objects randomly pushed back into boxes and the lids jammed shut. But the annex was just as the robbers had left it, with stuff all over the floor. There was jewelry missing, arrows with their metal points broken off, and a wooden pedestal from which a gold statuette had been ripped away. A shawl, tied into a knot with a handful of solid gold rings inside, had been dropped and left behind, suggesting the looters were disturbed during their plundering—perhaps even caught red-handed in the tomb.

≡

*Tut-ankh-Amen though dead yet liveth and reigneth in
Thebes and Luxor today . . . One cannot escape the
name of Tut-ankh-Amen anywhere. It is shouted in the
streets, whispered in the hotels, while the local shops
advertise Tut-ankh-Amen art, Tut-ankh-Amen hats,
Tut-ankh-Amen curios, Tut-ankh-Amen photographs,
and tomorrow probably genuine Tut-ankh-Amen
antiquities . . . Slight acquaintances buttonhole one and
tell of dreams they had yesterday of Tut-ankh-Amen.
There is a dance tonight at which the first piece is to be a
Tut-ankh-Amen rag.*

—*NEW YORK TIMES*, FEBRUARY 18, 1923

TO LEARN ABOUT what happened in the early days after finding Tutankhamun's tomb, Carter himself is the main source of information, along with accounts of a few other privileged observers. But once news of the discovery got out, that changed dramatically, and suddenly we can watch the events unfold through hundreds of different pairs of eyes. The newspapers took each day's developments to fascinated audiences around the world, and Tutankhamun's story was no longer just about what archaeologists were getting up to inside his tomb. He had become an international phenomenon.

Tourists and journalists flocked to Luxor. They came from Europe and the United States in the thousands, crossing the Atlantic on steamers with names like the *Homeric*, *Empress of Scotland*, and *Mauretania*. The telegraph office at Luxor was so deluged by newspaper dispatches that three direct lines had to be laid between Luxor and Cairo, while an emergency hospital was converted into a telegraph office for presswork. Tourist shops sold out of cameras, films, and books on Egypt's history. Luxor's two biggest hotels set up tents in their gardens, with their guests sleeping on army cots.

Each day, these visitors crossed the river on wooden sailing boats called feluccas. They headed into the Valley of the Kings by donkey, sand cart, or horse-drawn cab, and made themselves at home for the day, sitting on a wall around the top of Tutankhamun's tomb as they waited for something to happen. About once a day, Carter's team brought out the most recently retrieved objects and carried them in convoy to the lab—they looked like casualties of war on their wooden stretchers, wrapped in surgical bandages and fixed with safety pins. Reporters whipped out their notebooks, tourists aimed their cameras, and a lane had to be cleared for the procession to pass through.

Carter himself was bombarded with letters and telegrams—congratulations, offers of assistance from tomb planning to personal valeting, requests for souvenirs, offers of money for everything from moving picture rights to the copyright on Egyptian fashions of dress. He was given advice on how to preserve antiquities and how to appease evil spirits. Shoemakers wanted the design of the royal slippers, and provisions dealers wanted parcels of mummified foods—apparently they expected them to be canned.

Tutankhamun "is as well known now as the Kaiser used to be," announced the *New York Times* on January 27, "and while Mr. Ford may still be in the lead, the space between them is small."[13]

Beyond the race to cash in on newfound "Tutmania," there was also increasing excitement about the prospect of entering the king's burial chamber and finding his mummy—finally, a chance to find out how an Egyptian pharaoh was actually laid to rest. Experts speculated about what state the mummy might be found in: Winlock predicted that "it will be one of the most perfect examples of its kind which has come down to us,"[14] while others feared the body was already desecrated, or that ancient priests had hidden it elsewhere.

By February, Carter realized that what he had thought were rolls of papyri were actually folded loincloths. It was a blow for historians, as no other texts were found in the tomb. And it made a scientific examination of the king's body even more important. With no letters, journals, or archives that could throw light on Tutankhamun's reign or the times in which he lived, any historical information would now have to come from the mummy itself. For example, it wasn't known how long Tutankhamun ruled for, or how he died. Children's clothing and furniture in the tomb suggested he died young,* but some experts maintained that the burial chamber would contain the mummy of an elderly man.

There was also a heartfelt debate over what should be done with the mummy, if it was found. Although most other royal mummies had been

---

* Labels on wine jars from the tomb also suggest a short reign, as none of the wine dates from later than the ninth year of Tutankhamun's rule, but that wasn't known at this point (as the wine jars were in the burial chamber and the annex, which hadn't yet been cleared).

taken to the Cairo Museum, the locals, hoping that Tutankhamun would become a powerful tourist attraction, wanted him to stay in his tomb.

Celebrities from scientists to writers had other ideas. Henry Rider Haggard, a popular author of adventure novels, argued that the mummies of all the pharaohs, including Tutankhamun, should be sealed with concrete inside the Great Pyramid at Giza. "Presently [Tutankhamun] too, may be stripped like the great Rameses and many other monarchs very mighty in his day and laid half naked to rot in a glass case in the museum at Cairo," he wrote in outrage.[15] "Is this decent? Is it doing as we would be done by?" After examining the mummies, he said, archaeologists should "hide them away again forever, as we ourselves would be hidden away."

Eminent archaeologist Flinders Petrie's response to the suggestion was withering. "Why spoil the great pyramid by blocking up one of the chambers?" he asked, arguing that there was no point getting sentimental about the fate of the pharaohs and their tombs when almost all of them had been plundered by the ancient Egyptians themselves.[16] To take the remains to Cairo's damper climate would be devastating, argued Petrie, but he didn't think Tutankhamun's mummy would be safe if left in the tomb. He suggested building a museum for all the royal mummies in the dry mountains of Thebes—with the small matter of a garrison of fifty-plus men to protect it from thieves.

Other distinguished archaeologists argued that the mummy should stay put, while in London the debate reached the highest political circles. Questions in the British House of Commons included whether the government would push for Tutankhamun's body to remain in his tomb, and whether they had any proof that the body was really there. Ronald McNeill, undersecretary for foreign affairs, answered no on both counts.[17]

Eventually Carnarvon stepped in. Unless the Egyptian government insisted on taking the mummy to Cairo, "Tutankhamun's body will be treated with utmost reverence and will be left lying in the sarcophagus unmoved from the spot where he has lain for three thousand years," he wrote in The Times.[18] "I have not yet discussed the point, nor do I view with favor the somewhat unwholesome and morbid taste which some people seem to enjoy of looking at mummies exposed in glass cases in museums."

Ordinary people, however, seemed deeply concerned about the idea of disturbing Tutankhamun at all. A correspondent to the London Times compared the corpse to that of Britain's not-long deceased queen: "I wonder how many of us would like to think that in the year, say, 5923, the tomb of Queen Victoria would be invaded by a party of foreigners who robbed it of its contents, took the body of the great Queen from the mausoleum . . . and exhibited it to all and sundry."[19]

In the United States, a writer for the *New York Times* was even more upset: "It does not seem to have entered anyone's thoughts to be shocked at the desecration of the tomb of the great King Tutankhamun. Science having abolished the Supreme and given omniscience to the atom is no doubt suitably employed in the ghoulish task of rifling an ancient tomb. It would be more becoming to Christian nations to take the bodies of the priests and kings now lying in the defilement of their public museums and reverently restore them to their sacred resting places."[20]

As the cultural historian Christopher Frayling put it in his 1992 book *The Face of Tutankhamun,* "The balance of opinion was that the archaeologists were transgressing a deeply felt taboo, and they would surely pay for it. Like Drs Faustus, Frankenstein and Jekyll . . . the scientists who dug in the sand would be destroyed by the results of their researches, because they had gone *too far.*"[21]

≡≡≡

BUT CARTER HAD NO INTENTION of stopping. By mid-February, the antechamber of the tomb had been cleared and swept, except for the two guardian statues on either side of the sealed door. It was time to see what was beyond it. Carter arranged a grand opening on February 16, with a series of important figures invited to view the inside of an Egyptian king's burial chamber: the first time such an extraordinary spectacle had ever been witnessed by modern humanity.

Except that it wasn't. That morning, Carnarvon drove to the Valley for the opening with his half-brother Mervyn and his daughter Evelyn. According to Mervyn's diary,[22] Evelyn leaned over to him and whispered something "under strictest promise of secrecy . . . They had both been into the Second Chamber!"

After discovering the sealed doorway, Carter's little group had apparently been unable to resist reopening the sealed door where robbers had previously broken through, and had crept inside for a sneak preview. It's not clear when, but it was probably shortly after the tomb was discovered. Evelyn also alludes to the episode in a letter to Carter, written on December 26—six weeks before the official opening—in which she tells him of her father's continuing excitement about the "Holy of Holies" (the burial chamber). "I can never thank you sufficiently for allowing me to enter its precincts," she adds. "It was the *Great Moment* of my life."[23]

Carter never publicly admitted to the break-in, but many years later, Lucas wrote in a couple of scholarly articles that Carter told him he did indeed make a hole in the wall, then resealed it afterward, covering the area with a basket lid and reeds so that no one would suspect.[24, 25] After his faux pas with Lord Cromer at Deir el-Bahri twenty years earlier, perhaps Carter can be forgiven for wanting to check what was beyond the door before arranging the grand opening.

Now, what he and his friends had seen was to be revealed to the world. There were about twenty privileged spectators. As well as Carter and the Carnarvons, and the rest of Carter's team, there were Egyptologists, antiquities officials and politicians, including Pierre Lacau (the latest director of the antiquities service), Sir William Garstin, and a number of high-ranking Egyptian officials. After dining in the luncheon tomb, the party assembled in front of Tutankhamun's tomb at a quarter past two.

"We are going to have a concert, Carter is going to sing a song," announced Carnarvon, glancing nervously at the assembled journalists.[26] The VIPs removed their coats and filed down the steep passage into the small antechamber, where rows of chairs had been set up for them, and the guardian statues had been covered with wooden planking, with a raised platform between them that looked like a stage. Under the glare of two electric lamps, Carter mounted the platform and attacked the top of the sealed doorway with a chisel, carefully chipping away the plaster and small stones. Within about ten minutes, he had a hole big enough to shine an electric torch through. But all he could see, about two feet from the doorway, was a solid wall of gold.

After that, the going got tougher. The door was made of huge slabs of stone, some precariously balanced, which took about two hours to clear. The air was hot and close, and the atmosphere horribly tense. The clink of the hammer and chisel echoed around the walls. At one point, Carnarvon retreated outside for a cigarette, his face pale and his forehead dripping with sweat. But he couldn't bear to miss anything, and threw it away after two minutes to go back into the tomb. Not everyone was so excited, though—one elderly Pasha was heard to murmur that he would far rather be in his club in Cairo.

Once the door had been removed, it became clear that the golden wall was the side of a huge gilt shrine that almost filled the chamber, built to protect the king's mummy in its sarcophagus. The floor of the burial chamber was about four feet lower than that of the antechamber. Carter lowered himself down into the narrow space between the door and the shrine, carrying a lamp, and edged cautiously to the corner of the shrine. Two alabaster vases blocked his way, so he passed them back to the antechamber, at which point Carnarvon and the portly Lacau squeezed down to join him.

The shrine was around seventeen by eleven feet, leaving a gap of about two feet on each side. Its roof almost touched the ceiling. It was made of wood, completely covered with gold, with inlays of blue faience* on its sides and covered with magic symbols to ensure its strength and safety. On the floor on the far side, eleven oars were carefully laid out—the magic oars the king would need to ferry himself across the waters of the underworld.

The main concern was whether the ancient thieves had penetrated the shrine. At its eastern end, round to the right, was a pair of enormous folding doors, closed and bolted but not sealed. The three men drew back the bolts and swung open the doors with an ominous creak. Immediately, they saw a second shrine. Between the two were some alabaster ornaments, and a little painted pot topped by a cat with a pink tongue that Carnarvon couldn't take his eyes off. But more importantly, these doors were bolted, sealed, and tied up with string. The robbers had not made it beyond this point. Tutankhamun must still be lying there, intact.

Admitting to "a feeling of intrusion,"[27] the men reclosed the doors and carried on around the shrine. In the far corner of the chamber, they found yet another low doorway, leading into a fourth small room. There was no door and as they peeped in, they saw some of the greatest treasures yet. Facing the doorway, on the far side, was what Carter described as "the most beautiful monument I have ever seen."[28] It was a large, shrine-shaped chest, covered in gold, topped with a cornice of cobras. At each corner stood four golden statues, facing inward but looking out over their shoulders—slender, graceful goddesses, with their arms protectively outstretched.

---

* Sometimes described as the first high-tech ceramic, faience was a brightly colored glaze (usually blue-green) made by heating finely ground sand, lime, and salt or ash. It was probably intended to mimic hard-to-get gems and precious stones.

In front of the chest was the black figure of a jackal, the god Anubis, resting on a portable wooden sled and swathed in a linen cloth. Staring straight at them, he was elegant and alert, with golden eyes, curved claws, and huge bat-like ears. Otherwise, the room was filled with shrine-shaped boxes, caskets of ivory and wood, miniature coffins, and a profusion of model boats.

Carnarvon and Lacau returned to the antechamber, after which the other guests were admitted in pairs. Carter stood in the far room (which he named the treasury) to guide them, enjoying the succession of dazed, bewildered faces. As each pair peered in through the doorway, he lifted one of the box lids with a flourish, to reveal a sumptuous ivory fan, plumed with perfectly preserved ostrich feathers.

At a quarter past five, the party filed out of the tomb, hot, dusty, and disheveled. "The very Valley seemed to have changed for us and taken on a more personal aspect," wrote Carter.[29] "We had been given the Freedom."

The following days were given up to a succession of high-profile visits to the tomb, as Luxor hummed with excitement. According to the *New York Times*, "the west bank of the Nile was black with masses of vehicles and people."[30] Every horse- and ass-drawn carriage in the region had been commandeered to take the officials and guests from the river up to the Valley, with herds of donkeys and crowds of donkey boys and hangers on, not to mention no fewer than seven motorcars, and a motorcycle with a sidecar. The water was congested with feluccas and motor launches, and throngs of spectators lined the river on both sides to watch the various celebrities on their way past. One highlight was the passage of the queen of the Belgians, dressed in white with a gray fox stole, veil, and broad-brimmed hat.

Each eminent guest insisted on squeezing round between the shrine and the wall, with two or three of the least slender getting stuck and needing help. "Fortunately the tabernacle is admirably built of wood," said the *New York Times*.[31] "Not every similar structure built today would last 3,000 years and stand as much pushing."

On February 28, the tomb was closed for the season, and Carter's team focused on their work in the lab, cataloging and conserving the hundreds of objects retrieved from the antechamber so far. With no new discoveries, the excitement and press attention started to ease off. But in mid-March, something happened that changed everything. Lord Carnarvon got bitten by a mosquito.

CHAPTER FOUR

DEATH ON
SWIFT WINGS

═══

L ORD CARNARVON KNOCKED the top off the mosquito bite, on his left cheek, while shaving in his suite at the Winter Palace hotel. It became infected, and thanks to Carnarvon's already weak constitution, the infection soon developed into blood poisoning. On March 14, he traveled to Cairo, planning to head home from there, but his condition grew rapidly worse and he developed a high fever. Five years before the discovery of antibiotics, there was little that his doctors could do but watch and wait.

After seeming to recover slightly, the patient relapsed on March 28. His temperature rose again and the infection reached his lungs, causing pneumonia. At two o'clock in the morning on April 5, 1923, with his wife, daughter, and son at his bedside, Carnarvon died.

And so began the legend of Tutankhamun's curse. Even before Carnarvon's death, the newspapers were full of suggestions that he had been afflicted not by any natural illness, but by the mummy's dreadful revenge.

A mystical writer called Marie Corelli (her real name was Mary MacKay) was one of the first to capitalize on Carnarvon's misfortune. She declared that she had personally warned the Earl of the dangers of entering the tomb, and said she wasn't surprised that disaster might befall "those daring explorers who rifle the tombs of dead monarchs." She cited an ancient book in her possession on Egyptian history, which apparently stated that some of the pharaohs were buried with "divers secret potions enclosed in boxes in such wise that they who touched them shall not know how they came to suffer."[1]

Other psychics followed, also claiming to have warned Carnarvon against working in the tomb. He had apparently replied: "If at this moment of my life all the mummies of Egypt were to warn me I would go on with my project just the same."[2]

Stories began to spread about written warnings that Carter had allegedly found in the tomb and suppressed. One rumor said that a clay tablet found over the tomb's entrance had read: "Death shall come on swift wings to whoever toucheth the tomb of Pharaoh." Carter supposedly buried it in the sand in case it scared his laborers into stopping their work. Another story featured a reed torch that was indeed found at the entrance to the treasury, with an inscription: "It is I who hinder the sand from choking flame. I have set aflame the desert, I have caused the path to be mistaken. I am for the protection of Osiris."[3] A fictional extra line was added: "And I will call all those who cross this threshold into the sacred precincts of the King who lives for ever."

Although Lord Carnarvon's death irrevocably linked the "mummy's curse" with Tutankhamun, the idea itself is of course much older. It doesn't stem particularly from ancient Egypt though, and there are very few documented examples from real tombs. Most of the known written warnings are from the Old Kingdom, around the twenty-fourth and twenty-fifth centuries BC. They are found in nonroyal tombs rather than those of the pharaohs, and warn for example against removing stones or bricks. The threatened vengeance tends to be promised only for the afterlife, however.* In ancient times, the greatest deterrent against robbing a tomb was earthly reprisal, not fear of a curse—anyone caught looting was punished or executed for theft.

The curse myth as we would recognize it today began instead in nineteenth-century England. According to Egyptologist Dominic Montserrat, who investigated its origins, the trail leads back to a little-known English author in the 1820s called Jane Loudon Webb. After attending a bizarre

---

* But not always: a Sixth-Dynasty official, Meni, warned any potential tomb violator that the crocodile will be against him in the water, and the snake on land. This punishment was to come from the gods, though, not Meni himself.

"striptease" show near London's Piccadilly Circus, in which Egyptian mummies were publicly unwrapped, she was inspired to write an early science fiction book called *The Mummy*. Set in the twenty-second century, it featured a vengeful mummy who threatened to strangle the book's hero, a young scholar called Edric.

In 1869, the author of *Little Women*, Louisa May Alcott, developed the concept in a short story called *Lost in a Pyramid*. An explorer inside a pyramid uses a mummified princess as a torch, and by the light of the burning mummy, steals a gold box containing three strange-looking seeds. After returning home to America, he gives the seeds to his fiancée who plants them. She wears the flowers at their wedding, but as she inhales their scent, she transforms into a living mummy. The curse idea was subsequently copied by other novelists in Britain and America, until Corelli applied it to the real-life discovery of Tutankhamun's tomb.

The newspapers loved the story, running daily updates on the arguments surrounding Carnarvon's death. Ernest Budge, keeper of Egyptian antiquities at the British Museum in London, was quick to describe Corelli's tales as "bunkum," while his assistant, H. R. Hall, added that if there really were a curse on ancient tombs, "there would not be any archaeologists left today."[4]

Emotions ran high. The adventure writer Rider Haggard described the curse idea as "dangerous nonsense" because "it goes to swell the rising tide of superstition which at present seems to be overflowing the world. Do you suppose that God Almighty would permit a Pharaoh, who after all was only a man with a crown on his head, to murder people by magical means, thousands of years after his own death?"[5]

But Sir Arthur Conan Doyle, creator of the fictional detective Sherlock Holmes, supported the curse theory. Evil spirits associated with the tomb could have led Carnarvon to his death, he argued. "There are many legends about the powers of the old Egyptians, and I know I wouldn't care to go fooling about their tombs and mummies," he said.[6] "I didn't say that some Egyptian spirit did kill Carnarvon, but I think it is possible. There are many malevolent spirits."

Conan Doyle, as opposed to his rational hero Holmes, was a leading figure in the popular spiritualist movement, which held that spirits of the dead (sometimes called "elementals") could communicate with the living, for example through séances. He also had an answer to why Tutankhamun's curse hadn't targeted other members of the excavation team, such as Carter.

"It is nonsense to say that because 'elementals' do not harm everybody, therefore they do not exist. One might as well say that because bulldogs do not bite everybody, therefore bulldogs do not exist!"[7]

Carnarvon's son seems to have bought into the curse idea too, saying in interviews that at the moment his father died, Cairo suffered a mysterious power cut, and that Carnarvon's beloved terrier, Susie, let out a long howl back home in Highclere and dropped dead at exactly two in the morning, the moment of her owner's death. Of course, inexplicable power cuts were common in Cairo in those days, and it's unclear who would have been around to witness the dog's sudden death in the early hours (not to mention that 2:00 A.M. in the UK would actually be 4:00 A.M. in Cairo[8]).

On April 16, Lady Carnarvon left Egypt with her husband's remains, carrying him home on a P&O steamer. Several fellow passengers canceled their passage, fearing the body's presence might cause some misfortune to befall the ship. Meanwhile, back in Britain, Carnarvon's death caused panic among collectors of Egyptian antiquities. The British Museum was deluged by mummy-related parcels, containing shriveled hands, feet, ears, and heads, as well as wooden, limestone, and ceramic figures and other relics, posted to the museum by owners fearful that they too might become victims of the curse.

Even among those who didn't believe in the curse itself, Carnarvon's death strengthened a feeling that perhaps the dead were better left undisturbed. One letter to the *New York Times* quoted a story by H. G. Wells, *The Treasure in the Forest*.[9] Two British men steal gold from a dead Chinaman, only to find that it is poisoned, and it kills them too.

Carter himself had no time for any such nonsense, however: "It is rather too much to ask me to believe that some spook is keeping watch and ward over the dead Pharaoh, ready to wreak vengeance on anyone who goes too near."[10] He wrote in his notebook that if there was any curse, it took the form of "Messrs Creepy, Crawly, Biteum and Co.," the company of nasty insects that bit him when he was out in the desert.[11]

Carter had traveled to Cairo to be with Carnarvon before he died, but he returned to Luxor on April 15 to finish the season's work. While he was away, Mace, Lucas, Callender, and Burton had been photographing, recording, and conserving the rest of the objects from the antechamber, and over the next few weeks, they packed the full haul—around five hundred items—into cases for the trip to the Egyptian Museum by barge.

First, though, the treasures had to be carried across the five winding miles to the river. Carter and his workmen used the hand-pushed railway cars that had proved so useful in the grunt work of earlier seasons. There were only ten lengths of rail, so they had to pick up track from the back and move it to the front so the cars could move forward, in scorching temperatures that made the metal rails almost too hot to touch. But they covered the distance in fifteen hours (plus an overnight stop), and soon the cases were on the boat to Cairo.

After helping to unpack the objects for display, Carter traveled home to London after the most incredible archaeological season he could ever have imagined. And the mummy that had caused so much furor got to rest in peace for one more summer.

———

THAT PEACE WAS SOON disturbed by hammering and swearing in several different languages. Tutankhamun's burial chamber, for so long a black, silent sanctuary, was now infested with loud, sweaty men stripped to vests and trousers, their faces glistening white under the glaring electric lights. The mummy's golden shrines were systematically and very ungracefully being taken apart.

Work had restarted in November 1923. It turned out there were four shrines, fitting tightly inside one another. They formed reportedly the largest area of plated gold in existence in the world, and it took Carter's team two months of tense, back-breaking work to dismantle them. The men were working in a horribly confined space, squeezing like weasels between unyielding rock and fragile three-thousand-year-old wood. Gradually, they peeled away the pharaoh's protective layers, easing the delicate woodwork apart "as gently as a hospital nurse."[12]

Unlike other parts of Tutankhamun's tomb, which have bare walls, the walls of his burial chamber are brightly painted with scenes and inscriptions. As Carter removed the bulky shrines, he got his first proper look at these paintings.

One scene, on the east wall, shows the king's funeral procession, with twelve mourners in white tunics pulling his mummy to the tomb. The mummy lies on a wooden bed, or bier, which is in turn on a sledge, and is covered by a shrine decorated with strings of flowers (or "festoons of garlands," as Carter delightfully put it[13]).

The burial party would have walked from Tutankhamun's mortuary chapel on the riverbank, where his body was embalmed, accompanied by mourning women with disheveled hair and exposed breasts. The mummy would have been followed by the canopic chest containing Tutankhamun's internal organs, and servants carrying his possessions—furniture, clothing, jewelry, chariots—everything he would need for the afterlife. When the procession reached the entrance to the tomb, the mummy would have been placed upright on a small heap of sand and subjected to various rituals, traditionally carried out by the king's eldest son, who was to succeed his throne.

But Tutankhamun didn't have a son. On the north wall of the burial chamber, facing you as you look in, Tutankhamun's successor, King Ay, is shown dressed in a leopard skin, enacting one of the key parts of the funeral ritual—the Opening of the Mouth ceremony, in which the mummy is magically brought back to life. The scene is unique, because in most royal tombs, the priest carrying out the ritual isn't named. Ay wasn't of royal birth; he had been a high-ranking official under Tutankhamun's revolutionary predecessor, Akhenaten. The unusual scene suggested to Egyptologists that in order to legitimize his claim to the throne, he had needed publicly to act the part of the loyal son. And it led to the first suggestions of foul play in Tutankhamun's death—that perhaps the king had been murdered by a scheming, power-hungry Ay.

After the Opening of the Mouth ceremony, Tutankhamun was placed into his coffins and sarcophagus, and the golden shrines erected around him before the tomb was filled and the door sealed. On the west wall was an excerpt from the journey that the Egyptians believed Tutankhamun's spirit would then take.

A pharaoh's route through the underworld is commonly shown on the walls of royal tombs from the Eighteenth Dynasty, in a set of scenes known as the Book of Amduat (which translates as "that which is in the afterworld"). They tell the story of Ra, the Egyptian sun god, who travels through the underworld each night, from sunset in the west to sunrise in the east. The dead pharaoh was said to take the same journey, ultimately to become one with Ra and live forever.

The Amduat contains scenes from the twelve hours of the night, and details all of the challenges that the sun god will encounter, mapped out like the ultimate adventure game. Because Tutankhamun's tomb is so small, there was only room on the wall for the first hour, the transition between day and night on the western horizon. If there had been space, further scenes would show Ra—accompanied by various other deities and deceased souls—

rowing across the "Waters of Osiris" (hence the need for the magic oars around Tutankhamun's golden shrines), and navigating dark zigzag pathways on the sandy, snake-infested island of the hawk god Sokar.

Eventually, Ra reaches the tomb of Osiris, king of the underworld, where the two briefly unite, a key moment that rejuvenates them both. Then there's just the small matter of Ra defeating his archenemy, a giant serpent called Apep who is out to annihilate all of creation, before rowing back through the waters toward the eastern horizon, ready to rise again as the new day's sun.

=====

THROUGHOUT THIS TIME, Carter's work was impeded by having to show a constant stream of journalists and other visitors around the tomb, and make repeated trips to Cairo to discuss his project with the Egyptian government. Since Carnarvon's death, Carter was digging under the name of the Earl's widow, Almina, though she didn't take an active interest in what he was up to. The circumstances were difficult—Carter was upset at having to spend so much time as a tour guide, while much of the international, including Egyptian, press was waging a campaign against his team in protest at their policy of only talking to *The Times* of London. Without Carnarvon's clout and diplomatic skills to help smooth things over, Carter's relations with the government were rapidly falling apart.

By the beginning of February, though, Carter's men finally managed to remove the last shrine from the burial chamber, revealing a huge stone chest, or sarcophagus,* of a very tough rock called quartzite. The decoration on the pinkish stone was understated yet elegant, with reliefs of four goddesses (Isis and her sister Nephthys, plus two others called Neith and Selquet) carved onto each corner, their outstretched winged arms protecting the sides and ends of the casket. It was beautiful and in perfect condition. If you rapped the walls of the sarcophagus with your knuckles, it rang like a bell.†

---

* Ironically, the word "sarcophagus" derives from the Greek for "flesh-eater," after a kind of limestone that the Greeks believed would consume or decompose the flesh of a corpse interred within it, and hence was used for coffins.

† As described in a private letter from the anatomist Douglas Derry, who later carried out an autopsy on the mummy, to his son Hugh.

On February 12, Carter held another opening ceremony full of VIPs. The sarcophagus lid was a huge slab of stone weighing more than one and a quarter tons. Rather than quartzite, it was made of cheaper granite and had broken in two in ancient times—perhaps it was dropped during Tutankhamun's funeral. But with a delicate pulley system, Carter raised the whole thing as one piece. There was silence as the lid rose. Light shone into the sarcophagus for the first time in 3,300 years, but the spectators couldn't make out any details and struggled at first to make sense of what they were seeing. Then they realized that the contents were covered by linen shrouds. Carter rolled them back, and "a gasp of wonderment escaped our lips, so gorgeous was the sight that met our eyes."[14]

A glorious golden figure filled the sarcophagus: it was a man-shaped coffin, seven feet long and made of wood that was covered in gold. It lay on a wooden bier, just as shown in the tomb paintings a few feet away. Its arms were folded across its chest, hands clasping a flail and crooked scepter made of gold and faience. The twin heads of a sacred cobra and vulture—protectors of Upper and Lower Egypt, respectively, and important symbols of a pharaoh—were mounted on its golden forehead.

To the Egyptians, this was Tutankhamun as a god. It was a portrait of the king, but not as a man—it represented his transformed immortal state, physically perfect and eternally young, with flesh of gold.[*] But in contrast to this eternal, divine figure, there was also a sign of human grief and frailty. A tiny wreath of olive leaves and cornflowers had been placed on the king's forehead, with fragile petals that still had a tinge of blue.

To the observers at Carter's ceremony, this seemed far more than a mummy case; it felt as if they were in the presence of the actual body of some great golden person lying in state. In the world above, empires had risen and fallen; wars and natural disasters had wracked the land; civilizations had sprung up, developed, and disappeared; major religions had come into existence and been superseded by others. Through all of it, just a few feet beneath the earth, this forgotten king had lain here in his sarcophagus, his golden face and obsidian eyes staring up toward the sky.

===

---

* The gods are described in ancient Egyptian inscriptions as having golden flesh.

IT WAS AS CLOSE as Carter would get to Tutankhamun for over a year. The day after the opening of the sarcophagus, he had arranged for the wives of his team to view the coffin, but early that morning he received a letter from Pierre Lacau, who had succeeded Maspero as head of the antiquities service in 1914, saying that the government forbade the women's visit. For Carter and his colleagues, who already felt that the government was doing everything possible to hinder rather than assist them, it was one insult too far. Carter posted a note on the notice board of the Winter Palace hotel.

"Owing to impossible restrictions and discourtesies on the part of the Public Works Dept and its antiquity service, all my collaborators, in protest, have refused to work any further upon the scientific investigations of the discoveries of the tomb of Tutankhamun."[15]

In other words, they were on strike.

Carter had the keys to the tomb, but the government responded by putting its own locks on the door, meaning that no one could get in. In the meantime, the heavy sarcophagus lid remained suspended precariously above the golden coffin. A few days later, the antiquities service and police forced open the tomb doors with chisels, crowbars, and hacksaws, lowered the lid, and changed the locks.

A lengthy court case followed. Although Carter's strike was triggered by a fairly petty dispute involving his team's wives, the real problems ran much deeper. As well as the issue of how many visitors should be allowed in the tomb, and who owned the press rights, there was an argument over who would end up with its treasures. Under Maspero, foreign private excavators such as Carnarvon had commonly kept half of the antiquities they recovered in return for paying for excavations. Lacau was keen to clamp down on this practice, much to the horror of foreign archaeologists from both sides of the Atlantic.

Various parties were desperately trying to negotiate a settlement, figuring that in the end the two sides had to work things out. Carter couldn't continue his work without the permission of the authorities. And the antiquities service had no one else who possessed the skills or inclination to take on such a huge task as the tomb. In March 1924, Lady Carnarvon gave up any claim to the tomb's contents, and the two sides seemed close to agreement. But then Carter's lawyer, speaking in court, likened the antiquities service's actions in breaking into the tomb to the action of "bandits." It was an unfortunate choice of word. In Egyptian culture, this was considered a mortal insult, and all negotiations subsequently broke down.

Meanwhile, Carter sailed to the United States on the *Berengaria* to lecture on Tutankhamun—his Norfolk accent helping to dispel Americans' widespread belief that he was in fact American. He lectured to thousands in sellout events, for example at Carnegie Hall in New York, where he speculated about the state in which Tutankhamun's mummy would be found— he predicted that Tutankhamun was about eighteen years old when he died, and that the king's body would be "not wrapped but literally canned in gold."[16] He must have been wondering if he would ever get back into the tomb to find out.

In December, Carter finally signed an agreement with the Egyptian government to restart his work, and headed straight for the tomb to check its contents. Everything was in order except for a few tools missing from the antechamber and a linen pall, studded with gold rosettes, that had originally hung over the roof of the second shrine. It had been left on the ground outside the laboratory tomb and was now hopelessly charred and decayed.

Carter spent the end of that season conserving objects already removed from the tomb and packed off nineteen more cases of objects to Cairo before heading home to London. He returned in October 1925 with just one aim in mind. At last, he would reveal Tutankhamun's mummy.

===

THE LID OF THE GOLD-COVERED COFFIN was slowly hoisted without mishap to reveal a second coffin similar to the first, except that its gold coating was inlaid with colorful glass: tiny arrow-shaped blues and reds that imitated turquoise, carnelian, and lapis lazuli. Carter's men raised the outer shell and second coffin out of the sarcophagus together—a huge weight, much heavier than Carter had thought possible—then slid wooden planks underneath and laid it on top of the sarcophagus.

The second coffin had no handles, and fit so closely into the outer shell that you couldn't even slide a little finger between them. It took some ingenuity to figure out how to extract it. In the end, Carter eased out some bronze pins by which the second coffin's lid was fastened down, just by a quarter of an inch, and tied wire around them. He used the wire to hold that coffin in midair while he lowered the outer shell back into the sarcophagus, then quickly slipped a wooden tray under the suspended weight. Removing the second coffin lid revealed a third coffin of similar shape. For three millennia, a nest of four gilded wooden shrines, a quartzite sarcophagus, and three

tightly fitting coffins—his own miniature cosmos*—had protected Tutankhamun's mummy from an alien future. Now, only one layer was left.

The innermost coffin was different from the others. Just over six feet
long, it was made of solid gold. It was an enormous mass of pure bullion,
and an extravagance that the archaeologists had never dreamed of. It also
explained why the second coffin had been so heavy to lift. Based on the fact
that it took eight strong men to raise it, Carter estimated that the inner coffin
alone weighed at least eight hundred pounds. The body was elaborately
carved and inlaid, and the golden face was topped off by a blue beard,
cobra-and-vulture headdress, and a necklace glinting red, blue, and gold.
Covered in protective decoration, this coffin looked snug and safe at the
same time as impressive. It was the perfect spaceship for time travel.

Carter raised the lid to reveal—at last—the mummy itself. It was neatly
wrapped and decorated with a network of golden straps and bands, another
necklace, and a pair of golden hands, sewn to the linen wrappings, which
held a crook and flail.

And, of course, it was wearing a solid gold mask. Well, it's a helmet more
than a mask, as it covers the entire head as well as the top of the shoulders
and chest. Ancient Egyptians used to call this the "head of mystery." It allowed the wearer to see in the afterlife and to drive away any enemies or
hostile forces that might attack him, as well as giving the dead person divine
attributes—wearing it was described as "seeing with the head of a god."[17]

The golden face had eyes made of aragonite and obsidian, and eyelids
inlaid with blue glass to imitate lapis lazuli. The mask bore a blue-and-gold
striped headdress as well as a sad but tranquil expression, with its gaze set
firmly on the heavens. The features are recognizably those of Tutankhamun,
but as with the three coffins, they're also meant to show him as a god—
specifically Osiris, the ruler of the underworld.

Osiris was the prototype mummy. In Egyptian mythology, he was a
king whose jealous brother Seth killed him by putting him in a box—the
first coffin—and throwing it in the Nile, before later chopping his body up
and dispersing the pieces across Egypt. Osiris's devoted wife and sister Isis

---

* In his 2010 book *Egyptian Mummies*, John Taylor, a specialist in ancient Egyptian funerary archaeology
at the British Museum in London, argues that an Egyptian mummy's coffins were endowed with powerful
symbolic meaning that helped the occupant to be resurrected and to flourish in the life after death.
They provided a sacred environment for the eternal life of the occupant—a dwelling, shrine, body of
the mother-goddess Nut, and even a miniature replica of the entire cosmos.

tracked them all down and put him back together again; then the jackal-headed god Anubis wrapped the body in bandages and resurrected him. Osiris went on to become ruler of the underworld and judge of the dead. By associating himself with Osiris, Tutankhamun hoped to share his fate of resurrection, before joining Ra on his journey through the heavens.

On the second floor of today's Cairo museum is a side room with black-painted walls and a dusty, arched window, through which you can see the city's rooftops and hear the bustle of nearby Tahrir Square. This is where Tutankhamun's most precious treasures are now held. In the middle of the room, displayed at eye height on a dramatically lit pedestal, is his mask. It is without doubt the most recognizable image of this king; as a symbol of Egypt, it is rivaled only by the Great Pyramids.

And yet, when you look into this iconic face, the familiarity fades away—as do the urgent honks of gridlock traffic. It's truly beautiful, with a well-proportioned nose, gorgeous full lips, and the eternal blackness of those obsidian eyes, which stare right through you with placid resolve. I don't know if it's the rare experience of staring at so much solid gold, or the serene, exquisitely crafted features, but suddenly it's not so hard to believe in Tutankhamun as a god, still riding through the sky each day with the sun.

Back in 1925, though, it wasn't at all clear that the mask would ever make it to Cairo. During Tutankhamun's funeral, bucketfuls of sticky anointing resin had been poured over the mummy, which over the centuries congealed into a black, rock-hard mass. Thanks to this extremely effective glue, the mummy and mask were stuck fast inside the innermost gold coffin, which was in turn stuck inside the second coffin. The coffins and their contents were immovable. They might as well have been encased in a block of cement.

So Carter's next challenge was how on earth to get the mummy out. Lucas experimented on the black material in his lab but couldn't find anything that dissolved it easily; then he discovered that it melted with heat. It was time for Tutankhamun to fulfill his wish and come face to face with Ra. The workmen carried the two glued-together coffins up the tomb's sloping corridor, and left the whole lot in the blazing sun.

Safe underground, the mummy had enjoyed a constant environment of around 80°F for millennia. Now, its temperature soared to a roasting 150°F, atoms jangling in the heat. But Tutankhamun wasn't so keen on leaving his golden home. After several hours, the glue hadn't softened at all. It seemed there was only one way that the mummy was going to leave its coffin: in pieces.

CHAPTER FIVE

A BRUTAL POSTMORTEM

===

IT WASN'T YOUR AVERAGE AUTOPSY. Laid out in the dark, narrow entrance corridor to the tomb of Seti II, the subject was tightly glued inside his coffins, overlooked by impressively carved religious reliefs, and enveloped in the sweet, woody smell of resin.

A few feet away, the anatomist Douglas Derry stood upright, smartly dressed in a white jacket and spotted bow tie, and looked steadily into the camera. Alongside him, most of his companions were smiling—in particular Howard Carter, eyes gleaming, had the air of gleeful schoolboy struggling to contain himself. But Derry showed no hint of excitement; instead he looked solemn to the point of sternness. Which perhaps isn't surprising, seeing as he was about to cut open one of the world's most famous historical figures.

Maybe he was thinking of the time the royal mummy found in the nearby Amarna cache largely disintegrated at American excavator Theodore Davis's touch, with the loss of vital information about the identity of that king. Here the stakes were even higher. No one had ever seen an Egyptian pharaoh in his original burial trappings and finery. Probably no one ever would again. One wrong move from Derry and the only chance in history to study an intact royal mummy could be ruined.

The appointed day was November 11, 1925. At 9:45 A.M., the group had filed into this converted laboratory tomb, where Carter had laid out the mummy the day before, its coffins protected by a surgical-looking white sheet. This was a more modest affair than Carter's previous grand openings of the tomb and burial chamber, which had been full to the brim with royals and other notables and besieged by journalists desperate for a glimpse of the action. On this day, Carter and Derry were joined only by the big-bearded antiquities chief Pierre Lacau, anatomist Saleh Bey Hamdi,[*] the chemist Alfred Lucas, and a handful of Egyptian officials in fezzes and dark suits. But the glare of world's media was only a telegram away. And Harry Burton, hidden behind his bulky wooden camera, was capturing each important moment for posterity in black and white.

Once the first photo pose was over, the men gathered around the coffin. Derry removed his jacket and waistcoat—the powerful electric lights had pushed the temperature in the tomb well above 80°F—and hung them carefully over the back of a chair. He took out a blue school exercise book, and filled in the blanks on the front in neat pencil.

NAME: Tut Ankh Amon
CLASS: Royal
SUBJECT: Anatomy
SCHOOL YEAR: 1356 BC–1925 AD

The mummy was enclosed in an outer linen sheet, held in position by bandages passing round the shoulders, hips, knees, and ankles. But Derry saw immediately that he couldn't simply peel them off. The fabric was so badly decomposed, it crumbled to the touch. At Carter's suggestion he strengthened the wrappings by coating them in paraffin wax, and waited for it to cool.[1] It was time to make the first cut.

Nerves might have got to most people at this point. But it's unlikely that Derry allowed his hand to shake. During the First World War, he had served in the Royal Army Medical Corps; on the Western Front, in Belgium, he rescued wounded men under heavy shellfire with such gallantry and coolness that he was awarded the Military Cross. And when it came to study-

---

[*] Ex-director of the Kasr Al Ainy Medical School in Cairo, where Derry was professor of anatomy.

ing mummies, Derry was a world expert. He had arrived in the anatomy department of Kasr Al Ainy Medical School (now part of University of Cairo) in 1905 under the professorship of Grafton Elliot Smith, a brilliant but eccentric Australian anatomist who was pioneering the study of ancient human remains. As well as finding that the mummy from the Amarna cache was male—despite Davis's firm belief that it was Queen Tiye—Elliot Smith had carried out a tediously detailed but badly needed survey of all the royal mummies held in the Cairo Museum.[2]

One of Derry's first postings was with the Archaeological Survey of Nubia, in a remote area on Egypt's southern border, working with Elliot Smith and another young anatomist called Frederic Wood Jones. The project was a race against time to salvage as much archaeological information as possible about the ancient civilizations that had lived there, before the entire area was flooded by the raising of the first Aswan Dam across the Nile in 1907.

Between 1907 and 1911, the three anatomists worked in the barren heat of the desert, surrounded by evil swarms of dust and flies. Much to the bemusement of the Nubian locals, few of whom had ever seen a white person before, they used metal calipers to measure skeleton after skeleton excavated from the thousands of shallow graves that lined the Nile, noting the results on cards that were tinted blue to protect their eyes from the glare of the sun. In four seasons, living mainly on rice and canned sardines, the tiny team studied more than 20,000 sets of human remains. They noted the age, sex, and ethnic origins of the people who had lived there millennia before; cultural practices such as circumcision and attempts at embalming; and their causes of death, from childbirth and leprosy to beatings and battle wounds.

Two particularly gruesome trenches yielded the bodies of more than a hundred young men, hanged by the Romans, some with the noose still around their necks. The injuries they suffered caused the team to join the debate over the most humane methods of hanging, which at the time was raging back in Britain, with Wood Jones later carrying out a series of clandestine experiments that involved dropping cadavers down the lift shaft of St Thomas's Hospital in London.

When Elliot Smith subsequently took a job in London, Derry took over his professorship at the medical school in Cairo and soon became Egypt's go-to expert for any human remains discovered by archaeologists in the country, gradually amassing one of the largest collections of desiccated body parts in the world. He was particularly excited by his work at Giza, site of the Great Pyramids—he measured hundreds of mummies and skeletons in the nobles' graves there, and wrote enthusiastically to his ex-mentor about what he found.[3]

Elliot Smith was fascinated, if not obsessed, by the racial origins of these pyramid builders, because he saw them as the original creators of human civilization, who spread their cultural practices around the world. (Unfortunately for his theories, he didn't know that the pyramids and mummies being unearthed in other regions such as South America were separated from their Egyptian counterparts by thousands of years.) So Derry became very interested in such questions too. Unfortunately, his studies didn't say much about the origins of civilization. But he did find among other things that the eye orbits in the nobles' skulls were markedly elliptical—meaning that the slanted eyes shown in the artwork of their tombs weren't just an aesthetic style or the result of over-enthusiastic application of eyeliner, they reflected how the ancient Egyptians really looked.

When Carter needed someone he could rely on to unwrap King Tutankhamun, he chose Derry as the principal anatomist in Egypt—much to the annoyance of Elliot Smith, over in England, who thought he should have been asked ahead of his ex-student. Cheeks glistening with sweat, Derry leaned over and pushed his scalpel into the mummy's chest, just below the hefty golden mask, and slowly slid the blade all the way down to its toes. He peeled the two resulting flaps outward, and immediately saw the glint of gold.

Unlike the cached royal mummies, reburied with scarcely a scrap of jewelry, this king was smothered from head to foot in an awesome array of precious items, each precisely placed according to ancient beliefs and rites. Unfortunately, the bandages beneath the wax were in an even worse state of decay than those of the top layer. They resembled black crumbly charcoal, which made the operation a messy business—less orderly unwrapping, more treasure hunt in a barrel of ash.

It was a big disappointment. Derry had unwrapped mummies seven hundred years older than Tutankhamun, with bandages that were still so strong he couldn't tear them. And because the king had never been disturbed, hopes had been high that he might be pristine. The deterioration seemed to be caused by an unfortunate combination of damp conditions—from plaster still wet when the tomb was sealed and floodwater that had leaked in over the millennia—and the huge quantities of oils and unguents poured over the mummy at the funeral, which as well as gluing it inside the coffin, had eaten away at the bandages.*

Derry started at the feet and over the next five days worked slowly up toward the mummy's neck, delving through its protective cocoon layer by layer as Carter brandished his magnifying glass in delight. The economic value of the trinkets they unearthed was incalculable but what had Carter so enthused was their meaning—an unprecedented insight into the magic and rituals with which the ancient Egyptians sent a king to his grave.

Tutankhamun's feet sported gold sandals, with individual toe stalls engraved with nails and joints. Over his legs were gold bangles, a ceremonial gold apron, and, to Carter's surprise and excitement, a beautifully decorated gold dagger with an iron blade still bright and rust-free after three thousand years. It was one of three iron objects found on the mummy, which were the earliest examples of iron ever found in Egypt. The discovery suggested that iron was introduced into Egypt by the Hittites in Tutankhamun's time—an early indication of foreign influence, and as Carter saw it, an omen for the future: "one of the first steps in decline of the Egyptian Empire—the greatest empire of the Age of Bronze."[4]

Around Tutankhamun's waist was another golden girdle, and tucked under it, another dagger, this time with a golden blade. The king's arms, instead of being crossed over his chest in the traditional pose seen in other royal mummies, were folded over his tummy, the left hand slightly higher than the right. Bangles were hidden in the wrappings just above his elbows, including one carved with a distinctive bird. Carter, always keen to link the Egyptians' religious beliefs with the wildlife he saw around him in the Valley of the Kings, identified it as the Egyptian swift. These birds lived in huge colonies in the cliffs at the edge of the desert, as he noted in his journal. The swifts flew down to the Nile at sunrise, screaming, and headed home, even louder, as the sun set. Maybe the Egyptians associated them with the transformation of the sun god, he mused, or the souls of the dead, which come forth by day with the sun and return at night.

The mummy's slender forearms were coated from elbow to wrist with chunky gold bracelets, all of different designs, some inlaid with semiprecious

---

* It's still unclear whether Tutankhamun's unguent-pourers were particularly enthusiastic in this respect or whether other Eighteenth-Dynasty pharaohs were smothered as liberally. If the latter, the other royal mummies may only have escaped similar damage because they were stripped of their original coverings at a fairly early date—in a sense, the tomb robbers may have done them a favor.

stones and glass. Each finger and thumb was individually wrapped in fine strips of linen, then enclosed in a gold sheath. Over its wrists were clusters of finger-rings made of gold, lapis lazuli, white and green chalcedony, turquoise, and resin.

The chest was even busier—a gleaming jungle of thirty-five objects placed at thirteen different layers within the wrappings. Four magnificent gold collars featuring vultures, snakes, and hawks were piled on top of one another. Two golden hawks covered the lower part of the chest, with their wings extending up under the king's armpits, as well as three more collars made up of hundreds of individual pieces of gold and inlaid glass. There was another series of gold bangles, and nearer the body, personal jewelry that showed signs of having been worn during life. Three beautiful blue scarabs (dung beetles) made of lapis lazuli held the disks of the sun and moon in their forelegs. And underneath everything, close to the skin, was an elaborate bib, made of tiny beads threaded together in a pattern of golden waves on a blue background.

Around Tutankhamun's neck was a profusion of amulets and sacred symbols intended to protect and guide him on his journey through the underworld, each separated by layers of bandaging. They included a red jasper *teyet* charm (shaped like an ankh symbol with droopy arms) to ensure the protection of the goddess Isis, and an inscribed gold *djed* pillar, which depending on whom you ask might be intended as a tree trunk, or as Osiris's backbone, and symbolizes stability and durability. There was a tiny scepter made of green feldspar symbolizing power and eternal youth; a red carnelian snake's head to protect Tutankhamun's spirit against the snakes that infested the tunnels of the underworld; and figures of several gods including the baboon-headed Thoth, jackal-headed Anubis, and falcon-headed Horus.

Suspended on a long gold wire was one of the most important items of all—a large black-resin scarab, its wing cases inlaid with a *Bennu* bird, or heron, in multicolored glass. This is thought to have been Tutankhamun's heart scarab (normally placed over the heart, but in this case it was closer to his navel).

The ancient Egyptians saw the heart, rather than the brain, as the seat of intelligence and knowledge, and the final challenge for any soul wishing to pass into eternal life was to have it weighed. The heart was placed on a set of scales before Osiris, with a feather representing Ma'at (a concept encompassing truth, order, and justice) on the other side. If your pans balanced, you would live happily ever after. If your heart was heavier, indicating that you hadn't lived your life in accordance with Ma'at, it was fed to a monster called "The Devourer," a lion-hippo-crocodile hybrid that crouched waiting, and your spirit would be cast into darkness. A mummy's heart scarab played a key role, rather like a "get out of jail free" card, preventing the deceased's heart from testifying against them and thus guaranteeing a positive outcome.

The number and richness of Tutankhamun's amulets brought home to the investigators just how much the ancient Egyptians must have feared the dangers of the underworld. The other overwhelming impression was that this mummy seemed to have been wrapped with no expense spared, not to mention oodles of care, love, and respect.

According to the Book of the Dead,* when these charms were placed on the mummy, magic spells associated with them were to be uttered "in solemn voice."[5] Now Carter and Derry put the careful work of the embalmers into reverse, transforming the divine, protected king back into a fragile, mortal corpse. Along the way, they turned his magic into science. At each layer, after brushing away the charred bandages, they carefully labeled each item with a letter, while Burton took photos to record the exact position in which each was found.

In all, they unearthed 143 items, wading through the jewelry all the way down to Tutankhamun's gray skin, which was brittle as eggshell and laced with cracks. Here, Carter lost interest somewhat. He was desperate for biographical information about the king's life—his age, for example, or cause of death—to shed some light on the mysterious Amarna period. Otherwise, the body itself paled into insignificance beside the glorious treasures that adorned it. With the amulets gone, it was little more than an obstacle to retrieving the gorgeous gold coffin and mask into which it was glued.

Derry, on the other hand, was now in his element. He took the autopsy slowly and carefully, noting each tiny detail in neat pencil in his exercise book. As he had feared from the carbonized wrappings, the body itself was in a poor state too, horribly fragile and shrunk until little more than skin and skeleton remained. When some flesh on one leg flaked away down to the bone, the whole thing—what had once been plump muscle, tendons, fat, and skin—was no thicker than cardboard.

---

* A collection of spells, introduced shortly before the New Kingdom, that was often included in tombs to help the spirit safely navigate the dangers of the underworld.

The left kneecap came away at Derry's touch, exposing the lower end of the mummy's femur. This provided crucial information about the king's age because in children and adolescents, long bones like the femur are still growing, so the bulb of the bone isn't yet fused to the shaft (instead it's attached by cartilage). The end of Tutankhamun's femur was still free from its shaft, so Derry concluded that he died young—as Carter had thought— at perhaps no more than eighteen.

No pubic hair was visible but the king's penis was easy to spot. Bandaged in the erect position, it measured around five centimeters long. And on the left side of Tutankhamun's tummy, running from his navel toward his hip, was a ragged opening through which the embalmers had pulled out his internal organs.

Assisted by Hamdi, Derry cleaned the limbs and body, took as many measurements as possible, and painted the whole thing with more hot paraffin wax to stop it crumbling any further. By the morning of November 16, they had stripped the entire mummy down to the skin—and in some cases the bones—apart from the head and shoulders, which were still stuck fast inside their golden helmet.

In case you're imagining the body neatly laid out beneath the mask, though, the truth is rather more brutal. Carter glossed over this minor detail in his diary and published account. But Derry's notes, written as the examination was taking place,* are more revealing. Because the mummy was stuck to the bottom of the coffin with resin, the team weren't able to remove much of the jewelry. So they took drastic action, pulling the mummy's limbs apart to slide free the bracelets, and then cutting the body completely in two, like magicians at work on an unlucky assistant, before using a hammer and chisel to scrape out each dismembered piece.

This procedure revealed that the body cavity was filled with a tightly packed mass of resin-soaked linen, now caked into a solid black. It also had the happy side effect of exposing the ends of various other bones that helped Derry to determine the body's age, so he was able to firm up his previous estimate of eighteen. Finally, the coffin was empty except for Tutankhamun's head and neck, stuck inside the mask, its wide, obsidian eyes staring straight up toward the painted vultures that circled on the tomb ceiling.

---

* It took me a long time to track Derry's original notebooks down, but I eventually found them in the archive of University College London.

The hammer and chisel technique didn't work on the head, so finally Derry extracted it by sliding hot knives between the bandages and the metal, to soften the resin and work the head free. Inside the mask, the head lay on an iron headrest, which according to the Book of the Dead would help the mummy rise up from its supine state and overthrow its enemies.

On the head, under a few layers of bandages, was one of the most impressive items found on the mummy—a gold and carnelian crown with cobra and vulture heads standing to attention in the front, and more snakes sweeping downward like ribbons at the back. Down through a few more layers of bandages, Derry found a band of burnished gold, and further down still, fitting tightly over the king's shaved head, was a skullcap made of linen, embroidered in a snake design with tiny gold and faience beads. The fabric of the cap had deteriorated, meaning that trying to remove it would scatter the beads in all directions. So Carter decided to leave it in place on the king's head, coating it in yet more wax.

It was time to reveal the king's face. Derry removed the final wrappings carefully, brushing away the last decayed scraps with a sable brush. At last, they saw the man himself: long eyelashes, nose squashed into a triangle by the bandages, pierced ears, and parted lips, which revealed slightly protruding upper teeth. The flesh of Tutankhamun's face had dried and contracted, leaving prominent cheekbones. On his left cheek was a round scab, like a large spot or mosquito bite that had yet to heal.*

Carter described "the serene and placid countenance of a young male . . . refined and cultured, features well formed, especially clearly marked lips."[6] I guess that's all true, though I can't help seeing in him a slightly awkward, goofy teenager.

Derry estimated Tutankhamun's height in life as 5 feet 6 inches tall, exactly the same height as the two guardian statues that had stood either side of the sealed door to the burial chamber. Meanwhile, Lucas took samples from plugs in the mummy's nostrils, white spots on its shoulders, and some reddish material in its right eye, and analyzed them to see what they were (linen, salt, and resin respectively). His methods, though pioneering

---

* Curse enthusiasts loved the fact that the blemish on the mummy's left cheek could conceivably be an inflamed mosquito bite. Perhaps the vengeful pharaoh had knocked off Lord Carnarvon in the very manner in which he himself died. (Though you'd think that someone who had the power to carry out such an act three thousand years after his own death might have managed to avoid dying from a mosquito bite in the first place.)

at the time, seem today like a series of school chemistry experiments—testing whether a sample was soluble in alcohol or benzene, whether it left a greasy stain on paper, or whether it melted with heat.

Much to Carter's disappointment, neither Derry nor Lucas came up with any clues to the cause of Tutankhamun's early death. The autopsy did reveal one other important detail, though. Afterward, Derry wrote to his son Hugh at boarding school in England, telling him all about the tomb and the mummy.[7] Derry described the richness of the jewelry he had retrieved, and explained how he calculated the king's age from the ends of his bones. Then he added mysteriously: "I also made another discovery which is of great interest and which may help to make the history of that time clearer, but I am not permitted to make it public and Carter will eventually do so I expect."

He was probably talking about the shape of Tutankhamun's skull, which he recorded in his notebook and was later included in the second volume of Carter's book on the tomb.[8] Back in 1907, Derry's mentor Elliot Smith had examined the mummy from the KV55 Amarna cache, then thought to be Akhenaten. One of his key findings was that the skull was quite exceptional—it stuck out a long way at the back, and at 154 centimeters across, was one of the widest skulls ever discovered in Egypt.

When Derry made his measurements, he found that Tutankhamun's skull closely matched the unusual shape of the KV55 skull. In fact, it was even broader, at nearly 157 centimeters wide. Derry concluded that Tutankhamun must have been closely related to the KV55 king, perhaps his brother, or his son.

This was a big surprise. Until then, archaeologists had assumed that Tutankhamun became heir to the throne when he married Ankhesenamun, King Akhenaten's daughter. But Derry's finding suggested that Tutankhamun was himself of royal blood. For historians of the period, with so little information to go on, it was a huge discovery, and required much rewriting of textbooks. It explained why Tutankhamun had ended up on the throne at such a young age—he was the heir in his own right. But it raised a question that still exercises experts today: Who were his royal parents?

Derry finished his examination on the morning of November 19, and appears to have seen no reason to hang around. He and Hamdi left for Cairo straight after lunch.

≡

CARTER AND LUCAS were left with the "terrible job," as Carter described it,[9] of separating the two stuck-together coffins. With the mummy out of the way, it was time for extreme measures, not to mention nerves of steel. They lined the inside of the gold coffin with thick plates of zinc, then suspended both coffins upside down on trestles. They covered the outer coffin with wet blankets. Then they put several Primus paraffin lamps under the hollow of the gold coffin and set them burning full blast.

For several hours, nothing happened, despite the gold coffin reaching a temperature of nearly 1000° F. Then it shifted an inch. At last, the resin was starting to melt.

Carter and Lucas turned off the lamps and left the coffins suspended on the trestles. After another hour or so they began to fall apart, and eventually they were free, albeit covered in a dripping mass of what looked like gloopy molasses. Even then, the gold mask was still clinging steadfastly to the inside of the coffin. They pulled it away, and cleaned off the sticky mess with a blast lamp and cleaning solvents.

The heat caused the glass inlay to come away from the mask; weeks later they were still replacing the tiny pieces. But on New Year's Eve, they were finally finished and sent the mask and inner coffin—the largest golden relic ever unearthed from the ancient world—on the night train to Cairo. Meanwhile, the mummy itself stayed in the converted lab tomb, its pieces collected in a tray of sand.

Newspapers had followed the whole process. The solid gold coffin and mask brought home to everyone around the world just how wealthy Egypt was in the Eighteenth Dynasty. Even the wildest funeral extravagances of Rome and Byzantium hadn't gone beyond marble and alabaster coffins. Confirmation of the mummy's young age also helped to fill out a romantic tale of a king who came to power as a child and died while still a teenager. Some liked to end this tale with a suitably tragic death from tuberculosis, but murder was a popular theory too. As well as Ay, suspicion fell on Horemheb, the general of Tutankhamun's armies. The elderly Ay only reigned for a few years before he died and was succeeded by Horemheb, who ruled for at least fourteen years and laid the foundation for the great military empire that was the Nineteenth Dynasty.

Work on the jewelry and other coffins continued until early May; then Carter returned home for the summer. When he returned to Egypt in late September, he was horrified to find that rats had burrowed under the entrance to the laboratory tomb. It was pure luck that they spared the dismembered king.

Carter prepared the mummy for reburial—carefully arranging its pieces in the sand to give the appearance of an intact body, folding its arms across its chest, and calling Burton to take one last photo before covering it in wads of cotton wool. On October 23, 1926, he placed the whole tray into the outermost of the three coffins and put that back into the sarcophagus, which still stood in the middle of the burial chamber. Finally he placed a large glass plate over the sarcophagus instead of its original lid, so visitors to the tomb could look down on the king's golden face.

There was no ceremony or fuss. Carter regularly waxed lyrical in his diary about how overwhelmed he was at certain key moments, such as first entering the tomb, or revealing the golden coffins, but he appears to have been little moved by reinterring the king. His words on this occasion were curt: "The first outermost coffin containing the King's Mummy finally rewrapped, was lowered into the sarcophagus this morning. We are now ready to begin upon the investigation of the Store Room" (i.e., the treasury).[10]

Back in 1923, Carter had blocked the entrance to the treasury with wooden boards so that his team wouldn't be distracted by its contents while they worked in the burial chamber. As he pulled them down, he could never have predicted what he would soon find inside. Tutankhamun was not alone in his tomb.

CHAPTER SIX

PALM WINE, SPICES, AND MYRRH

———

THE BIG BLACK JACKAL that greeted Carter when he unblocked the door to Tutankhamun's treasury is probably my favorite object in the whole of the Egyptian Museum. It no longer wears its linen cloak and scarf, or the collar of blue lotus and cornflowers that adorned it when the tomb was first opened. But if anything, it's more striking without them.

The dog rests on a high wooden sled, lying on its tummy with head facing forward and paws out flat in front. I love its shape: the long, fluid lines of its neck, back, and haunches, and oversized nose and ears that should be faintly ridiculous but instead make the animal look hyperalert and ready to spring to life. The wood has been coated with a chalky primer called gesso and then painted jet black: a jackal-shaped hole in the universe, save for the gentlest sheen.

This is the god Anubis. His silhouette is punctuated with ears and eyes of gold and claws of silver, appropriately enough for one whose job is to watch over and guard the dead. In early Egyptian times, Anubis was the principal god of the dead, patron deity of embalmers and the Egyptians' most important symbol of death and the transition to the afterlife. He was probably envisioned as a jackal because these scavengers were often seen prowling around tombs (and would happily dig up shallowly buried corpses if given the chance).

During the Middle Kingdom, Osiris—the first mummy—usurped him as king of the underworld, and Anubis was rewritten in myths as the inventor of mummification. If you died as an ancient Egyptian, Anubis would preside over your embalming and guard your tomb. He would watch over the weighing of your heart, too, a job he apparently took very seriously, checking to make sure that the scales balanced exactly, and making sure that your heart was safely returned to you afterward.

Although there are many thousands of objects to see in the Cairo museum, there's something about this representation of Anubis that seems to lay the souls of the ancient Egyptians bare. It powerfully articulates emotions that are just as strong today: the fear of death, and the desire to have a powerful yet loyal companion who will watch over and defend us through whatever might lie ahead. If I could design such a guardian from scratch, I'd be very happy to end up with something like this great jackal.

Carter was fascinated by the figure too, not least because he was intrigued by whether the features of this god were inspired by actual jackals that roamed the Valley of the Kings in ancient times. The jackals in modern Thebes were smaller and brown, but on just a couple of occasions in the decades he spent in the Valley, Carter caught sight of a much taller, black animal, with a long muzzle and large, pointed ears, perhaps a throwback to an ancient variant now almost extinct.

═══

ONCE THE JACKAL was carried out of the tomb, it was time to investigate the rest of the treasury. Along its south wall, to the right as you look in, were rows of black sinister-looking chests. Carter had been wondering what was inside them since 1923, and now he got to find out: a multitude of miniature gods and kings. Stacked on top of these chests were piles of model boats, beautifully detailed, complete with cabins, lookouts, and thrones. On the opposite side of the room were more boats, the piled-up pieces of two hunting chariots, a row of treasure caskets decorated with ivory, ebony, and gold, and some white-painted wooden boxes. They contained jewels and other treasures, such as an ostrich-feather fan with an ivory handle.

At the back of the room—almost touching the ceiling—was the large gilded shrine protected by four gorgeous goddesses (Isis and her friends, just as on the sarcophagus) that contained the miniature golden coffins that held Tutankhamun's internal organs.

But the room also held some surprises, of which there had been no hint when Carter first briefly surveyed the room in 1923. In the far northeast corner, on top of a pile of black boxes, was a small wooden coffin, about two and a half feet long. Inside were three smaller coffins, nested like Russian dolls, and inside the last one, carefully folded in linen and bearing the name and titles of Queen Tiye, was a plaited lock of hair. Carter figured it must have been passed down the family as an heirloom, until when Tutankhamun died, the last in the line, it was buried with him; a sad symbol of the end of a dynasty.

Even more tragic were the contents of a wooden box just next to it. Two more tiny coffins were stuffed inside (literally, one of them had its toes hacked off to allow the lid to close), placed head to toe. Each contained a second gilt coffin, and inside them, surrounded by heaps of small, dead beetles, one of the most intriguing finds of the whole tomb: two mummified fetuses. One of them wore a small gilt mask several sizes too large for its tiny head.

Carter unwrapped one of the fetuses, then sent both to Derry, who later examined them in his lab in Cairo. Neat, blackened bundles, they were wrapped just like full-size mummies. They were beautifully preserved, both female, at around five and seven months gestation, respectively. They looked like little fragile aliens, with giant heads far too heavy for their skinny, wilted bodies, big dark holes for eyes, and pointed chins.

Carter concluded that they must be the stillborn offspring of Tutankhamun and his wife, the result of two miscarriages. If so, this shed light on why the king had died without an heir, a situation that ultimately led to the fall of the Eighteenth Dynasty and the rise of the Nineteenth, with its succession of strong military leaders including the mighty Rameses II. "Was that the result of an abnormality on the part of the little Queen Ankhesenamun," Carter asked (presumably the idea that the father's contribution might be anything less than perfect hadn't penetrated 1920s thinking), "or was it the result of political intrigue ending in crime? Those are questions, I fear, which will never be answered, but it may be inferred that had one of those babes lived there might never have been a Rameses."[1]

In November 1927, Carter finally got to perhaps the most daunting task of clearing the tomb: the jumbled, chaotic annex. Though necropolis officials had made a cursory attempt to tidy up other parts of the tomb after the break-ins, when it came to the annex, they didn't even try. It was a topsy-turvy tangle of bedsteads, chairs, footstools, game-boards, fruit baskets, vases, wine jars, toys, weapons, and pretty much anything else you care to think of. It was here, with the contents of boxes and caskets still callously strewn all over the floor, that Carter found it easiest to visualize the robbers' hurried scramble for loot. Inside some of the jars of sticky oil, he found fingermarks where the contents had been scooped out. The lid of one white-painted box still bore the bare footprints, dirty and black, of one of the thieves.

The annex floor was about three feet below that of the antechamber. There was nowhere to stand, so to clear floor space initially, Carter adopted the ungainly strategy of leaning in headfirst, with a rope under his armpits held by three or four men standing behind. This chamber seemed to be a storeroom that contained supplies for Tutankhamun's spirit in the afterlife, such as oils, unguents, wine, and food. Various other objects that wouldn't fit elsewhere in the cramped tomb were then stacked messily on top.

These included the king's personal possessions, which started to paint a picture of the actual man (or boy) behind all the golden rhetoric. One sturdy wooden chest was made up of complicated partitions and drawers, each with a sliding lid. These were stuffed full of what seemed to be knickknacks and playthings from Tutankhamun's youth—anklets and bracelets, pocket game boards made of ivory, slings for hurling stones, a fire-lighter,* some leather archer's "bracers" (used to protect the left wrist from the blow of the bowstring), mechanical toys, some samples of different minerals, and a set of pigments and paints. Turning a knob on the front of the box locked its lid—perhaps the earliest automatic fastening that had ever been discovered.

The collection gives a touchingly familiar impression of the joys of boyhood, or as Carter put it: "The sense of manliness imparted by possession of implements in connection with fire, hunting, or fighting . . . was evidently as pleasing to the youth of those days as to the boy of our era."[2] Other items found in the annex told of this adventure-loving boy turning into a man.

---

* This fire-lighting kit consisted of a rectangular slab of wood with a series of holes around its edge that had been treated with resin to promote friction. It also included a "bow drill," which was used to rapidly rotate a piece of stick in one of the holes, to create a spark. The thong of the bow wound round the shaft of a drill into which the stick was fixed, so that moving the bow backward and forward rotated the drill (and therefore the stick).

There was a large collection of sticks and staves—several of them forked, for fending off snakes—as well as clubs, throw sticks, boomerangs, bows and arrows, shields, and armor.

It took another three years to finish emptying the antechamber—the work was interrupted several times due to more arguments with the Egyptian government. But by November 1930, it only remained for an exhausted Carter to remove the great gilded panels of the shrines, which had been stacked against the antechamber wall (he had to widen the entrance to get them out), and to sweep the tomb clean, in time for the peak of the tourist season the next January.

Press attention naturally turned to what Carter was going to do next, and he obliged by telling journalists that he knew just where to search for the tomb of Alexander the Great.[3] It's unclear whether he seriously intended to look for it or was just telling reporters what they wanted to hear. After the publication in 1931 of his third and final popular volume on Tutankhamun's tomb, Carter was wiped out, physically and emotionally, and never embarked on another significant excavation.

He spent his summers in London haunting dealers' shops, and his winters in Luxor, living quietly in his house on the hill. Dressed in a three-piece suit and Homburg hat, he used to sit alone on the veranda of the Winter Palace hotel, eager to tell the story of his grand discovery to any passing visitor. His health quickly deteriorated and he died in his London home in March 1939, of what would now probably be diagnosed as Hodgkin's disease.[4]

In all, Carter had found a staggering 5,398 objects in Tutankhamun's tomb. He always promised to publish a detailed academic report on them all, but it never appeared, and once he died, there was no one else who could do it for him. Instead, the legacy of his giant excavation is held in the Griffith Institute's underground archive, with details of the unique objects he uncovered scribbled on more than 3,500 note cards and hundreds of journal pages.

Jaromir Malek, the archive's keeper until his retirement in September 2011, spent more than fifteen years overseeing a project to scan and transcribe every word and image that Carter and his team produced from the tomb, and to post the whole thing online. He says he started thinking about it in the early 1990s, "when the Web was just a baby." He realized that although there have been countless glossy publications on Tutankhamun, fewer than a third of the objects from the tomb had ever been properly studied and published, a situation he describes as "not acceptable" for such an important archaeological find.

The project was recently completed,* and Malek says he hopes that making the information available will spur Egyptologists into studying the artifacts from the tomb, as well as making the entire discovery—the thousands of objects behind that famous golden mask—more accessible to the public.[5] "This doesn't belong to Egyptologists only," he says. "It doesn't even belong to Egypt only. The discovery belongs to everybody."

Sitting in front of those gray rolling stacks, Malek tells me that after going through every single page of Carter's excavation notes, he has a new appreciation of the archaeologist's strength of character. "He was not easy to work with," he says. "He was quite often short tempered, perhaps not always tactful. But what I find really impressive is that there was this massive task, and in spite of all the difficulties, he finished it."

≡≡≡

AFTER WORK ON Tutankhamun's tomb was completed, Lucas and Derry each continued to live and work in Egypt—Lucas as the antiquities service's consultant on chemical matters, and Derry at the Kasr Al Ainy Medical School, which by this time was part of the University of Cairo. One interest they shared was trying to decode the process of mummification—working out how the ancient Egyptians managed to preserve such lifelike corpses over millennia.

The word "mummy" simply means a body for which at least some of the soft tissues become preserved—skin, flesh, and so on—as opposed to just a bare skeleton. Mummies can be made naturally—frozen in permafrost, for example—or artificially, when a body is purposefully embalmed to stop the normal process of decomposition. The oldest mummies in Egypt—including some of the remains Derry studied in Nubia—formed naturally. Buried in shallow graves in the fetal position, these bodies dried out before they could decompose, thanks to being in direct contact with the hot, dry sand. These corpses were preserved intact, even delicate structures like the eyes and brain, and ended up tough and brown like old leather.

---

* It's called *Tutankhamun: Anatomy of an Excavation* and you can see it here: http://www.griffith.ox.ac.uk /tutankhamundiscovery.html.

The idea of trying to preserve the body forever probably came from the Egyptians' occasional discovery of these perfectly mummified corpses. This evolved into the belief that if someone's body could be prevented from decomposing, their soul* could reinhabit it, essentially resurrecting the person in the afterlife.

As the Egyptians started burying their dead with the supplies and possessions thought necessary for the afterlife, it became essential to protect the body in the grave from theft, for example by burying the body deeper, or in the chambers of an underground tomb. But once they were no longer enveloped in the hot, dry sand close to the surface, bodies started to decompose.

This seems to have led to attempts to preserve the dead artificially. In the first two Dynasties, the Egyptians tried wrapping bodies in strips of bandage, and placing them in wooden coffins. The results weren't pretty. In the Third Dynasty, they started opening the body to remove the decomposable internal organs, and packed the cavity with linen. The organs were wrapped separately and placed in stone vessels (called canopic jars) near the body.

This worked better. But these early mummies still had a tendency to decay, so the embalmers reproduced certain key parts (the face and genitals being deemed particularly important) in linen or a resinous paste. In 1934, Derry was excited to be sent part of the foot of a Third-Dynasty pharaoh named Djoser, who lived around 2600 BC. The French Egyptologist Jean-Philippe Lauer explored the granite burial chamber of Djoser's famous Step Pyramid at Saqqara, a revolutionary structure that basically started the whole pyramid-building craze, and found the foot, which had probably been torn off the rest of Djoser's mummy by robbers stealing its anklets. When Derry studied it, he found that within the bandages, the foot had been faithfully represented in resin-soaked linen, even the tendons running to the toes.

Later on, the embalmers got better, until the art of mummification reached its peak in the Eighteenth Dynasty with some mummies that are today still strikingly lifelike and full of character, for example the amiable Yuya and Tjuiu. But exactly how they achieved this has been subject to

---

* The ancient Egyptians believed that the soul had several components, including the *Ba*, represented by a human-headed bird, which traveled within and beyond the tomb, and the *Ka*, which stayed with the body and needed offerings of food (real or metaphorical) to survive.

much debate among Egyptologists. Unfortunately, beyond a few instructions for things like what order to wrap the limbs in, or what spells to say when, the ancient embalmers didn't leave any how-to manuals.

The best we have is an account by Herodotus, a Greek traveler and historian, who described his impressions of mummification when he visited Egypt in the fifth century BC.[6] He's the only classical writer who described the process while it was actually practiced, but he visited relatively late in Egypt's history, in the Twenty-Seventh Dynasty, when much of the art had long since declined.

Herodotus said there were several different ways to mummify a body, depending on how much you wanted to pay. The most expensive sounds a bit like a gourmet recipe. First, draw the brain out through the nostrils using an iron hook. Then cut open the abdomen using a sharp Ethiopian stone and take out its contents. Clean the body cavity; rinse with palm wine and ground-up spices; fill the belly with myrrh, cassia, and other spices (but absolutely not frankincense, apparently); and sew it up again. Cure the body with salt for seventy days.* Wash the corpse, wrap it in linen bandages, and cover the whole thing with gum or resin. Finally, put it in a human-shaped wooden case, fasten it, and store it upright against a wall until the funeral.

If you couldn't afford that, though, there was a cheaper method, though it's not for the faint-hearted: syringe a strong solution of "oleo-resin" (a mixture of oil and resin produced by some trees, a bit like turpentine) into the rectum and leave for several days. When you drain the liquid out, it will bring the dissolved organs with it.†

Herodotus included one particularly telling (if gruesome) detail. Normally, the mummification process was begun as soon as possible after a person died, because in Egypt's hot climate, a body would quickly start to decompose. But Herodotus claimed that high-status or beautiful women weren't given to the embalmers until three or four days later, "in order that the embalmers may not abuse their women, for they say that one of them was taken once doing so to the corpse of a woman lately dead." Elliot Smith,

---

* Herodotus said to cure the body for seventy days, but this was probably the time required for the entire mummification process. The actual drying time may have been just forty days.
† John Taylor, a specialist in ancient Egyptian funerary archaeology at the British Museum in London, argues that this method wouldn't actually dissolve the organs. He suggests that Herodotus may have been mistaken, and the injection of resin was instead meant to preserve the organs inside the body.

Derry, and Wood Jones were reminded of this during their studies in Nubia. In later mummies in particular, they saw signs of decomposition such as long-dead maggots and beetles much more often in women than men, leading them to conclude that Herodotus's statement regarding the embalmers' necrophiliac tendencies may have had good foundation.[7]

As a chemist, Lucas was particularly interested in identifying the components of the embalming products used in mummification.* One material he didn't find was bitumen, an oil-like substance found in certain rocks. It had long been assumed that the black material found on mummies was bitumen—Greek, Latin, and Arab authors had all described the use of bitumen or pitch to preserve mummies, and modern experts had gone along with this assumption. Lucas seems to have been the first to actually bother to test what the black substance was, and when he did, he found no trace of bitumen or anything like it. Instead, the bodies were embalmed with plant-based materials—such as juniper resin, gum, and wood pitch.[8, 9]

This is ironic, as the very word *mummy* comes from the Latin word *mumia* (itself derived from the Persian *mūm*), meaning bitumen. In ancient times, *mumia*/bitumen had a reputation as a drug that could cure all manner of ills, from epilepsy and heart murmurs to tuberculosis. In the sixteenth and seventeenth centuries, the belief that mummies contained bitumen led to a bizarre cannibalistic craze for consuming them for medicinal purposes, and ground mummy became a popular item in apothecaries' shops in Europe. Dealers even started faking mummies, drying out corpses exhumed from local cemeteries, to try to meet demand. Lucas's work finally revealed that aside from being highly unethical (not to mention unpalatable), the entire *mumia* craze was built on a misconception. Not that this put everyone off, though. As late as the 1970s, there was still reportedly a New York pharmacy, catering to witches, selling powdered Egyptian mummy for forty dollars an ounce.[10]

Another topic that interested Lucas was the nature of the salt that the Egyptians used to dry bodies prior to embalming them. It is generally agreed that this was natron, a naturally occurring salt mixture deposited at the bottom of various lakes in Egypt when they dried up at the end of the annual river flood, for example at Wadi el-Natrun, about forty miles west of Cairo

---

* He had plenty of other interests too, though, and also wrote about other ancient Egyptian technologies from wigs and cosmetics to glassware and even poisons.

in what's now Libyan desert. But was it used dry, with the mummies cured like pieces of ham, or were they pickled in a salty natron bath?

Elliot Smith thought the Egyptians used a bath, arguing that the top layer of mummies' skin appeared to have peeled off, something you'd expect after immersion in corrosive natron solution, and that their finger- and toe-nails were often tied round with string, presumably to prevent them coming away too. Derry, on the other hand, argued that the interior of the body cavity showed no signs of having been submerged in such a bath, so where parts of the skin had come away, it was probably just the result of normal decomposition.

Lucas tested the bath theory, mummifying two chickens by soaking them in natron solution for seventy days, then drying them in air. He found that it works fine—five years later, the dry, shrunken birds hadn't deteriorated at all, as opposed to another chicken he soaked in common salt.[11]

It's an argument that still fizzles on today. Most scholars think dry salt was used, because in general the mummies' skin looks too good to have been immersed in natron solution, and because no mummy "baths"—the receptacles they would have been soaked in—have ever been found. In the end, though, both techniques were probably used, with dry natron being most common. In the 1990s, an American Egyptologist named Bob Brier made his own human mummy with a donated body, using dry salt and as many authentic details as possible, even down to chanting the appropriate spells.[12] It's still going strong and now serves as an experimental resource for scientists wanting to test out their techniques for working on mummies. Meanwhile, Stephen Buckley, a chemist from the University of York, UK, thinks that for a period during the Eighteenth Dynasty at least, the embalmers used a bath, and recently made his own human mummy—of a taxi driver named Alan—to prove it.[13]

It may have been Derry, however, who made the first Egyptian-style human mummy of modern times. Later in his life, he told his grandchildren that he once mummified a recently demised colleague in Cairo (who had volunteered use of his body after his death) to test out his theories. Unfortunately, there's no record of who this was or how the mummification turned out.*

---

* Derry's grandson, Ramsay Derry, suggests that it might have been his flatmate, Dr. Roy Dobbin, chair of the medical school where Derry worked and an obstetrician who pioneered safer methods of caesarean section, who died in 1939 on a trip with Derry to Port Said.

Meanwhile, Derry built on his collection of mummies from all over Egypt and beyond, and studied several of the royal mummies kept in the Egyptian Museum in Cairo. In 1931, he examined the mysterious KV55 mummy, concluding that this king couldn't be Akhenaten.[14] Like Elliot Smith in 1907, Derry said the ends of the bones suggested an age of early twenties—too young to have been Akhenaten. Elliot Smith had found a get-out clause, arguing that the king could have suffered from a condition that caused his bones to mature more slowly than normal, meaning that the body could have been older, and therefore might be Akhenaten after all.*

But Derry pooh-poohed this idea, and suggested that the body was much more likely to be Akhenaten's son-in-law and short-lived successor Smenkhkare. He published a paper with Rex Engelbach, curator of the Egyptian Museum, who had reinterpreted the objects found in the confused Amarna cache, and likewise concluded that the coffin actually belonged to Smenkhkare.[15] It is an argument that continues to run.

===

ON APRIL 17, 1939, the silence of the Egyptian Museum's huge hall was broken by a series of shrill, piercing blasts. It was the sound of two military trumpets from Tutankhamun's tomb, played after three thousand years by a British bandsman named James Tappern. The event was broadcast around the world to an estimated 150 million listeners, being heard in New York at 11 A.M. Before Tappern's performance, Lucas was interviewed about the trumpets, and explained that one was made of silver and the other of bronze. He didn't say that he'd been up all night repairing the silver trumpet, after the use of a modern mouthpiece (not by Tappern) during a test run the evening before had caused the instrument to split right down its length. Lucas was reportedly left as shattered as the trumpet, and needed hospital treatment from the stress.[16]

Within a few months, the world was at war.† Tutankhamun's coffins, jewelry, and furniture were temporarily taken from their display cases;

---

* Elliot Smith also interpreted the mummy's unusual skull shape as being caused by hydrocephalus—a build-up of fluid around the brain. Derry rejected this idea, particularly after finding that Tutankhamun's skull was so similar.

† Giving curse enthusiasts the opportunity to blame even the Second World War on Tutankhamun. According to the BBC, a curator at the Cairo museum claims the trumpet retains "magical powers" and was also blown before the first Gulf War, and the week before the Egyptian uprising in 2011.

Lucas helped the museum staff to pack the objects into boxes, and hide them in bombproof cellars thirty feet underground. In the Valley of the Kings, however, no such measures were taken. With most foreign antiquities officials posted elsewhere, security fell apart—with devastating consequences for Tutankhamun's mummy that wouldn't be discovered for another two decades.

Lucas traveled around Egypt during the war, lecturing to British servicemen in hospitals and military camps, and showing officers around the museum after it reopened in 1944. He died in December 1945, aged seventy-nine, after suffering a heart attack on a train to Luxor, with the medicine he needed stuck in a different carriage.

By the late 1940s, Derry had been in Cairo so long he was something of an institution (according to one of his colleagues, "Do you know Derry?" became a kind of test of social acceptability among British expats in Egypt[17]). Teaching at the medical school was a tough job, mainly because of the huge number of students—he taught in an enormous lecture theater, often to more than a thousand people at once—combined with a scarcity of bodies with which to teach them.

The body shortage was eventually solved by a cholera epidemic, but until then it motivated a number of thefts. One group of students (who Derry rather admired), stole a whole corpse, dressed it, and drove it out of the university in the back of an open car, talking to it as they passed the police guards.

Body theft wasn't the only disciplinary issue he had to face. In May 1950, a student brought a loaded revolver to his oral exam and, fearing he was about to fail, shot Derry's colleague in the arm. He then tried to shoot Derry but the gun jammed so he beat the professor round the head with it instead. After subduing the attacker and waiting for the police to arrive, Derry drove himself to the hospital.[*, 18]

But it was becoming impossible for even someone as tough as Derry to remain in Cairo. Egypt had been occupied by Britain's army since 1882, and nothing had changed with formal independence in 1922. The country had its own king, Farouk, but the British had humiliated him in 1942, sur-

---

* Another time, students at the university threw a bomb from the college roof into the street below, killing a policeman, and followed it up with bottles of acid from the chemistry lab. The enraged police swept through the building, beating up anyone they found, killing two orderlies and seriously injuring the physiology professor. A dissecting-room attendant stripped naked and lay on a dissecting table to escape the violence. Derry sat quietly in his room through the whole thing.[19]

rounding his palace with tanks and ordering him at gunpoint to appoint their chosen cabinet or abdicate (Farouk went into moral decline after that, and spent the rest of his life womanizing, gambling, and eating). Egyptians bitterly resented the intervention. Once the Second World War was over, there were increasing numbers of anti-British riots and demonstrations.

In October 1951, the government dismissed all British employees. Events culminated in "Black Saturday," on January 26, 1952, when violent mobs rampaged through the streets of Cairo, setting fire to many of its iconic buildings. Derry, along with all the other Brits in the country, was forced to go home. He left his beloved Egypt and retired to a thatched cottage in Essex, bringing his gung-ho driving habits—learned on Cairo's lawless roads—to the unsuspecting village of Saffron Walden.

At regular intervals, he gave interviews to the newspapers debunking the idea of Tutankhamun's curse, which resurfaced—even decades on— every time someone connected with the project died. "Look at me," he told journalists in 1952, pointing out that if anyone should be exposed to the curse it was surely him, as the person who actually cut open Tutankhamun's mummy.[20] "I have never suffered from and I have never been affected by ill effects from dissecting mummies."

But a few months after his return to England, the curse arguably caught up with him. Derry was incredibly proud of his youngest son, John, a famous test pilot who in 1948 had become the first British pilot to exceed the speed of sound. On September 6, 1952, John broke the sound barrier again, in front of excited crowds at a prestigious air show in Farnborough, Kent. A few seconds later, his fighter plane disintegrated and crashed into the crowd, killing him, the observer on board, and twenty-nine spectators. It was the worst air-show disaster in Britain's history.

Derry lived out his retirement in his picturesque cottage: watching birds, playing croquet, and entertaining his grandchildren with tales of Egypt. He remained alert and upright until he died, aged eighty-seven, in February 1961. He was the last surviving member of Carter's team.

Meanwhile, a new chapter in the life of Tutankhamun's mummy was just beginning. In the sleepy coastal town of Rhyl, north Wales, a terrible secret had just been found in a landlady's cupboard.

CHAPTER SEVEN

LETTERS
FROM LIVERPOOL

≡

NOTHING MUCH used to happen in the drab Welsh seaside resort of Rhyl. Then, in April 1960, a frail grandmother and landlady named Sarah Jane Harvey was admitted to hospital with a stomach tumor. While she was there, her son-in-law decided to decorate her home as a surprise for her return.

There was a locked cupboard on the landing that she had told him never to open, but to do a proper job of the painting, he forced the door with a knife. Inside, covered with thick layers of dust and wearing a blue nightgown, was a horrific-looking mummy.

The long-dead woman was shriveled and brown, with flesh and skin somehow still clinging to her bones. She lay on her back with legs bent up against the wall, her head facing the door with empty eye sockets and teeth bared in a chilling smile. There were traces of a cord around her neck, and on the floor next to her stood an empty bottle of disinfectant and some flypaper.

Harvey was arrested, and soon found herself at the center of one of the murder trials of the decade. As the trial progressed through the summer of 1960, the British press went wild over the case of the mummy in the cupboard. They ran stories of secret lab tests revealing gruesome embalming rituals, and speculated about whether she had been pickled in a bath of saltwater, or plunged into a vat of pitch. Meanwhile, holidaymakers poured off trains and buses at the sleepy coastal town. Armed with ice creams and box cameras, they queued around the block to get into the courtroom for the trial and catch a glimpse of the murderous grandmother.

The mummy wasn't like anything the local pathologists had seen before. The woman's flesh was as hard as stone; she had to be soaked in glycerin for a week before they could even do a postmortem. They called in a medical expert to help with the corpse: Ronald Harrison, anatomy professor at the University of Liverpool. He had a long-standing interest in Egyptian mummies and was tasked with helping to identify the victim, plus offering an opinion on how she was killed, how long she had been in the cupboard, and how she was preserved.

Harrison compared the corpse's condition to various reports on Egyptian mummies, to glean clues about the origins of their Welsh cousin. Despite the speculation in the newspapers, he saw no signs of artificial embalming; the state of the corpse was closer to the naturally dried remains previously studied by Douglas Derry. It must have taken the body a while to dry out, though, as it had started to decay before the tissues stabilized. Dead maggots filled the mummy's skull, and there was a gaping hole where her anus once was (Harrison speculated that gases produced inside the body as it decomposed had forced part of the alimentary canal out through the rectum, where it had been eaten away by maggots or bacteria).[1]

The woman's mummification was a freak accident caused by the location of the cupboard she was found in, Harrison concluded. It was next to a chimney flue, causing a draught of warm air to circulate, which had slowly dried the body before it could fully decompose.

The police thought that the victim was most likely a previous lodger of Harvey's, a divorcée named Frances Knight, who hadn't been seen for twenty years. Harrison found that the victim's height and physical attributes matched Knight's records. He clinched the identification by testing the blood group of the mummy and matching it with the blood of Knight's relatives. It was cutting-edge science for the time. He carried out the tests with the help of scientists at the British Museum in London, who sent him the necessary antiserum on ice on the 12:20 P.M. train from Euston.

But Harvey was acquitted of murder. Despite the cord—a cotton stocking—twisted tight around the victim's throat, the prosecutors were unable to prove how she died. Harvey claimed that wrapping a warm stocking round your neck is a well-known remedy for the common cold, and that when her sickly lodger died suddenly, she panicked and hid the body in case she got accused of murder. She did go down for fraud though—it turned out that she had been claiming the woman's two pounds per week maintenance for the entire twenty years that she had been missing.

For Harrison, the case cemented his interest in mummies, and showed him the potential—very much ahead of his time—for using molecular techniques to reveal family relationships of the long dead. It was the perfect approach for studying royal mummies.

═══

WHEREAS CARTER WAS always a bit awkward, defensive even, when it came to authority, Harrison was full of charm, supremely self-confident, and relished being part of the establishment. He wasn't born into it though. The son of a stationmaster, he was brought up fairly modestly in England's pretty Lake District, then won a scholarship to Oxford University and went on to become one of its youngest ever dons.

He was passionate about Oxford and its traditions, and was one of the last professors there to lecture in Latin. A member of the British Eugenics Society,* he initially specialized in research into fertility and contraception, writing papers on subjects like what happens to guinea pig testicles when you freeze them.[2] Harrison moved to Liverpool University in 1950, to take over an anatomy department left crippled by bombing during the Second World War, and thanks to his charismatic speaking style became something of a minor celebrity there. His lectures were jam-packed, and he was much in demand as an after-dinner speaker, addressing groups such as the Egremont Housewives Club and Liverpool's Hundred Best Ladies.

His interest in ancient Egypt seems to have started thanks to his friendship with one of his colleagues at Liverpool, the Egyptologist Herbert Fairman

---

* The field of eugenics advocates policies to "improve" the genetic composition of a population, and today tends to conjure horrific images of Nazi experiments and compulsory sterilization. It was more socially acceptable in the past, however, with advocates including some prominent Egyptologists. Scholars who saw evidence in ancient Egypt for the supremacy of certain races included Flinders Petrie, who worked closely with Francis Galton, the founder of eugenics, and Grafton Elliot Smith, who although not a eugenicist himself was convinced that a (light-skinned) racial group behind the pyramids then spread civilization throughout the world. Leslie Hall, archivist of the Eugenics Society (now renamed the Galton Institute), says that after World War II, it focused on promoting academic research, with members broadly interested in issues relating to population, genetics, and society. So Harrison's membership in the society probably had more to do with its ability to fund research than his political beliefs. "It doesn't mean he was a neo-Nazi," she says.

(usually known as H. W.). Fairman had worked at Amarna in the 1930s and had a strong interest in the tangled events that occurred at the end of the Eighteenth Dynasty.

In 1961, Fairman became the latest Egyptologist to study the inscriptions on the coffin found in the KV55 Amarna cache, and decided that it was originally made for Meritaten, the eldest daughter of Akhenaten and wife of his successor Smenkhkare.[3] He reckoned that Meritaten's body had been later taken out from the coffin and her husband buried in it instead, apparently not an unusual practice for the time. This suggested that the body wasn't Akhenaten but Smenkhkare—as Derry and Engelbach had earlier concluded, albeit by a different route. After the success of Harrison's work on the Rhyl case, Fairman asked him to examine, again, the mysterious remains of the mummy from KV55.

It was Harrison's first trip to Egypt, in December 1963, and he had a blast. He was treated like royalty—invited to lavish dinners, and even taken down the Nile on the luxury yacht that had belonged to King Farouk. (Farouk himself was in exile by this time. He was deposed by a revolution in July 1952 led by a young colonel named Gamal Abd el-Nasser, who became Egypt's most famous leader of modern times.) Harrison examined the KV55 bones in the Egyptian Museum, as Elliot Smith and Derry had done before him. Then he took them to the hospital at Derry's old medical school, now at the University of Cairo, to x-ray them.

It wasn't the first time that anyone x-rayed an Egyptian pharaoh. In 1903, just eight years after the discovery of this revealing form of radiation by the German physicist Wilhelm Röntgen, Elliot Smith and Carter tried it out on Thutmose IV. In a forerunner of Derry's favorite student theft, they surreptitiously slipped the rigid mummy out of the museum, put it in a horse-drawn cab, and took it to the only nursing home in Cairo that had an X-ray machine. They were able to estimate his age at around forty to fifty years, saw that his chest was packed with linen, and found some small pieces of jewelry in the wrappings that had previously been missed.[4]

Carter originally hoped to x-ray Tutankhamun's mummy too.[*] He arranged the procedure with a British pioneer of medical radiography,

---

[*] This seems to have been Derry's idea. As early as 1923, he suggested x-raying Tutankhamun so that he wouldn't need to be unwrapped. But Carter and Carnarvon argued that the mummy couldn't be left intact as any jewelry in the wrappings would make it a sure target for looters. "Therefore it was decided to unwrap the mummy and no one who knows anything of archaeology will question the wisdom of this decision which saved the King's body from ruthless desecration," Derry later wrote in his notebook, rather defensively. In the end, the fact that the mummy was stuck inside the golden coffin and mask—both extremely opaque to radiation—made x-raying it impossible anyway.

Archibald Douglas Reid, before the mummy was even found, but Reid died suddenly in February 1925, while recuperating from illness in Switzerland (and not, as several curse advocates later claimed, on his way home from x-raying the mummy). Then in 1932, Derry x-rayed Amenhotep I, the beautifully wrapped pharaoh that Maspero couldn't bear to spoil.[5] He found a middle-aged man whose hands and feet had been torn off by thieves. And that was it until Harrison looked at KV55 in 1963.

He reached very similar conclusions to Derry regarding the king's young age at death.[6] He estimated that the mystery monarch was a rather small man despite his enormous skull, around 5 feet 7 inches tall. He also reconstructed the king's face based on the X-rays, and was struck by the resemblance to images of Tutankhamun. Harrison agreed with Fairman, Derry, and Engelbach that the mystery body was Smenkhkare.

Harrison had one more tool at his disposal. Since the Rhyl case, he had taken on a young lecturer and researcher, Robert Connolly, who specialized in determining blood groups. Harrison carried one of the skeleton's toes home with him to Liverpool and gave it to Connolly to test.

Blood groups are determined by molecules called antigens on the surface of red blood cells. Which antigens are present determines what blood group you are. There are various different classes of blood group, but two of them involve antigens that stand a chance of surviving in a three-thousand-year-old mummy. One is the commonly known ABO system, in which you can be A, B, AB (if you have both types of antigen), or O (if you have neither). To complicate matters slightly, A comes in two versions—A1 or A2. The other class Connolly tested was the MN system, in which you can be M, N, or MN. Both involve molecules that are present on cells all over the body, not just blood cells, and that can survive for long periods of time.

Connolly took the toe and duly worked out the blood group: A2/MN. This didn't tell Harrison much on its own, though. To conclude anything about the identity or family relationships of the king from KV55, he needed someone else to compare it against. Harrison was now desperate to get his hands on an even bigger prize—the mummy of Tutankhamun.

But Tutankhamun was holed up in his tomb, shut away in the gold-plated coffin where Carter had left him in 1926. You couldn't just walk in and take a chunk. To get to this king, Harrison knew he'd need allies on the ground in Egypt. So he played a long game. He took on Egyptian students in his department in Liverpool, who later returned to influential positions at the University of Cairo. They included Ali Abdalla, whom he met in Cairo on his 1963 trip and soon afterward took on as a PhD student. Abdalla was sweet, hardworking, and devoted to his British mentor and Harrison's wife, June. "I can hardly keep the tears from my eyes," Abdalla wrote after he and his own wife returned to Egypt. "We'll always think of you as the best friends we have."[7]

Harrison set Abdalla to work, pulling strings and working contacts in the antiquities service to secure the go-ahead to study Tutankhamun. But even if they could get permission, another difficulty was where to x-ray the mummy. It wasn't clear if there was any suitable radiography equipment in the whole of Luxor, let alone in the Valley of the Kings. Undaunted, Harrison suggested that the authorities might save themselves the trouble of policing Tutankhamun's tomb if they moved the coffin and mummy to the Egyptian Museum. They didn't take him up on his offer.

Harrison also needed funds. The project didn't form part of his official duties at Liverpool, where he was supposed to be teaching anatomy. So he approached the BBC. In May 1967, a senior producer named Paul Johnstone,* agreed to fund the project, which Harrison estimated shouldn't exceed £400. They sealed the deal over a tasty lunch on London's Kensington High Street.

Johnstone wanted to film the project for a prestigious archaeology series called *Chronicle*—one of the first documentaries ever to be filmed in color. Initially, Johnstone and Harrison agreed to carry out the project that December, but had to postpone as "things were boiling up in the Middle East" after President Nasser's brief but ill-advised war with Israel.[8] And Abdalla still hadn't gotten written permission for the project from the antiquities service. "If you could procure this as soon as possible I would be more than grateful," Harrison wrote to him in December 1967, as if he was asking him to pick up some milk from the shops.

With the Suez Canal and half of its oil production in Israel's hands, Egypt was teetering on the brink of bankruptcy and riven by protests. Harrison received dramatic reports that Luxor was overrun with wild, rabies-infested dogs, and that hospitals in the area were lacking even basic supplies.

---

* Johnstone pioneered science and history documentaries for the BBC, helping to make the names of presenters like wildlife-documentary legend David Attenborough. He thought up the idea for an astronomy program called *The Sky at Night* and headhunted amateur astronomer Patrick Moore as its presenter—it went on to become British TV's longest-running show, still on the air (with Moore still presenting) more than fifty years later.

In March 1968, he decided to delay the project again—much to the relief of Johnstone, who was in the middle of filming at a prehistoric earthwork near Stonehenge, in a pioneering project to film a complete excavation from start to finish.

At the end of March, Abdalla finally came through with written permission from the antiquities service, but there was a snag. The permit included the condition that "the mummy should not be removed from its place." In other words, Tutankhamun could not be taken out of his tomb. Harrison would need to take an X-ray machine to the mummy, and hope that the electricity supply in the tomb was up to the job.

He didn't have the budget to fly heavy equipment from the UK—a hugely expensive undertaking in those days—so he wrote to Abdalla again, who eventually tracked down a portable machine in Cairo University's anatomy department. Unfortunately, it turned out to be a vintage contraption dating from the 1930s—presumably the one that Derry had used to x-ray Amenhotep I. Luckily, Harrison enjoyed the services of Lyn Reeve, his department's photographer and radiographer. Reeve was brilliant at improvising with mechanical devices, and at getting broken things to work.

By the beginning of December, everything was finally in place. The team flew to Luxor: Johnstone and his film crew, Harrison, Reeve, and an enthusiastic couple named Mr. and Mrs. Leek. Frank Leek was a retired dentist from Hemel Hempstead, and he had plans for Tutankhamun's teeth.

The group stayed in luxury in the Winter Palace hotel, right on the Nile, where Carnarvon had once had a suite. They would have just two days to study the mummy, and were not allowed to close the tomb or disrupt the flow of visitors. On the morning of Wednesday December 4, they crossed the river and drove to the Valley of the Kings in a green minibus, cameras rolling and spirits high. Harrison, despite the bright sunshine, had for some reason attired himself in a bright-red woolen jumper and white hat (at least on the resulting film it's easy to tell which one is him). None of them suspected that when they arrived at the tomb and finally opened Tutankhamun's coffin, they would find that someone else had gotten there first.

HARRISON'S LIFTING of the lid wasn't quite as dramatic as Carter's opening ceremony. But it was chaotic, tense, and brightly lit. The baking-hot burial chamber was filled to bursting with a crowd of men and boys—inspectors, workmen, hangers-on—in traditional robes and white turbans. Between their feet, a mess of cables snaked to floodlights squeezed up against the ancient stone. The work was supervised by Zaki Iskander, Alfred Lucas's successor as scientific director of the antiquities service. Meanwhile, the camera crew, a few passing tourists, and Leek's wife, Phyllis, looked down on the melee from a wooden gallery, built where the sealed doorway from the antechamber had once been.

Some of the workers held up electric lights, while others grabbed round every square inch of the great glass sheet that covered the sarcophagus. Easing it off was no easy task in such a cramped space, so perhaps it's impressive that all they broke was the corner (the plate was later replaced free of charge by Pilkington Glass).

There was another burst of activity, with Iskander at one point climbing into the huge sarcophagus alongside the golden coffin, as the workmen reached down to grasp the handles around the sides of the coffin lid, lifted it amongst much hubbub and shouting, and laid it on the floor to one side.* The sweet, almost sickly smell of resin once again floated through the tomb.

With Harrison a hovering red blob in the background, Iskander's men used ropes to lift out a small, flimsy-looking wooden tray, and laid it across the top of the sarcophagus to inspect its contents. What they saw was, frankly, a mess. Thick clumps of cotton wool were placed roughly over Tutankhamun's blackened remains, fixed on with just a few strips of bandage that were tied around the tray. On top was a small card signed by Carter, giving the date that the mummy had been reinterred.

When Harrison and Iskander lifted off the cotton wool, they were shocked to see that the mummy was in pieces. This was the first time anyone realized that Carter hadn't put the mummy back whole, as he and Derry fudged this detail in their published accounts. A reporter for the Egyptian newspaper *Al Ahram* was present in the tomb for Harrison's opening, and the next day the paper ran a front-page splash, slamming Carter for decapitating Egypt's king, then putting his remains in a tray that had been used for storing sugar. Carter's disrespect soon became worldwide news, with headlines like: "Britain Accused of Cutting Off Boy King's Head" and "Head of Pharaoh Found in Sugar Box."

---

* Harrison was particularly impressed by a detail that hadn't been noted by Carter—beautifully made silver flanges all around the lid, each embossed with Tutankhamun's name, which slotted precisely into sockets on the base of the coffin.

But the damage Harrison uncovered seems to go far beyond anything inflicted by Carter. Before the mummy was placed back in the tomb in 1926, Burton photographed it in the sand tray (see photo insert).[9] Although the picture has no date or caption, this portrait is widely assumed to show the condition of Tutankhamun's body as Carter replaced it. Considering that the corpse is in several pieces, it looks pretty good—carefully laid out with each piece in its place, right down to the fingers and toes, and its bony arms folded neatly across its tummy. The skin is pale gray, and you can see even delicate details of the king's youthful face.

The mummy shown in photos and footage taken by Harrison's team is in a much sorrier state (see photo insert). The remains are charcoal black, and they look ragged and battered. The mummy's arms are by its sides. The head is tilted instead of straight. The ears, previously almost intact, are mostly destroyed, the eyes are punched in, and the eyelids and eyelashes are gone.

Harrison also found pieces of the mummy scattered around the tray and its wrappings. For example, the right thumb and left hand were lying in the base of the tray, a collection of bones including a clavicle and femur were lined up in the sand next to the mummy's head, and the left forearm wasn't in the tray at all, but in a layer of cotton wool placed underneath it.

Mohamed Saleh, a member of Iskander's team who was to become director of the Cairo museum, later told Al Ahram that once the group had finished their study, they spent hours trying to find and return all the pieces to their proper position.[10]

That wasn't all. Two pieces of jewelry were still on the body in Burton's portrait: the beaded skullcap and wave-patterned bib. Carter says in his diary that he didn't try to remove the skullcap because it would have disintegrated, so he painted it over with wax and left it in place. It seems likely that he treated the fragile bib in the same way. But when Harrison opened the coffin, both items were gone. Only a few traces of colored pigment from the skullcap remained, and some scattered beads from the bib.

Strangely, Harrison never seems to have spoken about the mummy's poor state. He doesn't comment on it in the papers he published on the project apart from noting which body parts were found where. And in the resulting BBC film, the narrator talks only of the team's "excitement at the completeness of the mummy."[11]

The obvious—though little publicized—conclusion, however, is that modern-day looters broke into the coffin sometime between 1926 and 1968 and stripped the mummy of its remaining jewelry, in the process further damaging the body and scattering some of its parts. The first to suggest this in writing seems to have been John Harris, then Professor of Egyptology at Copenhagen University in Denmark, after Leek described the condition of the mummy in a letter to him in 1972.[12] He replied to Leek: "There can, I think, be no doubt that the coffin was opened and the remains mishandled at some unspecified date between Derry's examination and Harrison's. How else can the hands and forearms have been displaced, and how else can the beaded skull cap have been removed?"

The idea is now generally accepted by Egyptologists. As Aidan Dodson, an expert in Tutankhamun's burial who is based at Bristol University, UK, told me: "Somebody presumably paid a large bribe to see the mummy, saw there was some jewelry still there and thought, 'I'll have that.'" It has even been suggested that Tutankhamun's eyes were punched in on purpose by superstitious thieves, to prevent him from "witnessing" their crime.[13]

The looting may have taken place during the Second World War, when security in Thebes was practically nonexistent. European inspectors had been phased out or called up for service (Egyptologists, because of their expertise in arcane languages, were particularly in demand as code-breakers), and the Egyptian inspectors who remained were demoralized.

Consequently, there was severe plundering and vandalism of the region's tombs and antiquities. Harrison's Liverpool colleague Fairman worked for the British embassy during the war, and reported back from Luxor that antiquities were being stolen from local storehouses, and reliefs hacked from the walls of nobles' tombs, presumably with the knowledge of the local guards. Fairman didn't mention the royal tombs, but they were easily accessible too—a favorite tourist attraction for British servicemen on leave from fighting German and Italian troops in the north of the country.*

When Harrison opened Tutankhamun's coffin in 1968, the mummy was covered with cotton wool, so someone had at least gone to the trouble of crudely restoring its rewrappings. Dodson suggests that local officials had an incentive to cover up the theft, as admitting it "would have been the end of someone's career," so after they discovered the plundered body, they may have tidied it up as best they could and placed it back in the coffin.

---

* For example, in a letter to his family now held by the Egypt Exploration Society, Bill Mountain, an engineer with the Royal Air Force, describes entering Tutankhamun's tomb in 1943—"there he was in his tomb, all covered with a gold plate, beautifully coloured, and well kept"—and photos taken by Eric Budd, of the First Bedfordshire and Hertfordshire Regiment, show the golden coffin in its sarcophagus during a visit the same year.[14]

Who carried out the daring theft—local looters and British servicemen have both been accused—is something we're unlikely to ever find out. There's one small mystery I can solve for you though: the whereabouts of Tutankhamun's penis. It is a distinctive feature in Burton's photos of the mummy but is nowhere to be seen in pictures from 1968, and Harrison doesn't mention it in the BBC film, or in his published papers on the project. The missing member has since sparked a raft of conspiracy theories that the looters made off with this too, perhaps stealing it to order for some eccentric private collector. (The mind boggles—a fan of desiccated genitalia? Creator of the ultimate virility potion?)

Decades later, in 2005, Egyptian researchers reported finding what they described as "probably" the penis in the sand of the mummy's tray.[15] But no photos or details were released, leaving many unconvinced that their identification was correct, or even that the organ's apparent recovery wasn't simply a face-saving publicity stunt.

So does Tutankhamun still have his penis or not? In the end, I found the answer in an unexpected location: a cardboard box in Liverpool. The box is part of the archive of Harrison's papers, held at the university. Among other things, it contains a thick pile of yellow handwritten pages: the draft manuscript of a book on Tutankhamun, that Harrison wrote but never published.

On page two hundred, Harrison says that "the penis and the scrotum had been removed and were found in the cotton wool underneath the sand tray." In other words, the king's crown jewels were never lost. Harrison knew where they were all along—he just didn't bother to mention them in his paper. Presumably, they were dislodged by the looters and (along with the forearm) were dropped into the coffin beneath the lifted-out tray. In 1968, rather than attempting to replace or reattach Tutankhamun's genitals, Harrison moved them into the sand, where the Egyptian researchers would later find them.

CHAPTER EIGHT

SECRETS FROM BLOOD AND BONE

===

L YN REEVE, HARRISON'S JOLLY but deathly pale radiographer, had a habit of playing German military marches as he labored in his darkroom. On this occasion, however, his working conditions were rather different from usual. After spending the first day at Tutankhamun's tomb taking a series of test exposures, Reeve converted a bathroom in the Winter Palace hotel, aided by the "dense blackness of the Egyptian night,"[1] into a makeshift darkroom. The hotel's luxurious bathroom furniture was perfect for the job, allowing him to develop these test films in one receptacle, fix in another, and wash in a third, while other members of the team guarded the doors.

Optimum exposure times established, the team had just one day left to get all the X-ray images they needed of Tutankhamun's remains. Here the mummy's dismembered state was an advantage, as it could be x-rayed piece by piece. Harrison grasped each fragment in turn and carried it over to the rickety X-ray machine: a foot; a black, clawlike hand; the famous head. He propped the pieces into position under the machine's steel dome with bits of plastic and rolled up cardboard. Reeve then planned to take these crucial films back to Liverpool, to develop in an actual darkroom. Harrison would have to wait a while to find out what they showed.

Meanwhile, it was Leek's turn. Leek was a small, spritely man with a mischievous smile and seemingly boundless energy, who always wrote in green ink. After retiring early from dentistry, he applied his professional knowledge to his hobby, Egyptology.* He had examined the teeth of thousands of ancient Egyptian skulls in various collections around the world, finding for example that although the Egyptians didn't suffer from tooth decay (thanks to a low-sugar diet), their teeth were horribly worn from grit in their bread, sometimes all the way down to the pulp.[2, 3]

Leek was in Luxor to take a dedicated X-ray image of Tutankhamun's teeth. The tricky part was that he wouldn't be able to open the rock-hard mummy's mouth to do it. So before the trip, Leek worked with staff at the UK's Atomic Energy Authority, developing a method that used a hypodermic needle to inject a tiny bead of a radioactive X-ray source, Iodine-125, through the underside of Tutankhamun's chin. The idea was that X-rays would then flood out of the mummy's mouth, making a detailed image of its teeth on a film wrapped around its jaw.[4]

Leek was proud of the pioneering technique, and carried his precious radioactive nugget all the way to the Valley of the Kings in a small cardboard box. But when his big moment came, he found that the area under the king's chin was covered in a shiny, brittle layer that the needle couldn't puncture. His carefully worked-out plan had to be abandoned.

It wasn't until Leek got home and checked Derry's autopsy report that he realized what must have happened. Derry had described the mummy's wisdom teeth, using them to help establish Tutankhamun's age. How did he do it without X-rays to look inside the clamped-shut mouth? Leek concluded that Derry must have subjected Tutankhamun to an extra procedure, not mentioned in his report. There's a technique routinely used in postmortems to examine a corpse's teeth when rigor mortis makes it impossible to open its mouth: you cut out the entire floor of the chin, and push down the tongue with a spatula to see the teeth. Derry must have done exactly this, then put back the cut-out flesh and covered his damage with a brittle

---

* Leek and a group of friends, including the Egyptologist Peter Clayton, often traveled to Egypt to visit ancient sites. According to Clayton, they once went to Saqqara to see some ibis catacombs there, and found some lids from the mummy cases in the sand. Leek's wife, Phyllis, walked off the site with them tucked in her bra.

layer of resin.[5] A few years later, Leek demonstrated the method on a human mummy held at the University of Manchester, UK.[*],[6]

The team flew home from Cairo on December 11, Harrison carrying a small piece of Tutankhamun's skin packed in an envelope, so that Connolly could test the mummy's blood group. After a four-in-the-morning start, the plane was late arriving, and they had a long wait on the plane before taking off—one member of the film crew was convinced it was all connected with the curse. But once they were finally airborne, said Harrison afterward, "We could hardly have had a more pleasant flight home."[7]

Back in Liverpool, Reeve got to work on the X-ray films, while Connolly tackled the skin sample, looking for evidence that Tutankhamun and the mummy from tomb KV55 were from the same family. Harrison's examination so far supported the idea that the pair were closely related. Both were of similar height, had similar skulls, and died at similar ages. And the X-rays showed that both men had a hole through each humerus (upper arm bone), just above the elbow joint, an inherited condition called epitrochlear foramina.

But a matching blood group would provide an independent line of evidence. The established method to test someone's blood group—whether a long-dead mummy or a living patient—is called the agglutination technique. Each antigen on the surface of a person's cells causes an immune reaction in someone who doesn't have that antigen (this is why blood transfusions between people have to be closely matched). The immune reaction causes the cells to clump together, or "agglutinate." In the test, you mix the cells you're testing with extracts, or antisera, derived from people with different blood groups to see which ones trigger a reaction.

It worked on the Rhyl mummy, and on the KV55 skeleton. Connolly had confidently told his boss that using a modification of this method, he'd be able to determine Tutankhamun's blood group too. But when the young lecturer saw the skin sample that Harrison had brought back, he was dismayed. It was tiny. The agglutination technique needs a sugar-lump sized piece of tissue to work, around a gram. Connolly had just ten milligrams to work with—one hundredth of the usual amount.

---

* Another time, the industrious Leek tested whether it really is possible to remove someone's brain through their nose with an iron hook, as ancient Egyptian embalmers apparently did. After trials on two sheep heads, he found that you can't exactly hook the brain out, as had been assumed. But if you whisk the hook around enough, it reduces the brain to a gloopy liquid, which can then be drained out through the nose.

Harrison wasn't going to take no for an answer though, and the BBC were counting on the blood result for their film. Connolly had to come up with another way. He had been researching antigens and immunity, for example, trying to identify the molecules on the surface of pollen that cause hay fever. So he was good at handling red blood cells, and he knew that under the right conditions, antigens spontaneously stick onto them if you mix the two together.

That gave him an idea. He would stick the antigens from Tutankhamun's mummy onto modern human blood cells, to give himself a larger sample to test. In effect, he would bring the pharaoh's blood type back to life.

It sounds simple, but it took months to get it to work. Connolly himself was blood group O, meaning that his own blood cells didn't have any of the relevant antigens attached. They would make the perfect clean slate for a mummy's ancient molecules. First, he tried out his idea on an anonymous mummy held at Liverpool University. In an experiment that would surely make the perfect starting point for a mummy-related horror film, Connolly took a tissue sample from the mummy, purified the antigens from it, and mixed them with his own blood.[8]

It worked, reviving the Egyptian's ancient blood type and converting Connolly's O blood into group A. Then Connolly moved on to the pharaoh himself, this time using control panels of modern blood helpfully provided by the Blood Transfusion Service.[*] When he tested his Tutankhamun-ized blood using the agglutination technique, he found that it was A2/MN—just the same as the KV55 mummy.

Previous studies on mummies suggested that this was a rare blood type among ancient Egyptians—one study of twenty-three mummies from the New Kingdom found that only two were blood group A.[9] So Harrison concluded that the identical blood group was unlikely to be a coincidence. Tutankhamun and Smenkhkare must be closely related—father and son, perhaps, but Harrison thought they were most likely brothers.[10]

═══

CONNOLLY IS NOW in his seventies and an honorary lecturer in anatomy at Liverpool University. As the last surviving member of Harrison's team,

---

[*] According to Connolly, human tissue legislation in the UK means it would no longer be permitted to use donated blood for this type of research.

he is the guardian of all the X-ray images and tissue samples from the Tut-ankhamun project, so I take the train to Liverpool to see him. "I'll be wearing a brown suit with yellow tie and pocket square," he texts, and meets me on the platform, holding a copy of the British science journal *Nature*.

His office in the anatomy department is a little box of a room with a sloping ceiling and walls lined with crowded bookshelves. On his deep, dusty windowsill, a collection of blackened skulls sits just behind the kettle. Around the room, family photos are interspersed with boxes of tiny bones, old-fashioned Cadburys tins, a picture of an armadillo, and a box of Royal Ceylon tea.

I've asked Connolly to show me what Harrison saw, once Reeve had developed his precious X-ray films. He slides the black-and-white trans-parencies out of a series of stiff A3 envelopes, and clips them to a light box, one by one.

A series of Tutankhamun's disembodied parts flicker to life in front of us. A bright, perfectly focused foot, floating in darkness where it ends at the ankle; then a femur, with the desperately thin layer of flesh that coats it barely visible. Next, we look at a side-on view of Tutankhamun's head, nicely showing the teenager's protruding top teeth, and a delicate, pointed chin (see photo insert). Immediately obvious are two dense shadows inside the skull cavity, one at the top and one at the back, which together form a right angle or L-shape. Connolly explains that these represent layers of solidified resin. After removing his brain, the pharaoh's embalmers must have poured in molten resin and allowed it to set on two separate occasions, once with the body lying on its back, and once with the head hanging upside down, perhaps with the body on its front, its top half hanging off the end of a table.

Another detail stands out—a faint smear of white at the back of the skull cavity. Connolly tells me it's a piece of bone. At first, Harrison figured it was dislodged when the embalmers poked their hook up the king's nose to remove his brain. But on closer examination, he thought the fragment was fused to the skull, so he guessed that it was from a depressed skull frac-ture (where a bit of broken bone gets pushed inward) at the back of the head, which had subsequently begun to heal over. If so, whatever blow caused the fracture didn't kill him immediately, but perhaps it triggered a brain hemorrhage that finished him off several weeks later.

Harrison also noted a second suspicious feature in this image: an area at the base of Tutankhamun's skull that looks unusually thin. Such "eggshell thinness," as he put it, can be caused by a tumor or brain hemorrhage, either of which could put pressure on the skull and cause the bone to become thinner over a period of weeks. He suggested that Tutankhamun (and perhaps Smenkhkare, too) might have suffered from an inherited disorder called a congenital aneurysm, where a weak spot in the wall of one of the arteries supplying the brain causes it to bulge like a balloon. These can burst—often in young adulthood—causing a fatal bleed. Or, such a hemorrhage could also have been caused by a blow to the head.

Last up on Connolly's light box is Tutankhamun's torso, with ribs sprouting left and right from a slightly curved spine. His chest cavity looks cloudy white—not the evidence of major lung cancer but where the embalmers packed it with rolls of cloth soaked in resin, now rock hard. The spine looks healthy, says Connolly, ruling out tuberculosis as a cause of death, as the advanced disease usually eats away at the vertebrae. Toward the bottom of the image there's an ominous gap, where Carter and Derry cut the entire torso in two. And there's a scattering of white spots—tiny beads, presumably the last remnants of that stolen bib.

Then Connolly points out something truly dramatic. Tutankhamun's heart and chest—his sternum and the front part of his ribs—are completely gone. Harrison didn't comment on the cause of this gigantic omission, apart from describing the damage as "post-mortem." Perhaps he assumed that the ribs were sawn off by Carter, or by looters in their efforts to remove the beaded bib. Today, however, some experts, including Connolly, think that by refusing to consider the mummy's absent chest, Harrison missed the most important clue of all to determining Tutankhamun's cause of death.

But we'll come to that later. X-ray tutorial over, there's one more thing I've come to Liverpool to see. "So, do you want to see the bits?" Connolly says, eyes twinkling. He opens a drawer in a small chest on his worktop and pulls out a thin cardboard box, inside which is a collection of glass screw-cap tubes with yellowed labels. One of them says *Smenkhkare*, but it's empty—a few years ago, Connolly gave this mummy's toe back to the Egyptian government. Then the one I'm looking for, scrawled with the name of Tutankhamun, containing what's left of the sample that Harrison brought home from the Valley of the Kings more than forty years ago.

Today, it's unthinkable that a British professor could walk off with such a prize. The Egyptian authorities are understandably very defensive about their heritage being taken abroad, and it's illegal to remove any archaeological sample from the country—particularly from something as precious as a royal mummy. I peer into the tube, and right at the bottom I spot some tiny brown-black fragments of Egypt's most famous ever king. They look just like toast crumbs.

=====

HARRISON IS STANDING in his plush office, wearing a black suit, and speaking to the camera in clipped, plummy tones. This is Johnstone's film, *Tutankhamen Post Mortem*, and when it was originally shown, on BBC2 on October 25, 1969, it was watched by nearly a million and a half people— an exceptionally large audience for that channel on a Saturday night.

This is the moment during which one of the most persistent and popular myths about Tutankhamun was created. Harrison stands next to the X-ray image of the skull that Connolly showed me. He points to the bit that's eggshell thin and says the following: "This is within normal limits. But in fact it could have been caused by a hemorrhage under the membranes overlying the brain in this region. And this could have been caused by a blow to the back of the head, and this in turn could have been responsible for the cause of death."

Within that convoluted mouthful was the story that the world's media had been waiting for. No one really cared who may or may not have been Tutankhamun's brother, or about the identity of some little-known mummy from tomb KV55. But the violent death of Egypt's favorite pharaoh—that was news. From the *New York Times* to the *Sydney Morning Herald* to the *South China News*, in Dutch, Arabic, Spanish, and French, giant headlines splashed the same story: "Tutankhamun Met with Violent End" . . . "Tutankhamun Murdered" . . . "Teoria sobre la Muerte de Tutankamon."

The story turned Tutankhamun into a global celebrity all over again, injecting new life into the story of the boy king and sparking fevered speculation about his death. Maybe he fell from a chariot, or was kicked in the head by a large beast. But the most popular theory was murder. Because Tutankhamun died so young and was eventually succeeded by a general, journalists around the world jumped to the conclusion that he had been assassinated in an army coup.

Harrison himself described the way the story was sensationalized in the press as "complete rubbish."[11] Murder was "most unlikely," he wrote later in his unpublished manuscript on Tutankhamun, as the degree of healing seen in the skull suggested that if there was an attack, it wasn't immediately fatal, and "a murderer would surely not have risked retribution by failing to complete his work!" He preferred the theory that a congenital aneurysm finished off both Tutankhamun and his brother Smenkhkare.

But no one ever got to read Harrison's book. Every publisher he sent it to turned it down. Unfortunately for Harrison, British publishers already had a glut of Tutankhamun-related books planned, to time with a huge exhibition of the king's treasures—including the famous golden burial mask—that was to open at London's British Museum in March 1972. It was the first time that such high-profile items from Tutankhamun's tomb had left Egypt, and the excitement it caused took everyone by surprise, attracting well over a million visitors and inspiring a generation of Egyptologists. But by the time Harrison's manuscript was ready, in 1971, he had missed the boat. It didn't matter that his was the only book to include new information based on an actual study of the mummy—publishers were already bored of Tut.

So Harrison found it particularly galling when his dentist friend Leek then published a book on Tutankhamun, even if it was only an academic monograph. *The Human Remains from the Tomb of Tutankhamun* was published by the Griffith Institute in 1972. In it, Leek went back to Derry's personal notes and became the first person to reveal publicly what that first brutal autopsy had really entailed. Leek also tried, unsuccessfully, to track down the mummified fetuses from the tomb. The antiquities service gave him permission to X-ray them, but when the time came, in January 1971, their tiny coffins in the Egyptian Museum turned out to be empty, with their bodies nowhere to be found.

Meanwhile, Harrison put his unwanted manuscript aside and moved on. He had a new goal—to study the other known royal mummies from Tutankhamun's time, and untangle their confusing family relationships. In particular, he was interested in Amenhotep III (Akhenaten's father, thought to be either Tutankhamun's father or grandfather) and the elderly couple Yuya and Tjuiu, parents of Amenhotep III's wife, Tiye.

By this time, Harrison had a new helper, a young female anatomist named Soheir Ahmed, who worked in Harrison's department in Liverpool for a couple of years starting in April 1970. With her assistance, the project to x-ray these three mummies in the Egyptian Museum took place in December 1972. This time Harrison was accompanied to Egypt by a film crew from an independent channel called ITV—the BBC turned him down as they had already commissioned fourteen programs on ancient Egypt to time with the British Museum exhibition. "I think it would be more appropriate if [ITV] did the Tut left-overs," Johnstone wrote to Harrison, rather sniffily.

The X-ray images didn't throw up any huge surprises. But Harrison was most interested in getting his hands on tissue samples. It took a lot of persuading, but eventually he was given some scraped-off pieces from each mummy, the remains of which now sit in more little glass jars in Connolly's collection.

Connolly found that Amenhotep III's blood group was A2/M, while Yuya and Tjuiu were both A2/N.[12] Tiye, therefore, would most likely be A2/N like her mother and father. This meant that Amenhotep III and Tiye could be the parents of Tutankhamun and Smenkhkare (both A2/MN), if that's who the KV55 mummy was, which would make those two kings Akhenaten's brothers.

Unfortunately, the results fit just as well with Akhenaten being their father. Or even with Akhenaten and Smenkhkare being brothers while Tutankhamun was either's son. In short, nothing much had been ruled out at all—Tutankhamun's family tree was as confusing as ever.

Harrison needed more family members. And he had a good idea where to find them, thanks to Ahmed el-Batrawi, Derry's old assistant, who was appointed professor of anatomy when Derry was thrown out of the country. While Harrison was in Cairo in 1963, Batrawi had shown him around a neglected storeroom in the university's old anatomy department—a dusty space stuffed floor to ceiling with a bewildering mass of human remains, from feet to skulls to whole bodies. It was Derry's forgotten mummy collection. In a plain wooden box, Batrawi showed Harrison a tiny, preserved figure: one of the missing fetuses from Tutankhamun's tomb.

CHAPTER NINE

X-RAYING
THE PHARAOHS

===

IF YOU GO TO THE VALLEY OF THE KINGS today, chances are that among the buzz of tourists and tour guides, you'll find a kindly gentleman named Kent Weeks sitting quietly in a little dust-colored caravan just opposite the entrance to a tomb called KV5.

After studying archaeology and anthropology at the University of Seattle, Weeks started work in Egypt in 1963, aged twenty. But his first few days didn't go too well. "I arrived in Cairo in November 1963," he tells me. "Within eighteen hours, I was in the hospital having my appendix out." Five days later, he flew south to the stiflingly hot town of Aswan, and when he saw the local youths swimming in the Nile, he unthinkingly jumped in to join them. "I pulled all my stitches," he says sheepishly. "I didn't realize how strong the current was."

However inauspiciously Weeks's career in Egypt began, it developed into greater things. He's now one of the most respected archaeologists in Egypt, and director of the Theban Mapping Project, an effort to survey and catalog all of the tombs and monuments of Luxor's west bank, particularly in the Valley of the Kings. He started in 1978 and has since used a variety of methods, from hot air balloons to laser scanning, to map the area and make accurate three-dimensional plans of every royal tomb.

He's now working on KV5, a tomb built by Rameses II for his many sons. The rubble-filled hole was first discovered in 1825, then dismissed by Howard Carter as uninteresting in 1902. Its location was forgotten until Weeks rediscovered it. He started clearing its chambers in 1994, and soon found that it is much larger than previously believed; in fact, it's by far the most extensive tomb in the Valley. So far, Weeks's team has revealed more than 130 corridors and chambers dug deep into the hillside (compared to an average of eight or nine for other royal tombs) taking up more than 1,200 square meters, and they still haven't determined its full extent. They have also found four mummies, whom Weeks believes are Rameses's sons.

But all of this was a long way off in 1963. Weeks's first trip to Egypt, when he pulled his stitches, was for something quite different. He didn't know it, but the project he was about to embark upon would ultimately become a major effort to unlock the secrets of the royal mummies, including Tutankhamun.

Weeks was following in Derry's footsteps, as part of another mission to salvage information from an area in Nubia that was soon to be flooded. In 1960, President Nasser announced the construction of the Aswan High Dam, a billion-dollar project that would dwarf the old Aswan dam. In fact, at more than two miles long, it dwarfed all the other dams in the world. The resulting lake now extends three hundred miles to the south, through all of Egyptian Nubia and well into Sudan.

Virtually the entire population of Egyptian Nubia had to be relocated. And all trace of the ancient people who lived there was soon to be lost forever. The United Nations led a hugely expensive international effort to rescue a number of ancient monuments, including a project to move the massive twin temples of Abu Simbel, piece by piece, to higher ground.

Like Derry, Weeks's job was to study and measure skeletons excavated from Nubian graves—as many of them as possible. After a short stretch clearing a cemetery at Armina, about twenty-five miles north of Abu Simbel, he went to work at the Citadel of Gebel Adda, one of the most important ancient cities in southern Nubia.

It was a remote desert area, about ten miles from the border with Sudan. Weeks was working on the east bank of the Nile, on a sandy plain about half a mile wide, with hills in the distance, and beyond that nothing until you got to the Red Sea. He lived in a tent, with an assistant, a Nubian cook, and a dog, in temperatures—at up to 125°F in the shade—that can only be described as brutal. "It was so, so hot," he recalls. "In the afternoon when we could bear it no longer, we would stop measuring skulls and jump into the river. But the water was so warm it didn't help. It didn't cool you down, it just meant you were wet."

He worked through six thousand skeletons and mummies, making more than a hundred measurements of each. He was interested in who the ancient Nubians were, in particular how they lived, how their genetic composition changed over thousands of years, and what pathological conditions they suffered from. As well as measuring the skeletons, he photographed them, described any abnormalities he found, and took hundreds of tissue samples for later analysis.

Thousands of miles away, a scruffily dressed orthodontist named James Harris was trying to understand why so many American children end up with crooked teeth. A professor at the University of Michigan, he wanted to tease out the different factors involved, including environmental factors such as diet and family dental history, as well as long-term shifts in the genes of entire populations. Ultimately, he hoped such studies would help him to predict whether the crowded teeth in his young patients were best corrected by braces, extraction, surgery, or just time.

To test his theories, he needed to study how the teeth of individual patients developed as they grew up, but also to compare different people from the same population over several centuries, to see how their teeth changed over long periods of time. U.S. dental records didn't go back far enough, but then Harris heard about Weeks's work. This ancient Nubian population sounded perfect. People had lived at this major crossroads of civilization for more than four thousand years, and their teeth were still perfectly preserved in their graves.

In the spring of 1965, Harris traveled to Nubia to x-ray the skulls that Weeks had previously examined and left in numbered boxes. As he would have no power source to produce X-rays in the middle of the desert, he decided—as Leek did a couple of years later—to use a chunk of radioactive metal that produced the radiation spontaneously as it decayed. Harris chose Ytterbium-169, which has a half-life of about thirty days.

Taking X-rays in the desert wasn't straightforward. The amount of radiation being produced by the ytterbium fell throughout the project as the source decayed, so Harris constantly had to adjust his exposure times. Keeping dust out of his equipment and keeping his developing solutions cool enough were also major problems. But he had it slightly more luxurious than Weeks, living not in a tent but in a boat moored on the Nile.

That spring, Harris x-rayed nearly a thousand skulls, all of which now lie at the bottom of Lake Nasser. In subsequent seasons, he also studied more than two thousand living schoolchildren at Aswan. He found that modern Nubians have smaller faces, smaller jaws, and more crowded teeth than their ancestors, suggesting that overcrowded teeth are so common today because our jaws have been getting smaller as we evolve.

As with Derry, studying Nubian skeletons soon led to higher things. Most of the skeletons that Harris and Weeks examined in Nubia belonged to commoners. They wanted to find out what was happening in the upper classes of Egyptian society too, which meant they needed to x-ray a set of high-status bodies, ideally belonging to related individuals over many generations. The royal mummies in the Egyptian Museum would be perfect. The two researchers submitted a proposal to the antiquities department, and it was approved.

Given such a valuable opportunity, Harris widened his approach beyond the mummies' teeth. He decided to use the study to estimate the royals' ages at death, something that he hoped would resolve various arguments over the chronology of different pharaohs' reigns in the New Kingdom. And he introduced a newfangled technique, popular among orthodontists, called cephalometrics. When taking an X-ray image of someone's skull, you stick a pair of rods into the person's ears, to line up their head perfectly with the X-ray beam. Aligning the images in this way allowed use of a computer to compare images of different jaws, or different images of the same person's jaw over time. That might sound simple today, but in the 1960s, when the microchip had only just been invented, this kind of analysis was cutting-edge.

The royal mummies represented individuals from the same family who had lived over three hundred years. So Harris and Weeks decided to use the technique to track the inheritance of facial resemblance down the family line, trying to pin down how the different pharaohs were related.

They started work on the royal mummies in December 1966, while Ronald Harrison was still chasing permission to study Tutankhamun. It took three seasons to get through them all. Harris, Weeks, and their team arrived at the museum each morning at nine, signed the guard's register, and trooped upstairs to Room 52, where the royal mummies were kept. They averaged four pharaohs a day. One by one, the museum workmen took one of the huge display cases, slid it into a narrow passage, and removed the glass lid. Inside, the mummy lay in a solid oak coffin, which the workmen gingerly carried over to the X-ray machine.

It was a tense working environment. After all, if you dropped and smashed an Egyptian king, you couldn't exactly run out and replace him. "We were surrounded by people who were frightfully concerned—rightly so—about the mummies," says Weeks, not to mention a constant crowd of curious tourists. But the garrulous Harris did his best to lighten the atmosphere and calm everyone's nerves. The mummies didn't break so much as a toe.

The normal orthodontists' technique had to be adapted slightly. The mummies were too fragile to stick metal rods into them, and anyway their ears were plugged with resin. So the researchers rigged up an ingenious contraption involving a right-angled gun sight to line up the mummies' heads perfectly without touching them.

Another bathroom was adapted for use as a darkroom, this time in the Nile Hilton hotel just across the street, where the team was staying. Harris's young technician had to make regular dashes there to develop his film, to check the images were suitable before each mummy was returned to its case.

The results revealed various items that had been wrapped with the mummies, such as three wax figures inside Rameses III's rib cage, and a gold plate placed over Yuya's embalming incision, as well as various maladies from which the royals had suffered. Amenhotep III, despite his fine-looking statues, apparently died a fat, diseased, sedentary man, while the attractive mummies of Yuya and Tjuiu were hiding awful teeth.

There were some bizarre findings too. Mysteriously, Merenptah, the son of Rameses II, had his testicles removed shortly before or after his death. Ahmose, founder of the Eighteenth Dynasty, wasn't circumcised—strange because this was customary for all males at puberty, even described as a "symbol of Egyptianness."[1] Harris wondered if perhaps Ahmose was a foreigner, or suffered from a physical disorder such as hemophilia that would have made the operation impossible.

A Twenty-First-Dynasty high priestess named Maatkare was long thought to have died in childbirth, partly because she shared her coffin with a miniature mummy—assumed to be her stillborn child. But the X-rays showed that her companion was actually a baboon.*

---

* Aidan Dodson, Egyptologist at the University of Bristol, explains that the other reason Maatkare was thought to have died in childbirth was her distended abdomen and large breasts. "Comparison of Maatkare's mummy with that of her brother, the high priest Masaharta, quickly explains her apparently 'pregnant' physique," he told me. "The pontiff was a man of massive girth closely resembling a 'Michelin man.' A family tendency toward obesity, together with the Twenty-First Dynasty practice of packing the body during embalming, is the most likely origin of Maatkare's appearance. Had the 'baby' not existed, it is unlikely that there would ever have been a diagnosis of pregnancy."

After the museum staff saw the successful results, they took Harris and Weeks to a small attic room, which they said had been locked for as long as they could remember. "Stepping over the threshold into two inches of choking dust, we felt like excavators entering a tomb that had been sealed for millennia," the pair wrote in a book about their project, *X-raying the Pharaohs*, published in 1973.[2] The room was filled with coffins, stacked three deep along the walls. It contained nearly forty mummies dating from the late New Kingdom: high priests, officials, and others. It took another two seasons to X-ray them all.

Back in Michigan, Harris used a computer program to compare the "craniofacial structure" (the bone structure of the face) of the different pharaohs, a process that involved painstakingly plotting 177 coordinates on each skull. Working with Egyptologist Ed Wente from the University of Chicago, Harris hoped to piece together how the different mummies were related, in other words to produce a family tree for the Eighteenth and Nineteenth Dynasties. But they soon realized there was a problem: many of the mummies seemed to be suffering from cases of mistaken identity.

Out of all the royal mummies in the Egyptian Museum, only Yuya and Tjuiu were found in their own, nearly intact tomb, so their identity is pretty much certain. The others are identified from notes written on them by the priests who rewrapped and reburied them in the Twenty-First Dynasty, or from the name on the coffin they were placed in. Maybe, when the priests were rewrapping and labeling all of those plundered Eighteenth- and Nineteenth-Dynasty bodies, they got some of them mixed up.[3]

For example, the mummy identified by Gaston Maspero as Thutmose I (who ruled at the beginning of the Eighteenth Dynasty) seemed to be just twenty-two—far too young for a king who had supposedly campaigned vigorously in Nubia and Asia. This mummy didn't have any inscription on the bandages themselves, and though its face resembled the mummies of Thutmose II and III, its arms were by its sides rather than folded across its chest—not what you would expect for a king. Harris concluded that this man wasn't Thutmose I at all, but another member of his family.

The mummy thought to be Seti II, of the Nineteenth Dynasty, didn't look anything like the other heavy-jawed pharaohs of his family line. But he did bear a striking resemblance to kings of the Eighteenth Dynasty, and was most similar to Thutmose II and III. The throne names of Seti II and Thutmose I look similar in the hieratic script used by the priests to label the bodies, suggesting that perhaps this mummy is really the missing Thutmose I.

Harris also became intrigued by the mummy identified as Amenhotep III, which showed a few unusual features. This mummy was smashed to pieces before being rewrapped by the Twenty-First-Dynasty priests, suffering far more than the damage usually inflicted by tomb robbers. It also showed signs of a special embalming process—with stuffing under the skin of its legs, arms, and neck, a method that wasn't otherwise seen until much later mummies. Harris concluded that the owner of this mummy would have been a strange-looking figure (rather like the KV55 mummy)—short, with a very large head for his body—and thought his face looked a lot like surviving statues of Akhenaten. Was he not Amenhotep III at all, but his son, the heretic king?

Harris suggested various complicated schemes to reshuffle the mummies' identities to try to explain the inconsistencies he found, but there was no single theory that fit all the facts. It didn't help that the methods he was using to compare the mummies' faces and estimate their ages at death were themselves subject to error, and raised almost as many questions as answers. In most cases, the mummies in the museum are still labeled with their original identities, and the doubts Harris raised are on their way to being forgotten.

===

REMEMBER THOSE THREE naked mummies that Victor Loret found in a side room of Amenhotep II's tomb? There were two women, nicknamed the Elder Lady and the Younger Lady,* and a boy with a cheeky face and a long sidelock of hair. Elliot Smith had described them in 1912 as part of his survey of the royal mummies. But no one had paid them much attention since.

Egyptologists had previously assumed they were included in Amenhotep II's tomb as part of his original burial, and were probably minor members of his family. But Harris and Wente wondered if they might be more important than anyone realized. In particular, they were interested in the haughty-looking Elder Lady, whom Elliot Smith described as "a middle aged woman with long, brown, wavy, lustrous hair."[4] Her left arm was bent

---

* Loret initially thought the Younger Lady was a man, as her head was shaved, but Elliot Smith corrected him in his 1912 report. "It requires no great knowledge of anatomy to decide that the excellently preserved naked body is a young woman's," he wrote, witheringly.

over her chest, a pose that had been seen in Egyptian queens, so perhaps she was an important queen herself.

When Harris was x-raying the mummies in the Egyptian Museum, he was particularly keen to add the Elder Lady to his collection. But she wasn't anywhere to be found, and the museum staff had no idea what had become of her. Eventually, Harris tracked her down hundreds of miles away in Luxor, still lying in the side room of tomb KV35 with her two companions.

In 1975, he got permission to open this side chamber and x-ray the Elder Lady. Initially, Harris had suspected that she might be the female pharaoh, Hatshepsut. But when he compared her facial structure with all the other female mummies studied, he found that she most resembled Tjuiu, the mother of Queen Tiye. In fact, the faces of these two mummies were more similar than any other two women in the study. The images revealed that this woman died in her forties, about the right age for Tiye. Could the Elder Lady be this missing queen?

Based on this result, Harris persuaded the antiquities department to give him a sample of the Elder Lady's hair, as well as a tiny piece—three hairs, flown from Cairo to Ann Arbor—from the lock of Tiye's hair found in Tutankhamun's tomb. In the summer of 1976, he analyzed both with a scanning electron microprobe, a technique in which you bounce a beam of electrons off the hair. This causes the hair to emit X-rays at frequencies that depend on the elements it contains, in effect giving you a chemical fingerprint.

The two samples matched almost perfectly: Harris announced that Queen Tiye had been found.[5]

——————

SOHEIR AHMED, A YOUNG MOTHER teaching anatomy at the medical school in Cairo, was suffering from some of the same problems as Derry had, two decades earlier. It was a far cry from the conditions she had enjoyed when working for Harrison in Liverpool. "The students don't have enough bodies to dissect," she wrote to him in 1974.[6] "We have 40 students on one limb . . . we need traffic wardens not teachers in the dissecting rooms!"

But she found time, at Harrison's request, to search for Tutankhamun's mummified fetuses. Derry's successor, Professor Batrawi, had died suddenly in 1964. And no one else in the anatomy department had ever heard of the tiny body that Batrawi had shown Harrison. Ahmed scoured the mummies held in the old collection, many of which had lost their labels, but couldn't find it. Then in November 1975, she finally tracked it down—the larger fetus, in a wooden box with a handwritten label: *Tomb of Tutankhamun*. There was no sign of the child's smaller companion.

The next obvious step was to x-ray the fetus. Ahmed was able to organize this almost immediately, but getting the resulting radiographs to Harrison in Liverpool was more difficult, as posting the bulky scans to Britain was prohibitively expensive. She first hoped to send them in December, with a university professor who was flying to Scotland for a meeting, but she missed him when her diabetic husband, Samir, became seriously ill with hepatitis.

In the end, the scans had to wait until Harrison visited Cairo again in September 1976, but when he got home, he wrote with bad news—the scans weren't clear enough and would have to be repeated. In the meantime, Ahmed had given Harrison a tiny piece from the fetus's head, but Connolly was having trouble getting any results from it. She would also need to send a second sample.

Soon she had riots to worry about, too. As a country, Egypt was struggling, with nine out of ten Egyptians living in poverty and half of the male population unemployed. The president, Anwar el-Sadat (one of Nasser's generals, who took over in 1970 after Nasser died from a heart attack), went to the International Monetary Fund for help with the country's spiraling debts. In January 1977, the IMF imposed austerity measures that ended generous subsidies on flour and other basic supplies. Hundreds of thousands of people took to the streets, with Cairo's Tahrir Square, right next to the museum, one focal point for the protests.

"I'm sorry to hear of the troubles in Cairo," Harrison wrote to Ahmed. "I saw a film of the riots last night on TV—attacking a VW car. I hope it wasn't yours."

Ahmed finally sent another sample of the fetus and a second set of X-ray images to Harrison in September 1977. He concluded that the infant had suffered from a congenital deformity called Sprengel shoulder, in which one shoulder is higher than the other, perhaps shedding some light on why she didn't survive. But was she Tutankhamun's daughter?

When Connolly saw the piece of the tiny mummy, he was again dismayed by what he had to work with. The sample had been packed in wool-fiber for transport and on the way had crumbled almost to dust. He had to use a microscope to pick out the individual fragments, piece by piece. But by

December he had a result, concluding that the fetus was group O/M.[7] It was indeed possible that Tutankhamun, with blood group A2/MN, was the father.[*]

Throughout all of this, Harrison and Harris were aware of each other's work, but didn't collaborate, and don't seem to have held each other in particularly high esteem. In 1972, when trying to arrange to x-ray Yuya, Tjuiu, and Amenhotep III, Harrison wrote to Abdalla,[8] saying that although "a man called Harris from Canada" had apparently x-rayed some of the mummies already, "I think it would be necessary to do this ourselves." Harris felt similarly, complaining that Harrison's X-rays of Tutankhamun weren't aligned in a way that enabled him to take anything useful from the data.[9]

In 1978, Harris decided to repeat the job, and x-rayed Tutankhamun for himself. It was a brief, low-profile project, with no press present as far as I've been able to determine, probably the most anticlimactic opening ever of Tutankhamun's coffin. Harris stayed only long enough to x-ray the mummy's head, and to add his details to Carter's little record card. Microfilms of the two resulting images are included in a 1980 academic publication, *An X-ray Atlas of Royal Mummies*;[10] if you get it out from the library you can find them stuffed in a little pocket in the back. They are barely mentioned in the book itself though, and Harris never separately published any results on Tutankhamun. It seems he couldn't add much to Harrison's study after all.

Meanwhile, Harrison had set his sights on Harris's newly identified queen. In November 1976, when Harrison heard about Harris's claim to have identified Tiye, he immediately added the Elder Lady to his wish list—he wrote to Ahmed asking if she could get him a sample of that mummy as well.

The Elder Lady was more difficult to access than the mummies in the Egyptian Museum as, like Tutankhamun, she was still in Luxor, so taking

---

[*] We inherit our blood group from both of our parents. As far as the ABO system is concerned, if Tutankhamun was A2 (in other words, he had the A2 antigen but no B antigen), this could mean that either he inherited the A2 antigen from both parents, or that he got A2 from one parent and O (i.e., no antigen) from the other. If the former, his children would have to inherit the A2 antigen. But if the latter, his children would have a fifty-fifty chance of inheriting from him either A2 or O (in addition to whatever they inherited from their mother). For the MN system, if Tutankhamun was MN, then he must have inherited the M antigen from one parent and the N antigen from the other. This means that he would pass on either M or N to his children.

a sample required special permission to open the tomb. It took Ahmed months to persuade Gamal Mokhtar, the head of the antiquities service, to approve the project. In the end, Mokhtar decided that if anyone was going to take a sample it would be him, which he did in the summer of 1977.

When Connolly worked out her blood group, it was O/N.[11] This wasn't what Harrison expected for Tiye. Her parents were both A2/N, so although the N fit, he had assumed that she would be A2 also. Finding this blood group would have been strong supportive evidence for Harris's identification. Finding a group of B, on the other hand, would have ruled the Elder Lady out as Tiye. Group O was annoyingly inconclusive. It was possible for Tiye,* but it wasn't a ringing endorsement of Harris's result. (Further doubt was cast on the hair result a few years later, when a German scientist argued that any hair sample tested by the method Harris used would have looked the same, in other words, all the electron probe study did was to produce a chemical fingerprint for "hair.")[12]

In February 1982, Harrison went to Egypt to reexamine the mummy of Queen Tiye. When he got home, he wrote to Ahmed.[13] The weather is "very cold," he said. "I wish I was back with you in Cairo." But he never visited Egypt again. He died on New Year's Eve 1982, aged sixty-one, from a tumor in the frontal lobe of his brain—possibly caused by regular use of an X-ray microscope, a contraption that enabled him to look at a light image of a sample at the same time as the equipment took an X-ray, giving him a beam of radiation right between the eyes.

═══

If I'd a known they would've lined up just to see 'im;
I'd a saved up all my money, and bought me a museum!
—STEVE MARTIN, 1979[14]

"IT'S MORE THAN A HULA-HOOP," remarked a Los Angeles storeowner in March 1978.[15] "Tutmania is going to go on for years."

---

* It would require both Yuya and Tjuiu to have inherited both the A2 blood groups from only one of their parents and O from the other, and for Tiye to have inherited the O group from both of them.

While Harrison and Harris vied for supremacy over the royal mummies in Egypt, Tutankhamun had been taking America by storm. The touring exhibition of the king's treasures that had been so popular in Britain a few years earlier was now making waves across the United States too, after opening in Washington DC in November 1976.

It almost didn't happen. When Thomas Hoving, director of the Metropolitan Museum of Art in New York, which eventually organized the tour, first applied to Egypt to host the treasures, he was turned down. The Egyptian government wasn't at all keen on America, friend of its archenemy Israel. After the exhibition finished its run in London, Egypt instead sent the artifacts to its long-standing ally, the Soviet Union.

But President Sadat was keen to reposition his country after the socialist years of Nasser. He threw Soviet troops out of the country in 1972, and after a brief war against Israel in 1973 (in which he regained the territory Nasser had lost in 1967, making him a hero in Egypt), he started talking to the United States, and indicated his willingness to negotiate toward a peace treaty with Israel.*

President Nixon, dependent on Middle Eastern oil, was keen for political stability in the region (and to strengthen his own influence there), and he saw the Tutankhamun exhibition as a way to cement links between Egypt and the United States. He visited Egypt in 1974 and personally asked Sadat to allow the treasures to travel to America—with one more city, and several more objects, than had been included in the Soviet tour.

Sadat agreed, but then the Metropolitan Museum had second thoughts, concerned about taking responsibility for so many priceless items. It turned out that withdrawing from the exhibition wasn't an option. The chair of the museum's board received a phone call from Nixon's secretary of state, Henry Kissinger, who told him that the show was "a vital part of the Middle East peace process." If the Met didn't organize the tour, he said ominously, the government would be "disturbed."[16]

The resulting exhibition triggered a frenzy of excitement across the United States, with sold-out tickets, long lines, and overcrowded galleries, and it smashed attendance records for a temporary museum show. Between 1976 and 1979, cities including Los Angeles, Seattle, Chicago, and New

---

* The process he started ultimately led to the Egyptian-Israeli Peace Treaty, signed by Sadat and the Israeli Prime Minister Menachem Begin in March 1979, after a series of 1978 meetings—the Camp David Accords—facilitated by U.S. President Jimmy Carter.

York saw more than a million visitors each—of whom it was estimated that more than a quarter had never set foot in a museum before.

The episode forever changed the way that U.S. museums did business. It also sent journalists rushing for appropriate superlative comparisons. According to the *New York Times*, "Egyptian fever is spreading faster than Asian flu," with sellers of Egyptian-inspired artifacts "proliferating faster than aspirin manufacturers."[17] Department stores and newly opened specialist Tut shops offered Egyptian motifs on bed linen, clothing, wallpaper, and furniture, along with Tut-inspired jewelry, appointment books, jigsaw puzzles, and paint-it-yourself funeral masks. A custom car show in Los Angeles featured a $10,000 car with a fiberglass grill in the shape of Tutankhamun's head, a cobra-head stick shift, and sphinxes adorning the running board.[18] At a specialist store in Seattle, you could buy a vibrating King Tut pillow that plugged into the wall.

The comedian Steve Martin wrote a parodic song about the phenomenon (which went on to sell more than a million copies), while women wore T-shirts featuring twin images of Tutankhamun's golden mask, and the slogan "Hands off my Tuts!"

Sociologists now cite this exhibition tour as a key moment in defining the "King Tut" we know today. Melani McAlister, a cultural historian at the Elliot School of International Affairs in Washington DC, says the press coverage and trinkets created Tut as a "significant cultural phenomenon," noting among other things the unique alliance it forged between "the high-culture world of museum exhibits and the popular traffic in celebrity icons."[19]

At the time, commentators scratched their heads over why this particular exhibition was causing such a sensation—was it the appeal of buried treasure, the intrigue of a murder mystery, or that fascinating story about the curse? One theologian described the exhibition as "an antidote for America's cultural amnesia," which appealed to a universal thirst for knowledge about human origins. The story of the royal mummies fascinates people, he said, because it isn't just the genealogy of a single family, but "the collective genealogy of the human race."[20]

Unfortunately, not everyone in Egypt shared America's enthusiasm for the pharaohs, or for peace in the Middle East. Under Nasser, Egypt had been an icon of Arab nationalism, and many in the Arab world now saw Sadat as a traitor for talking to Israel. On October 6, 1981, Sadat sat in a viewing stand in front of the pyramid-shaped Tomb of the Unknown Soldier, surrounded by layers of security as well as dignitaries from around the world. They were there to watch the interminably long victory parade held annually to celebrate the war with Israel in 1973.

As the crowd's attention was distracted by a flyby of air force jets, an army truck stopped in front of the stand and a group of soldiers jumped out. Expecting a salute, Sadat rose to greet them but instead they riddled his body with gunfire and threw hand grenades into the stand, killing him and at least seven others. Their leader, Lieutenant Khalid al-Islambouli, only stopped shooting when he ran out of bullets. Then he shouted: "I have killed the pharaoh."[21]

Sadat was succeeded by another army general, his vice president, Hosni Mubarak, who had been sitting next to him when the assassination took place. In coming decades, Mubarak's regime would be intimately involved with a new generation of multimillion-dollar studies on Tutankhamun and his family that would bring unprecedented sums of money pouring into Egypt, and turn the mummies into international TV stars.

But Tutankhamun would be making plenty more headlines before then.

CHAPTER TEN

LIVING IMAGE
OF THE LORD

≡

HOW'S THIS FOR A DRAMATIC REVELATION: Tutankhamun was none other than Jesus Christ himself. With so much popular interest in King Tut, I guess it was only a matter of time before someone made the claim. And in 1992, an Egyptian historian named Ahmed Osman did the honors, publishing a lengthy (and bestselling) account of how this ancient king was actually the son of God.

This is just one of many strange theories that cling to Tutankhamun. Perhaps it's because he's ultra-famous, yet we know so little for sure about him. He has become a sort of universal blank slate, onto which people from different backgrounds and cultures can project their own beliefs and desires without having to take too great a risk of being proved wrong.

This has happened ever since the tomb was discovered, of course. But between the 1970s and 1990s, the imaginations of Tut enthusiasts ran particularly wild. With Tutankhamun's coffin unopened after James Harris's visit in 1978, there were no new scientific data regarding the mummy to feed people's interest in the king. The headlines had to come from elsewhere, and they centered on three crowd-pleasing themes. There was Tutankhamun's curse, and his murder, and we'll look at both in the next chapter. But the biggest one was God, with multiple claims of links between the Egyptian royal mummies and high-profile religious figures such as Jesus and Moses—much to the disquiet of the authorities in Cairo.

Scholars and amateurs alike have tried to link archaeological information coming from discoveries in ancient Egypt with biblical accounts since long before Tutankhamun's tomb was discovered. In the West at least, the Bible was the only reference point that many people had for this time period and part of the world. The accounts in it were assumed by many Christians to be literally true, so there was intense interest in a second source of evidence that might help to confirm the details.

Egypt is frequently mentioned in the Old Testament, with several key figures ending up close to the Egyptian royal family. The most important is Moses, seen as a lawgiver and prophet by Christians and Muslims alike. In the Bible, the Book of Exodus describes a time when the Israelites were a tribe living in Egypt as slaves. Their numbers were multiplying, so the pharaoh ordered all newborn Hebrew boys to be drowned. Moses's mother hid him in a basket and floated it down the Nile, after which he was found and adopted by the Egyptian royal family.

Moses later fled the country after killing an Egyptian, but returned many years later, when a new pharaoh was on the throne, to demand the release of his people (after receiving instructions from God, in the form of a burning bush). It took the Ten Plagues to persuade the pharaoh to agree, after which Moses led the Israelites out of Egypt and across the Red Sea (some experts say this is a mistranslation of a smaller body of water called the "Reed Sea"). Going back on his promise, the pharaoh chased with his army. God divided the waters to allow the Israelites to pass safely, but when the Egyptian army followed, the waters returned and drowned them. After much wandering in the Sinai desert, the Israelites finally reached their promised land.

Unfortunately for those trying to prove that these were actual historical events, the religious texts describing them don't tend to give definite dates, or identify the rulers concerned; the Bible describes them all simply as "Pharaoh." And strangely (or not, depending on your views on the veracity of the Bible), none of this seems to have made much impression on the Egyptians. There's no hint of these events in the extensive record we now have from ancient Egypt, not even of the supposedly devastating plagues, and only one mention of Israel, on a black granite slab from the reign of Merenptah in the Nineteenth Dynasty.

So when Tutankhamun's tomb was discovered, scholars were excited about the insight it might provide into their biblical heroes. Several experts, including Egyptologist Arthur Weigall (previously the chief inspector of antiquities at Luxor), believed the tomb would prove that Tutankhamun himself was the pharaoh of the Exodus.[1] They argued that Akhenaten's monotheistic revolution must have been inspired by Moses, when he was a prominent figure in the Egyptian court. So Tutankhamun, who reversed those religious changes, was clearly the one who chased Moses out.

Unfortunately, the tomb, with its lack of written records, didn't offer a scrap of evidence for the theory. And now, most historians and archaeologists reject the idea that biblical stories represent actual historical events. Some dismiss the story of the Exodus completely, or consider it to be a distorted account of Ahmose I's expulsion of the Hyksos. Others suggest that waves of migration occurring over long periods of time later became condensed and dramatized into a single narrative. Such a movement of people may have occurred on a grand scale, but the individuals named are metaphorical, not real.

Despite this, however, there's no shortage of people who remain convinced that the characters described in the Bible—and related accounts in Jewish and Islamic texts—did exist. Not only that, but their mummified bodies are still with us, on display for all to see.

One of them was Maurice Bucaille. A French medical doctor who died in 1998, he was brought up as a Catholic in the little town of Pont l'Évêque. After studying various religious texts, he became convinced that the Qur'an represents a scientifically accurate description of the world, including hints of facts not discovered until centuries after the text was written, for example that the universe is expanding, or that man would one day travel into space. In the Bible, on the other hand, he saw major scientific errors, such as the claim that humans had only been around for six thousand years, or that the animals of the earth were created before the birds.

His conclusion was that while the Bible contains many details that can't be trusted, the Qur'an is the true word of God, and should therefore be embraced by Christians. In 1976, he published a book on his ideas called *The Bible, the Qur'an and Science*,[2] which became a best seller. The practice of using science to try to prove the truth of religion, particularly Islam, is still known as "Bucaillism."[3]

Bucaille took a great interest in the royal mummies, including Tutankhamun, and in 1990 published another book called *Mummies of the Pharaohs: Modern Medical Investigations*.[4] My copy has a red stamp: "Discarded by the Kalamazoo Public Library," which I imagine to be quite an achievement.

In it, he repeated for a much wider audience Leek's account of the sorry state of Tutankhamun's mummy. But he went much further than Leek, claiming that Carter had willfully destroyed the body, then "lied blatantly"[5] to cover up the damage he caused. He also accused a whole line of other Egyptologists since of assisting in the deception, by glossing over the mummy's condition in their accounts of Carter's work. According to Bucaille, the story of Tutankhamun's mummy could be summarized as: "33 centuries of the sleep of the dead—a week of dismembering—a quarter of a century of misleading narratives."[6]

There's no doubt that the mummy did suffer at Carter and Derry's hands, with the loss of valuable information. And their failure to disclose exactly what they did—from cutting the torso in two, to fixing up areas such as the chin and skull with resin—has caused complications and confusion for later scholars trying to piece together the details of Tutankhamun's life and death from the state of his body.

But I don't think that Carter was engaged in outright deception. It seems more likely that he just wasn't very interested in the body itself, and didn't see such details as particularly relevant. It's also important to judge Carter and Derry by the standards of their own time. Only a few years previously, archaeologists were destroying mummies out of curiosity or in the hunt for gold without making any proper records. Several royal mummies were unwrapped in as little as fifteen minutes each, whereas Carter and Derry took eight meticulous days. Some of the details make us cringe today, but the pair set the standard for how such a mummy should be treated, at a time when archaeology was only just turning from a treasure hunt into a science.

Beyond his rant about Tutankhamun, Bucaille's main interest was identifying the pharaoh of the Exodus, by comparing the royal mummies held in the Egyptian Museum with details of the story given in the Bible and Qur'an. He focused on two prime suspects: Rameses II and his son Merenptah. In the Exodus story, Egypt controlled a vast empire, which fits the period that followed Rameses II's conquests. It even mentions a city called Rameses. Almost all of the Eighteenth- and Nineteenth-Dynasty pharaohs have been implicated as the pharaoh of the Exodus at one time or another, but most scholars to express an opinion have plumped for one of these two kings.

Largely due to his friendship with President Sadat's wife (he successfully treated a member of her family), Bucaille was given permission to study the royal mummies in the 1970s. He was shocked to find that many of the mummies were rotting away. The bodies were surrounded by bits of dead insects, covered with colonies of whitish fungus, and emanated various sour smells. The accepted method of conservation appeared to be spraying them every so often with insecticide.

Bucaille described lifting the lid of one particular case that lay on a pedestal in the well of a staircase. Inside, he found a badly damaged mummy exuding an "indescribable stench of putrefaction. . . . The woman from the museum who had accompanied us implored us to finish photographing as quickly as we could, because the air was becoming quite unbearable. Before the cover was replaced on the sepulchre the mummy was sprayed with a cloud of goodness knows what from an extremely ancient-looking can."[7] When he consulted the museum inventory, it turned out that the mummy was thought to be that of Merenre I, who reigned in the Sixth Dynasty, around a thousand years before Tutankhamun—the oldest and most complete royal mummy in the museum.[*]

Other experts, including Harris, argued that conditions for the mummies weren't as bad as Bucaille claimed. But in September 1976, after the Frenchman raised the alarm, the museum's most prized mummy was sent to Paris for urgent conservation. Rameses II was flown by the French Air Force and given full military honors on his arrival: the first and only trip of an Egyptian pharaoh outside Egypt (if you don't count the crumbs that went to Liverpool).

Researchers there found that Rameses was infested with fungus. After much discussion about what to do—there were concerns that chemical or heat treatment might damage the mummy, though it's hard to imagine what could be worse than decades of insecticide—it was decided to sterilize him using gamma rays. Scientists at the French Atomic Energy Commission carried out a series of trials on less valuable mummies, to make sure, for example, that their hair didn't fall out. Then the pharaoh was placed into a smart new case and irradiated, before being flown back to Cairo the next May.

Rameses survived the treatment unscathed, but unfortunately his display case, made of an advanced type of Plexiglas, had been wiped with a cleaning product just before the irradiation. This caused the gamma rays to react with the glass, which became cracked and yellowed. After the entire lengthy rescue process, poor Rameses wasn't fit for display.

---

[*] On the other hand, other Egyptologists now consider it to be a later (New Kingdom) body subsequently buried in the king's pyramid, and thus not a royal mummy at all. Today it is on display in the Imhotep Museum at Saqqara.

Meanwhile, Bucaille decided that he wasn't happy with Harris's X-ray plates, and worked with staff at the museum to x-ray, again, several royal mummies including Rameses II and Merenptah. He concluded that Rameses II was an old man when he died and suffering from excruciating pus-filled abscesses in his teeth, so was unlikely to have taken off across the desert chasing the Israelites shortly before his death.

Merenptah, on the other hand, had a hole in his skull—evidence of a blow to the head that killed him. Bucaille took this as proof that Merenptah came to a tragic end, and must therefore be the king he was looking for. You might think that someone swallowed up by the extensive waters of the Red Sea is unlikely to have been retrieved and mummified in order to end up in the Egyptian Museum. But Bucaille found a passage in the Qur'an that says the body was recovered—saved by God "to act as a sign for future generations."

This would mean that Rameses II, Merenptah's father, was the pharaoh who originally ordered the killing of Jewish babies, and subsequently welcomed Moses into his court. Bucaille got quite carried away when looking at Rameses II's face, noting that the embalmers had removed his eyes: "Those eyes had enabled one of antiquity's greatest sovereigns to see one of the greatest figures of religious history—Moses . . . Having looked at those closed eyelids, I was certain beyond the shadow of a doubt that Rameses II knew Moses personally." It's a quote that seems to sum up Bucaille's scientific approach rather well.

Other authors have identified Moses himself from among the pharaohs. The prime candidate is Tutankhamun's predecessor Akhenaten, who thanks to his religious revolution has been often described as the world's first monotheist. Back in 1939, the psychoanalyst Sigmund Freud suggested in his final book, *Moses and Monotheism*,[8] that Moses was inspired by Akhenaten's devotion to the Aten. Then in 1990, Ahmed Osman went one step further, claiming in a book called *Moses and Akhenaten*[9] that the heretic king was in fact Moses himself.

Osman is an Egyptian-born writer and self-taught historian, now based in London. He had previously argued that Yuya, the smiling elderly mummy found with his wife, was none other than Joseph, famous for his multicolored coat. The Book of Genesis tells how Joseph was sold into slavery by his jealous brothers. He ended up in an Egyptian prison, but used his God-given talent for interpreting dreams to become the most powerful man in Egypt next to the pharaoh. He's also highly regarded by Muslims, with a whole chapter of the Qur'an dedicated to him.

Most modern biblical scholars date the story in its current form to the fifth century BC at earliest. Osman's alternative theory is based largely on convoluted wordplay and coincidences. For example, he sees in Yuya's name the shortened form of the Hebrew Yahweh, God of the Israelites, and concludes that Yuya was a foreigner in Egypt, nicknamed after his God.

Then, in 1992, Osman went even further and in a mind-bending re-interpretation of accepted history, decided that Tutankhamun was Jesus. In *Jesus in the House of the Pharaohs*,[10] Osman follows a trail of clues of which Dan Brown* would be proud. For example, he points out that the biblical word *Messiah* comes from the Hebrew *Mashiach*, which he claims can itself be traced back further to ancient Egypt, to a word meaning crocodile. Mean-while, the English name Christ derives from the Greek Christos, meaning the Anointed One, or King. It was an Egyptian custom to anoint kings not with oil but the fat of the holy crocodile. So, Christ must have been an Egyptian king.

But which king? It could only be Tutankhamun, says Osman, because his birth name—Tut-Ankh-Aten—translates as "Living image of the Lord."† Osman isn't concerned by the fact that Tutankhamun lived more than 1300 years before the supposed birth of Christ. He concludes that Judaism and Christianity derive from an ancient Egyptian mystery cult that was later suppressed and transformed by the Roman authorities in a triumph of fic-tional propaganda. In other words, the roots of the entire Western religious belief system lie in Egypt, with biblical personalities simply fictitious versions of various Egyptian kings.

Sound far-fetched? As you might expect, the idea of a divine Tut has been largely ignored by conventional academics. But scholars have felt the need to rebut Osman's work in publications such as the *Biblical Archaeology Review*,[11] while his ideas have been covered positively in leading Egyptian newspapers including *Al Ahram*.[12] And he has sold a lot of books. We all love a good cover-up.‡

---

* Author of the bestselling 2003 novel *The Da Vinci Code*.

† Other Egyptologists point out that "Aten" actually means not Lord, but "globe of the Sun."

‡ Osman isn't the only one to claim that Tutankhamun was Jesus. In 1997, a Cairo-based author named Moustafa Gadalla published a book called *Tutankhamun: The Living Image of the Lord*[13], in which he claims Christianity as "the world's greatest conspiracy and cover-up, which re-created the character of Jesus, living in another time (Roman era) and another place (Palestine, Israel)." As late as 2008, a Cana-dian-based online magazine called *The Ambassadors* issued a public letter to a hundred scholars[14] chal-lenging them to respond to Gadalla's hypothesis. Judging from the lack of mention of the topic in subsequent issues, they did not answer the call.

═══

ON THE EDGE of the Faiyum oasis, in the desert around eighty miles south-west of Cairo, is an early Christian cemetery called Fag el-Gamous. In the early 1990s, two scientists were excavating there: Scott Woodward and Wil-fred Griggs from Brigham Young University in Utah. Griggs is an archaeol-ogist and Woodward is a geneticist; both are high-ranking members of the Church of Jesus Christ of Latter Day Saints, otherwise known as the Mormons.

Woodward was a pioneer of the new field of ancient DNA research, and around this time he published a groundbreaking paper in the U.S. journal *Science*, reporting DNA from an 80-million-year-old dinosaur[15] (though read Chapter 15 before you get too excited about this). In Egypt, he was using his cutting-edge techniques to isolate DNA from the mummies at Faiyum.

In 1993, Nasry Iskander of Egypt's antiquities service asked Woodward to test six intriguing mummies held in the Cairo Museum. Known as the "Akhmim" mummies after the site north of Luxor where they were found, they dated from Dynasty Four or Five. Two were of grandparent age, two were of parent age, and two were children. X-ray images revealed broken necks—they had all been hanged. Using DNA, Woodward was able to con-firm the mummies' sex, and show that they represented three generations of the same doomed family.[16]

The success of that work led to an even more exciting project. After Bu-caille's complaints about the conditions in which the royal mummies were being kept, they were all being moved into new climate-controlled cases, designed by the Getty Conservation Institute in Los Angeles. With Iskander's permission, Woodward used the opportunity to take samples of the royal mummies' DNA. Like Harris, he hoped to tease out the murky family rela-tionships of the Eighteenth-Dynasty kings. His work was featured in a U.S. documentary series called *Secrets of the Pharaohs*, shown on PBS in 2000. He collected scraps of loose tissue from the mummies (he wasn't allowed to use more invasive methods) and took them back to Utah for lab tests.

Woodward hoped to test Tutankhamun too, but his project came to an abrupt end, after coming what he later described as "tantalizingly close" to sampling the boy king.[17] The PBS documentary says that the authorities decided Tutankhamun was "too precious to disturb." But Egyptologists widely believe the termination of the project was triggered by concerns of an ulterior—religious—motive.

To anyone on the outside, Mormonism looks like a pretty strange religion. Its followers believe that in 1827 an angel named Moroni led Joseph
Smith, the movement's founder, to a set of golden plates buried in a hillside
near his New York home. The plates contained divine writings in a strange
language described as "Reformed Egyptian." God provided Smith with a
pair of glasses and seer stones that allowed him to translate them, producing
the "Book of Mormon: Another Testament of Jesus Christ." Among other
things, it claims that a forgotten tribe of Jews sailed from Jerusalem to the
New World in 600 BC, and became the ancestors of the Native Americans.*

There are now around 13 million Mormons around the world and they
are massively into genealogy. The Church has the largest genealogical library
in the world, in Salt Lake City, Utah. It contains more than 2 million names,
on everything from fourteenth-century English church records to African
oral histories, and more than two thousand people visit every day. The
Church also has a website, FamilySearch.org, that contains over a billion
names from over a hundred countries, and is working on a huge project to
digitize microfilm and other records, which it says could potentially add
billions more.

They're not just doing this out of curiosity. A central Mormon belief
is that if you can identify your dead ancestors, you can posthumously convert their spirits to the cause. As the Mormon.org website puts it: "Discovering that you're related to a renaissance nobleman could be a lot of fun. It
could also mean giving him and his family an opportunity to receive the
gospel of Jesus Christ."

The Mormons are particularly interested in Egypt, because they believe
that the Jews who supposedly traveled to America in the sixth century BC
were descendants of the biblical Joseph, who lived in Egypt and was close
to the royal family (or was part of the family, if you believe Osman's claims).

---

* This claim has helped the Church to convert huge numbers of people in Central and South America,
and the Pacific Islands. But it has caused controversy in recent years,[18] since studies of native peoples
in the Americas show no sign of the DNA markers that are found in Jewish people throughout the
world. According to their DNA, the ancestors of Native Americans came from Asia, not the Middle East.
The finding has caused some prominent figures, such as Australian biochemist Simon Southerton, to
leave the Church. By contrast, Scott Woodward has been a high-profile proponent of a controversial
explanation called the Limited Geography model, which says that rather than the Hebrew tribe being
the principal ancestors of Native Americans as had previously been claimed, they must have represented
a relatively small number of people in just one part of Central America, which is why there is no trace
of their DNA left today.

So Woodward and Griggs's presence in Egypt raised a few eyebrows, with some Egyptologists wondering whether they might be looking for distant ancestors to convert to Mormonism. "There was a feeling that they wanted to baptize the bodies," one prominent Egyptologist (who asked not to be named) said to me about their work at Faiyum. "It was odd: there was no need to excavate the cemetery. There weren't going to be any grave goods there." Meanwhile, Ahmed Saleh, an Egyptian Egyptologist working for the antiquities service, complained to *Egypt Today* that Woodward was looking for links between Egyptian kings and Jewish prophets.[19] "They are trying to say that our Egyptian history belongs to them," he said.

Whereas Osman claimed Judaism and Christianity for Egypt, the fear was that Woodward aimed to do the reverse, and prove that the Egyptian rulers were in fact Jews. Did he even plan to convert the pharaohs?

Woodward has since left Brigham Young University to run an organization called the Sorenson Molecular Genealogy Foundation (SMGF). Funded by a Mormon billionaire, it combines genealogy with DNA tests—on a huge scale. The aim is to create a large, searchable database of DNA sequences from different individuals, linked to their corresponding family trees, "to help people make new family connections."[20] Since it was founded in 2000, the SMGF has collected more than 100,000 DNA samples, with corresponding pedigree charts, from volunteers in more than 100 countries.

Woodward didn't respond to my repeated requests for comment about his work and motivations (although when I called the SMGF, a helpful young man who answered the phone scanned the database for my ancestors before I'd even had a chance to explain what I wanted). He hasn't commented publicly either on why his project was cut short. But in a lecture to the Egyptian Study Society in 2001,[21] he said that among the questions he was trying to answer at the Faiyum cemetery at least was whether the individuals buried there have any living descendants, and whether they can be genetically tied with living peoples in Egypt and elsewhere.

So on the one hand, it would perhaps seem strange if someone with Woodward's beliefs wasn't interested in finding direct ancestors among the Egyptian mummies he studied. But then maybe it's a bit lazy simply to assign religious motivations to his work. After all, presumably he wasn't looking for souls to convert when he analyzed those dinosaur bones.

Whatever Woodward's intentions, little useful information has come out of his project. In that 2001 lecture, Woodward said he took tissues from eleven mummies and had sequenced DNA from seven of them, including Amenhotep I, the so-called Thutmose I, and the queens Seknet-re and Ahmose-Nefertari. The PBS documentary also showed samples being taken from Thutmose III and the two fetuses from Tutankhamun's tomb (Woodward and Griggs are shown tracking them down in the medical school, under the care of anatomy professor Fawzi Gaballah—it seems that despite Soheir Ahmed's searches for Harrison during which she found only the larger fetus, both of them were there after all). Some claim that Yuya—who Osman had identified as the Mormons' ultimate ancestor Joseph—was included in the study too.

In the documentary, Woodward said that although his analysis wasn't complete, preliminary data suggested several brother-sister marriages in the early part of the dynasty (with Ahmose marrying his sister Seknet-re, for example), followed by a break in the maternal line during which new genetic material was introduced. But Woodward has not published his results, nor submitted any data to the Egyptian authorities. So it's impossible to know whether these preliminary hints can be trusted or not.

In 2000, another attempt was made to DNA test Tutankhamun's mummy. The project was coordinated by Iskander at the antiquities service and led by a respected Egyptologist named Sakuji Yoshimura, director of the Institute of Egyptology at Waseda University in Japan. The researchers hoped to determine Tutankhamun's royal lineage by taking samples from his mummy as well as Amenhotep III (thought to be his father or grandfather). They also planned to test the Elder and Younger Ladies in the side room of KV35, to investigate whether the Elder Lady was really Queen Tiye (Amenhotep III's wife and just possibly Tutankhamun's mother) as James Harris's hair analysis suggested.

In November 2000, the researchers announced that they would carry out the tests the next month.[22] But at the beginning of December, the plans were postponed without explanation. According to press reports, the idea of testing the mummies had provoked controversy among archaeologists in Egypt, who saw it as "meddling" with Egypt's history, trying to alter the established view of the pharaohs and their succession.[23]

An antiquities service inspector named Zahi Hawass, who was in charge of the Giza Pyramids, was one of those who took this view: "I have refused in the past to allow foreign teams to carry out such tests on the bones of the Pyramids builders," he said, "because there are some people who try to tamper with Egyptian history."[24]

The plans were rescheduled for February 17, 2001, but at a press conference a couple of days later, Yoshimura announced that the Egyptian government had abruptly canceled the project, citing "security reasons."[25] According to the newspaper *Al Ahram*, this happened just an hour before the researchers were due to begin taking their samples.[26]

Like Woodward, Yoshimura declined to speak to me about what happened. But many archaeologists believe that this project was ultimately stopped for similar reasons to Woodward's earlier attempt. There's no suggestion that Yoshimura himself had any hidden religious motive. But the editor of *Archaeology* magazine, Mark Rose, wrote that the work was canceled "due to concern that results might strengthen an association between the family of Tutankhamun and the Biblical Moses."[27]

"There was a fear it would be said that the pharaohs were Jewish," agrees another Egyptologist with close links to the antiquities service, speaking to me off the record.

But if the Egyptian authorities harbor a certain defensiveness, or even paranoia, about their history being co-opted by other cultural groups, perhaps that's understandable after the unbridled treasure hunts of the eighteenth and nineteenth centuries. Some sociologists argue that Europeans took not just physical artifacts, but have been stealing the intellectual heritage of the ancient Egyptians ever since, with western press coverage, museum exhibitions and books all claiming Egyptian civilization as "universal," belonging to all humanity, rather than being anything particularly to do with Egypt.[28]

The royal mummies have been at the heart of that battleground, with many different groups—racial as well as religious—keen to claim the pharaohs as their own. Robert Connolly's blood group results are still the focus of bitter arguments on certain online forums, with far right groups claiming, however erroneously, that the pharaohs' blood groups prove that the civilization that built the pyramids was "white Nordic."[29]

Others have been equally desperate to define the pharaohs as black African—the 1970s Tutankhamun exhibition triggered widespread demonstrations that the king's African heritage was being denied, for example, while decades later in 2005, a reconstruction of Tutankhamun's face had to be removed from a Los Angeles exhibition after protests that it was not sufficiently "black," and therefore disrespectful to Egypt's African roots. "We do not need modern scientists to reconstruct the bust and tell us what to see," Los Angeles historian LeGrand Clegg told the news agency AFP.[30] "Do not deprive black children of their heritage."

It's hard to think of any other group in history with whom so many people are so keen to identify themselves. Owning the pharaohs, it seems, means getting to lay claim to a privileged place in history—to being the founders of civilization, and to somehow being better than everyone else.

Well, except where being related to the pharaohs is intended as a mortal insult. In 2009, a few months after Barack Obama was inaugurated as the first black president of the United States, a bonkers but nasty crop of videos started doing the rounds that showed images of Akhenaten and members of his family morphing into photos of Barack Obama and his wife and daughters. The makers of these videos claimed a family resemblance that supposedly proved Obama was a secret clone of the heretic pharaoh—with the implication that he could be counted on to betray his country in the same way.[31]

"Was the First Family created in test tubes using DNA from Akhenaten, his daughters, and Queen Tiye?" asked one.[32] Which has to be the strangest story of all.

CHAPTER ELEVEN

EVIL PYRAMIDS
AND MURDEROUS MOLD

═══

WHEN THE ANCIENT PRIESTS closed Tutankhamun's tomb for what they hoped would be eternity, they left behind a daunting series of booby-traps intended to punish any future intruder with a quick and painful death. After carefully locating the tomb in a remote site particularly susceptible to harmful cosmic radiation, and designing its chambers to magnify the earth's magnetic field in a way guaranteed to drive unlucky visitors to madness, they lined its floor with radioactive uranium. Then, they drenched the mummy's bandages in cyanide extracted from peach pits, and laced its surroundings with liquid mercury and scorpion venom. To make extra sure, they armed the tomb with laser guns.

By the 1970s, the myth of Tutankhamun's curse had evolved somewhat. The idea itself was as popular as ever, providing inspiration not just for novels and horror films but a continuing stream of supposedly factual books and documentaries. But instead of the revenge-seeking spirits and walking dead favored by 1920s séance enthusiasts like Marie Corelli and Arthur Conan Doyle, the focus shifted to physical mechanisms by which the Egyptians might have booby-trapped a tomb—with all of the above ideas, as crazy as they might sound, being suggested.

The basic draw of the curse was no longer the fearsome power of the spirit world, which had fallen out of fashion. Like the myth of Atlantis, the curse fed instead on a thirst for lost knowledge, the idea that ancient civilizations had access to sophisticated technology that is long forgotten in the modern world.

Such ideas were made popular partly by Erich von Däniken, a Swiss writer who has sold more than 60 million books, starting with *Chariots of the Gods?*[1] in 1968, which argued that Earth was visited thousands of years ago by intelligent extraterrestrials. Using an artful blend of exaggeration, insinuation, and a tiny bit of fact, he suggested that these aliens built many ancient monuments, including the Great Pyramids at Giza, and provided ancient civilizations with sophisticated technology (such as the electric light-bulb, which von Däniken sees represented in ancient Egyptian reliefs), as well as providing the inspiration for their gods.

Accordingly, some of the explanations put forward for the curse were barely less magical than the idea of murderous ghosts. For example, following in von Däniken's footsteps in 1975 was a book called *The Curse of the Pharaohs*[2] by Philipp Vandenberg (described by his publishers as "an internationally acclaimed archaeological writer").[3] With a similar ability to build tall tales upon the shakiest of foundations,* he suggested a range of enticing yet implausible ways in which the pharaohs might have ensured the death of future intruders, from pyramids that induce mental imbalance to uranium-lined tomb floors.†

But such wild stories soon gave way to a more scientific approach, in which curse-related deaths were explained not by the murderous abilities of the ancient Egyptians, but by a new kind of culprit altogether.

First on this particular bandwagon was Geoffrey Dean, a doctor in Port Elizabeth, South Africa. When he read about Ronald Harrison's work

---

* The following passage on page 103, regarding Derry's examination of Tutankhamun's mummy, is typical: "Tutankhamun's autopsy at the Anatomical Institute of Cairo University on November 11, 1925, had tragic consequences: Alfred Lucas died soon after from a heart attack, and a little later Professor Derry died of circulatory collapse." Quite apart from the fact that the mummy has never been anywhere near Cairo, Lucas died twenty years after the autopsy in 1945, and Derry nearly forty years later, in 1961.

† The rocks of the Valley of the Kings do contain a significant amount of naturally occurring uranium, however. In 2011, scientists measured concentrations of radon—a radioactive gas produced when uranium decays—in twelve tombs in the Valley, and checked the radon exposures of guards working in the tombs each day.[4] They estimated that the guards were receiving a radiation dose of up to 66 milli-Sieverts (mSv) over a six-month period, well above the U.S. safety limit of 50 mSv per year.

in Tutankhamun's tomb, it brought back memories of a strange medical case. In November 1955, Dean was asked to take a patient who was desperately ill with pneumonia. The patient, John Wiles, was a geologist, and five weeks earlier, he had spent the day in a complex of caves in the Urungwe Reserve in what's now Zimbabwe. These caves were home to thousands of bats, and Wiles wanted to see if the huge piles of guano inside could be used as fertilizer.

Two weeks after entering the caves, Wiles started to feel ill, with severe fever and headaches, and trouble breathing. By the time Dean saw him, Wiles was desperately sick, but blood tests for parasites came back negative, and antibiotics had no effect, suggesting a bacterial infection wasn't to blame either.

Dean was at a loss to explain Wiles's condition, until a retired colonel from the British South African Police, Alexis Surgey, insisted on seeing him. The officer told Dean how two members of his police staff had died mysteriously thirty years earlier. Local witchdoctors, or *njanga*, had been stirring rebellion among the local Africans, claiming that their magic was more powerful than the white man's. As proof, the witchdoctors pointed to local bat-infested caves, which they said were bewitched, and that anyone who was not a *njanga* and went down into the caves would die.

To break the spell, one of Surgey's African constables entered the caves. Three weeks later, he became ill and breathless, and in another three weeks he was dead. A few months after that, a Londoner joined Surgey's staff. Dismissing the idea of black magic, he went down into the caves and collected some of the bones used by the witchdoctors for their ceremonies. He also became ill, and died six weeks after his visit.

Surgey had never solved the mystery, but his story reminded Dean of a talk he once heard, in which a microbiologist described the fate of an unfortunate group of caving enthusiasts called the Transvaal Speleological Society. Most new members became ill with a pneumonia-like illness shortly after joining, and several of them had died. But once a member recovered, they did not get ill again.

The illness was eventually traced to a fungus called *Histoplasma capsulatum,* which grows in bat guano. Inhaling the fungus-laden dust that filled the region's bat-infested caves generally ensured an episode of potentially fatal disease. But a victim lucky enough to recover would be immune to further attacks.

Dean tested Wiles for histoplasmosis (or "cave disease" as it had been dubbed), and sure enough the result was positive. After that, the patient slowly recovered, though his lungs were permanently scarred. When Dean next visited Zimbabwe, he interviewed two *njanga*, who told him that witchdoctors were given great power and wealth, including several wives and many cattle. Anyone who wanted to join their ranks had to attend a meeting down in the caves. Many aspirants died afterward, but those who recovered from their illness were rewarded with *njanga* status.

The whole episode reminded Dean of the infamous death of Lord Carnarvon, shortly after entering Tutankhamun's tomb. Could cave disease be responsible for the legendary Pharaoh's Curse?

In 1974, after hearing of Harrison's work on Tutankhamun's mummy, Dean wrote to him in Liverpool to ask if bats had ever infested Tutankhamun's tomb. Harrison checked with Gamal Mokhtar, chairman of the Egyptian antiquities service, who in turn asked "old people who were present at the time."[5] The elderly witnesses confirmed that for the first six months after the tomb was opened, it was protected only by a temporary iron door made of bars. Bats flew in at night, to the extent that Carter's workmen had to clear them out each morning. (It's quite surreal to think of bats roosting and pooing on the precious artifacts—not something Carter mentioned in his official accounts.) Dean subsequently published a paper suggesting that Carnarvon was killed by the *Histoplasma* fungus.[6] The theory explained why Carnarvon, with his weak lungs, was affected, but not, for example, Howard Carter, who as an experienced archaeologist might well have been immune to the disease already.

In 1993, scientists came up with another deadly mold that could have finished Carnarvon off. An Italian doctor named Nicola Di Paolo treated a farmer's wife from Siena who felt dizzy and had trouble breathing after sieving wheat stored inside a cold barn. The granary had been closed for two years, and some of the wheat had gone moldy. She subsequently developed acute kidney failure, but recovered after six weeks in hospital.

After putting some guinea pigs and rabbits into a cage with the suspect wheat (several of them died, almost all suffered severe kidney or liver damage), Di Paolo diagnosed the culprit as a fungus called *Aspergillus*, which produces a poison called aflatoxin.[7] Di Paolo happened to be an amateur Egyptology enthusiast, and subsequently suggested that *Aspergillus* growing in Tutankhamun's tomb was responsible for Lord Carnarvon's death. In several more studies carried out during the 1990s—mostly for TV documentaries, and unfortunately not published in the academic literature—various *Aspergillus* species were apparently found growing on Egyptian mummies (as they had been on the unfortunate Rameses II, on his trip to Paris in 1976[8]).

You can be at risk from *Aspergillus* even if you've been nowhere near a tomb. In 2007, a British gardener died of kidney failure after inhaling spores of the fungus while dispersing bags of rotting mulch in his backyard.[9] But the most dramatic example of *Aspergillus*'s deadliness is the case of Casimir IV, who was King of Poland from 1447 to 1492. If anyone deserves their own curse myth, it's him.

The remains of Casimir and his wife, Elizabeth, were interred in a tomb in the chapel of Wawel Castle in Krakow, Poland. In 1973, with the consent of the Archbishop of Krakow (who later became Pope John Paul II), a team of twelve scientists entered the royal vault—the first time it had been opened since the king's funeral. They aimed to examine the remains to decide how best to restore them and the tomb. Inside, they found rotting wooden coffins containing what was left of the king and queen.

Within weeks, ten of the twelve researchers were dead.[10] When one of the survivors, Boleslaw Smyk, tested samples taken from the tomb, he found several species of fungus including *Aspergillus*.

These mold-related explanations for the curse are ingenious, and certainly a big improvement on evil spirits and ancient aliens. They have been taken seriously by the academic community: for example, the idea that Carnarvon was killed by *Aspergillus* toxin, perhaps from fungus growing in stores of grain in the tomb, was discussed in a series of letters to the medical journal *The Lancet* in 2003.[11] But it seems unlikely to me that Tutankhamun's tomb could have hosted a hefty enough dose of spores or toxin to cause any medical problems.

In the Urungwe caves, the piles of fungus-laden bat guano were up to six feet deep. And *Aspergillus* needs damp conditions to grow. There was some humidity in Tutankhamun's tomb at intervals over the millennia, probably from small amounts of floodwater seeping through the rock, but when Carter and his team entered, it was desert dry. Carter's chemist, Lucas, tested various small fungus colonies found in the tomb (for example, some brown spots on the walls of the burial chamber) and concluded that all were long dead by the time the tomb was opened.[12] In the absence of any direct evidence whatsoever for a fungal killer, the most plausible explanation still seems to be that Carnarvon's death had nothing to do with Tutankhamun's tomb, and that he succumbed, as stated on his death certificate, from the complications of his infected mosquito bite.

In 2002, an epidemiologist named Mark Nelson, from Monash University in Australia, took a different approach to the curse—using science not to explain it but to debunk it. It wasn't the first time this had been tried. After Carnarvon's death, the press blamed every tenuously related death on the curse, including Richard Bethell, Howard Carter's private secretary, found dead in a club in Mayfair, London, in 1931; his father, Lord Westbury, who jumped out of a window in his grief; and a boy who was subsequently knocked over by the Lord's hearse. In 1934, the Metropolitan Museum Egyptologist Herbert Winlock decided it was time to take action, after journalists started hounding the family of his seriously ill colleague Albert Lythgoe.

"The Boston hospital in which he is a patient has been so harassed by so many persons telephoning about the Tut-ankh-Amen superstition that others with legitimate business to transact can hardly get in touch with the hospital," Winlock wrote angrily.[13] "Mrs. Lythgoe's privacy is disturbed at all hours." Winlock put together a chart, published in the *New York Times*, of forty people present in the tomb when various parts of it were opened, of whom only six had died in the intervening years. If there was a curse, it certainly didn't seem to be a very powerful one.

Nelson went one step further, designing a formal trial of the curse based on protocols for testing the efficacy (or determining the side effects) of medical drugs. He compared people who were in the tomb at four key times—the openings of the burial chamber, sarcophagus, and coffins, and the examination of the mummy—with people who were in Egypt at the time but not in the tomb. In total, he included forty-four people in the study, who had received anything from 0 to 4 "doses" of the curse, and compared how long they all lived.

He concluded what many might say was the blatantly obvious—that being in the tomb did not significantly hasten death.[14] The average survival time was 20.8 years for those "exposed" to the tomb, compared to 28.9 years for the controls, but this difference was mainly due to the fact that there were more women (who tend to live longer) in the control group. The exposed group—twenty-four men plus Lady Evelyn—lived to an average age of seventy-five, not bad for men born late in the nineteenth century, who had a life expectancy of a little over fifty years.

But like Winlock, Nelson hasn't succeeded in banishing the curse myth, which remains perennially popular—a quick Google search for "curse" and "pharaoh" returns nearly 4 million results, for example. And in a way, such efforts miss the point. Tutankhamun's curse has always been a social phenomenon, not a medical one, far more influenced by people's unspoken, instinctive feelings and concerns than any amount of logic or scientific evidence. Besides, it really does make for a great movie plot.

=====

LORD CARNARVON'S DEMISE wasn't the only source of dramatic stories constructed from evidence that some might consider rather thin. Attention also focused on Tutankhamun's own death, or to be more specific, his murder. The idea that the king was violently killed started with Ronald Harrison and the "eggshell thinning" he saw at the base of the mummy's skull. But in 1996, thanks to a parapsychologist turned Egyptologist named Bob Brier, Tutankhamun's murder hit the big time.

After making his human mummy in 1994, Brier, of Long Island University, was asked to make what he thought would be a low-profile documentary about Tutankhamun for the Learning Channel. But the resulting film caused a storm of interest, so Brier followed it with a book in 1998, called *The Murder of Tutankhamen: A True Story*, which itself became a best seller.[15]

What was so explosive? As part of his research, Brier had persuaded Robert Connolly, in Liverpool, to send him a copy of Harrison's X-ray image of Tutankhamun's skull. Brier showed the X-ray image to Gerald Irwin, a trauma specialist at nearby Winthrop University Hospital. Irwin scrutinized the area of eggshell thinness noted by Harrison, and agreed it could be caused by a brain hemorrhage. He also saw a faint line just above the affected area, which he interpreted as a hardened membrane that had formed over the hemorrhage. Such membranes are slow to form, suggesting that if the bleed was caused by a blow to the head, Tutankhamun had lingered on for weeks.

If so, reasoned Brier, the injured king must have been conscious for most of that time and able to eat and drink; otherwise, he would have died of dehydration or starvation before the membrane had time to form. The site of the supposed bleed was a very unusual one for such an injury—a well-protected spot at the back of the head, right where the neck joins the skull. The king must have been struck from behind, perhaps while sleeping on his front or side. Brier then added a large dose of dramatic imagination to these hints in order to construct what is still probably the most widely known version of Tutankhamun's death. After the king went to bed alone, the door to his room silently opened and a man crept through:

Stealthily the night intruder made his way to Pharaoh's bed, the sound of his steps perhaps obscured by the drip, drip of a water clock. He found the king sleeping on his side, his head supported by an alabaster headrest. From under his clothes the man drew out a heavy object, possibly an Egyptian mace that joined a solid three-inch stone to the end of a substantial two-foot stick. After a single deep breath, he swung the heavy object at Tutankhamun's skull.[16]

The next morning, continues Brier, servants discovered the unconscious but not yet dead pharaoh and summoned a physician who regretfully announced that there was nothing he could do. Tutankhamun regained consciousness but then gradually weakened over the following weeks, and despite drinking wine laced with powdered eggshells (so that his damaged skull would heal smooth as an egg), he finally succumbed to his injury.

Following this account, Brier considered who could have been behind the brutal attack, including Tutankhamun's young wife, Ankhesenamun, and his two successors, the grand courtier Ay, and the chief army general Horemheb, before finally pinning the blame on Ay.

The most senior official in Tutankhamun's government, the elderly Ay had the uniquely privileged title of "God's father." He had served under Amenhotep III before Akhenaten moved everyone to his new city at Amarna. When Tutankhamun moved the court back to Thebes, records of most of the officials serving at Amarna disappear—their names aren't found in subsequent records at Thebes. But Ay continued his career. Brier interprets this as evidence of Ay's great influence over the king, and his willingness to switch his allegiance, even change his religion, as circumstances required.

Brier finds his smoking gun in a collection of records known as the Hittite letters. Excavations in Turkey have yielded thousands of clay tablets from the Egyptians' archenemies, the Hittites, which record everything from land deeds to military exploits. At the beginning of twentieth century, archaeologists unearthed some tablets chronicling the reign of the Hittite king Suppiluliuma. They mention an Egyptian king named Nibhuriya, which is thought by most experts to be the Hittite transliteration of Tutankhamun's throne name, Neb-kheperu-re.

The tablets quote an extraordinary pair of letters from a queen named Dahamunzu (probably the Hittite version of the generic Egyptian phrase meaning "the king's wife"). The queen writes that her husband is dead, and asks the Hittite king to provide one of his sons for her to marry, so that he might become king of Egypt. As the king is thought to be Tutankhamun, the queen writing the letter is presumably his widow, Ankhesenamun. A skeptical Suppiluliuma sent his chamberlain to verify the story, who eventually returned with a second letter and an envoy from Egypt, who confirmed that the queen indeed had no heirs and wished to marry a Hittite prince. Finally (some ninety days after the first letter), the king sent a son, but he mysteriously died on the way. Ay became the next pharaoh.

In her second letter, Ankhesenamun hints that she is under pressure, if not in danger, from someone in her court. "Never shall I pick out a servant of mine and make him my husband," she says. "I am afraid." But according to Brier, this is exactly what happened. In 1931, the Egyptologist Percy Newberry came across a faience ring found in a Cairo antique shop, which featured the royal names of Ay and Ankhesenamun, suggesting that she had married the old man and become his queen. Newberry copied the design and sent it to Carter, but didn't buy the ring, and it subsequently disappeared. As decades passed, some Egyptologists began to doubt it even existed, but in the early 1970s, another ring sporting the same two names was purchased by the Egyptian Museum in Berlin.

This is the last known mention of Ankhesenamun. Ay died after four years on the throne but the artwork in his tomb shows only his first wife, Tiy.* The whole thing was masterminded by an evil Ay, suggested Brier, who was desperate to become king before he died. He had ordered the murders of Tutankhamun, the Hittite prince (perhaps with some help from general Horemheb), and finally Ankhesenamun—after marrying her to cement his claim to the throne.

Brier says he was completely unprepared for the popularity of his 1996 documentary, which was covered in the *New York Times*, and then by newspapers around the world, with headlines like: "Professor Proves Boy-King Murdered": "Documentaries about Egypt are common, but the idea that this 18-year-old pharaoh was murdered touched the public," he wrote afterward.[17]

His book, published two years later, set off an even broader wave of interest. But this time he wasn't surprised: "By now I realized that the story had all the elements of an Agatha Christie murder mystery."[18] These included a spectacular backdrop of temples and palaces; a cast of characters including young, orphaned lovers and a deceitful prime minister desperate for power;

---

* Not to be confused with Amenhotep III's wife, Tiye.

and, of course, the discovery of the greatest archaeological treasure of all time. *The Murder of Tutankhamen* was translated into more than a dozen languages, inspired a gaggle of other documentaries and, Brier claims, created a new interest in the study of Tutankhamun.

One of the films inspired by Brier was *The Assassination of King Tut*,[19] shown on the Discovery Channel in 2002. It featured a couple of ex–FBI agents, Greg Cooper and Mike King, who stomped through Tutankhamun's tomb, attempting to reassess the clues surrounding his death. Heavy-set Americans with big, chubby heads and suits to match, the pair were billed as expert criminal profilers, used to dealing with homicides. After much talk about crime scenes, victim profiling, and a rather baffling "Tutankhamun risk continuum," they cited the Hittite letters to reach a very similar conclusion to Brier: Tut was murdered, and the culprit was Ay.

Cooper and King had medical experts too: Richard Boyer, Ernst Rodin, and Todd Grey of the University of Utah in Salt Lake City. Connolly sent them copies of several of Harrison's X-ray plates, whereas Brier's expert had worked from a single photograph. Grey was a pathologist who had worked with Cooper and King on cases before. He found no clear evidence for foul play, but thought that the features noted by Harrison and Brier—the bone fragment at the back of the skull, and the thinned region—were suspicious enough that murder was possible (a possibility that suddenly becomes fact in the film's subsequent narration).

Meanwhile, neuroradiologist Boyer saw something else odd in the X-ray images—the vertebrae at the very top of Tutankhamun's spine were fused to his skull. Boyer diagnosed a rare congenital disorder known as Klippel-Feil syndrome, which would have left the king unable to able to bend or turn his neck. "His head is like it's on the end of a broomstick," he commented in the film. This added a new dimension to the dramatization of Tutankhamun's death. The condition would have made the young king particularly unsteady on his feet—perhaps all that the assassin needed to do was to push him over.

The next year, however, Boyer, Rodin, and Grey published an academic paper including the X-ray images of Tutankhamun's skull, and disowning the conclusions they reached in Cooper and King's documentary.[20] The academics complained that the film crew gave them only a few hours to look over the X-ray images on the day that their interviews were filmed. There was no time for a detailed examination, and no chance to compare notes.

A dawn flight in a hot air balloon is perhaps the most breathtaking way to experience how the Nile valley is laid out. The river is bordered by a mile or two of fertile fields, which turn abruptly to the lifeless desert hills that conceal the Valley of the Kings.

Hatshepsut's great mortuary temple is built into the base of the rocky amphitheater known as Deir el-Bahri. The village of Gurna is perched on the far (south) side of this basin, close to the hidden cache of royal mummies entered by Émile Brugsch in 1881.

Only a few houses remain of the village of Gurna, once home to those talented tomb robbers, the Abd el-Rassuls. The houses are built onto ancient nobles' tombs, using their outer chambers as extra rooms.

The striking Elder Lady mummy was discovered by Victor Loret in 1898. Originally found lying on the floor of tomb KV35, she has since been identified as several different queens, including Akhenaten's wife, Nefertiti, and his mother, Tiye. She is now in the Egyptian Museum in Cairo.

A view over the Valley of the Kings. In this photograph, the entrance to Tutankhamun's tomb is located on the left-hand side of the Valley's flat central floor, just opposite the large visitor center.

Howard Carter glances at the camera during the opening of Tutankhamun's burial chamber on February 16, 1923. Just behind the stone blocks stands a wall of gold—the king's outer shrine, which almost fills the chamber. The wooden platform that Carter stands on hides a hole through which he and his colleagues secretly entered the chamber ahead of the official opening.

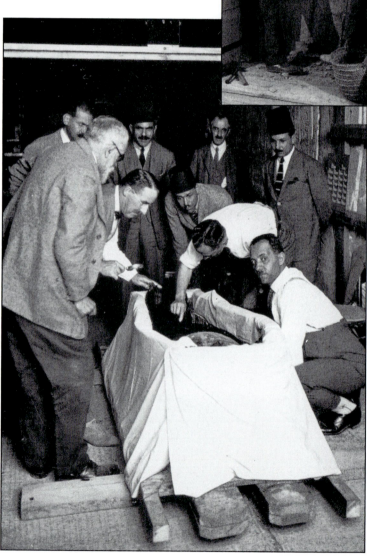

Preparing to autopsy Tutankhamun on November 11, 1925. Howard Carter is on the left, holding a magnifying glass. On the right of the coffin, anatomist Douglas Derry bends over the mummy, perhaps about to make the first cut.

The anatomist Douglas Derry (left) surveys the harsh Nubian landscape, ca. 1909, accompanied by the eminent Egyptologist Flinders Petrie.

Douglas Derry in his office at the Kasr Al Ainy Medical School in Cairo, ca. 1930.

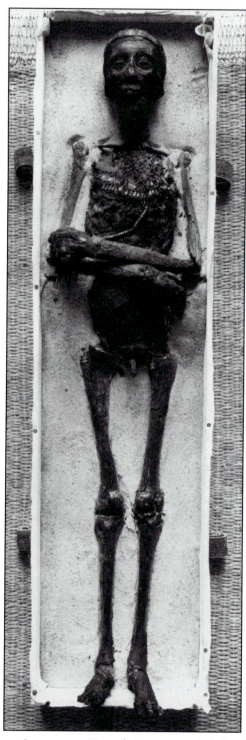

Tutankhamun's mummy, as Howard Carter arranged it before he placed it back into the tomb in October 1926. The mummy is in pieces, held in place in a tray of sand. A beaded vest is visible on the mummy's chest.

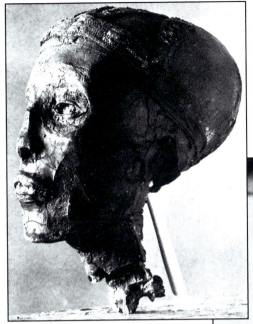

The head of Tutankhamun's mummy, as it looked after Carter and Derry's autopsy in November 1925. A beaded skullcap is still in place.

The larger fetus, discovered in the tomb's treasury in 1927. The female mummy is of around eight months' gestation and was accompanied by a second fetus of around five months' gestation. They are presumed to be Tutankhamun's stillborn daughters.

When workmen opened Tutankhamun's coffin for Ronald Harrison's X-ray examination of the mummy in December 1968, they broke the glass plate that Howard Carter had placed over the sarcophagus. It was replaced free of charge by the glass manufacturer Pilkington Brothers in St. Helens, Lancashire, UK.

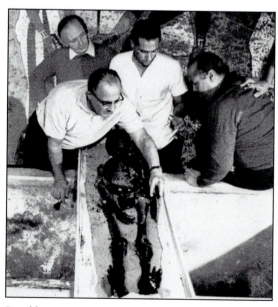

Ronald Harrison with members of the Egyptian Department of Antiquities in the tomb of Tutankhamun in December 1968.

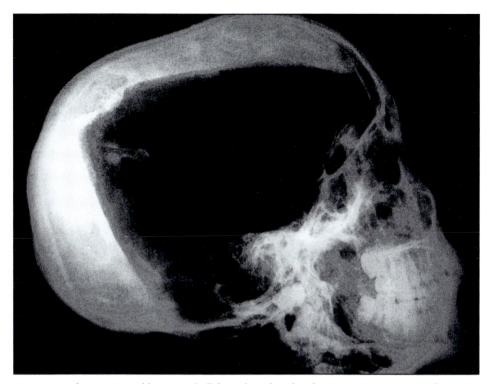

X-ray image showing Tutankhamun's skull from the side, taken by Linton Reeve in December 1968. The white material at the top and back of the skull is solidified resin, poured in by the ancient embalmers. Near the corner of the two layers is a fragment of bone, dislodged when Douglas Derry checked inside the skull in 1925.

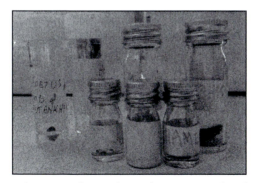

Robert Connolly now keeps these tiny samples of the royal mummies—obtained by Ronald Harrison in the 1960s and '70s—in his office at the University of Liverpool, UK.

Egyptologist Kent Weeks, director of the Theban Mapping Project (www.thebanmappingproject.com), can often be found in his little dust-colored caravan, just outside the entrance to KV5 tomb in the Valley of the Kings.

The Museum of Egyptian Antiquities, commonly known as the Egyptian Museum, is a huge, neoclassical building located just off Tahrir Square in the center of Cairo. Opened in November 1902, it is estimated to hold around 120,000 artifacts, many of them stored in the basement.

A statue of the revolutionary king Akhenaten, now on display in the Egyptian Museum in Cairo.

The famous bust of Queen Nefertiti, wife of Akhenaten. It was discovered at Amarna in 1912 and is now held in the Egyptian Museum in Berlin, Germany.

An Egyptian postage stamp showing King Tutankhamun's burial mask, printed ca. 1994.

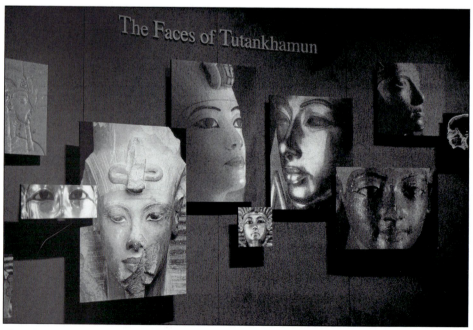

The different faces of Tutankhamun, on display as part of "Tutankhamun and the Golden Age of the Pharaohs" at Los Angeles County Museum of Art in 2005. The touring exhibit smashed museum attendance records and sparked a wave of Tutmania.

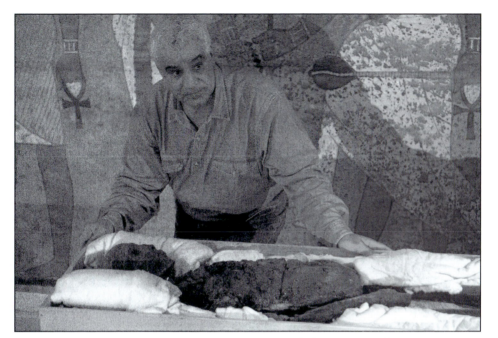

Zahi Hawass stands with Tutankhamun's exposed mummy before sending it for a CT scan on the evening of January 5, 2005.

Zahi Hawass speaks to journalists in the Egyptian Museum on February 17, 2010, during a press conference to announce the latest DNA and CT scan results on the royal mummies.

Pharaonic imagery was frequently used by protestors against President Mubarak's regime, as this graffiti in central Cairo shows.

Soldiers in an army tank look on as antigovernment protestors gather to protect the Egyptian Museum from looters on January 29, 2011. Behind the museum, smoke billows from the headquarters of the ruling National Democratic Party.

A soldier guards King Tutankhamun's golden burial mask in the Egyptian Museum in Cairo, shortly after the museum was looted during the January 2011 protests.

I visited Zahi Hawass in his private office in the Mohandessin area of Cairo in November 2011. Having recently lost his position as Egypt's antiquities chief, Hawass told me that he was working on two books—one on the revolution and one on Tutankhamun.

How the entrance to Tutankhamun's tomb in the Valley of the Kings looks to visitors today. The steep passage unearthed by Carter and his men in 1922 is hidden inside.

Once the experts studied the images properly, they realized that all of the strange-looking features had perfectly normal explanations. Tutankhamun didn't suffer from Klippel-Feil syndrome—his vertebrae were fused not because of a congenital disorder but because of the glue and resin that Carter and Derry had used to stick the mummy's skull back onto its spine.

The bone fragment turned out to consist of two bits of bone, not one. After a suggestion from Connolly, the researchers matched these to pieces missing from the vertebra at the very top of the mummy's spine. So they weren't caused by a skull fracture at all. Instead, Derry must have dislodged them in 1925, when he poked through the back of the skull to have a look inside. Further evidence for this came from the fact that Harris's 1978 X-ray images of the skull show the fragments in a different position to Harrison's, proving that they are loose in the skull. This means they must have broken off after Tutankhamun was mummified; otherwise, they'd be embedded in the resin that the embalmers poured into the king's cranium.

The eggshell thinning that Harrison had seen, and the ghostly second line noted by Brier's expert, had nothing to do with a brain hemorrhage. They were an optical illusion, caused by the fact that the skull was at a slight angle when Harrison x-rayed it. This meant that the two sides of the floor of the skull were at slightly different heights in the resulting image, so instead of one thick line, they appear as two thin ones.

In other words, there was nothing remotely pathological or suspicious about the skull whatsoever, just signs of how the mummy had been handled by previous excavators. Evidence for murder: zero.

But Boyer, Rodin, and Grey's paper, published in an academic journal, did not filter through to the general public. A subsequent edition of Cooper and King's documentary, produced after 2003, still claims murder, and still includes the footage of these scientists expressing the old conclusions that they have since disclaimed.

To finally kill off the murder theory would take a much more powerful voice. And newly appointed as head of Egypt's antiquities service was just the man—someone who, it seemed, would not rest until he had become as famous as Tutankhamun himself, and as full of contradictions. He would single-handedly change the face of Egyptology, and his meteoric rise—and fall—would have profound consequences for Tutankhamun and the other royal mummies. His name was Zahi Hawass.

CHAPTER TWELVE

SLICED, DICED, BROUGHT BACK TO LIFE

⸻

EXCITEMENT WAS USUALLY the only emotion Zahi Hawass felt when he was about to embark on an archaeological investigation. This time was different. As he landed at Luxor airport early in the morning of January 5, 2005, he did not relish the task ahead. He wrote later that he hadn't slept at all the night before. And instead of giving any interviews to journalists, usually a favorite pastime, he went straight to his hotel and stayed there until the afternoon. "I was so nervous, I turned all the phones off."[1]

Hawass is known for telling stories with the utmost dramatic flair. But on this occasion, it's quite reasonable that he did feel particularly apprehensive. As head of the antiquities service, he was about to remove Tutankhamun from his tomb for the first time since Carter replaced him there in 1926. The plan was to run the mummy through a multimillion-dollar scanner that would provide a detailed three-dimensional image of its insides, to settle the outstanding questions about the king's life and death. The whole thing was to be filmed by National Geographic for a glossy TV documentary.

Although this was the sort of thing that Hawass normally looked forward to with great anticipation, this time he was under attack from Egyptian scholars who did not want to see the king disturbed. Just a week before, the head of his scientific team, Saleh Badeir, had quit, accusing Hawass and his team of unprofessional and reckless behavior, and claiming that the project to image Tutankhamun had no chance of revealing any useful information, instead being just "another zero to add to the group of zeros we have obtained already."[2]

"People were watching me carefully, hoping for a disaster," says Hawass.[3] He needed that evening to go off without a hitch.

———

LIKE HOWARD CARTER, Hawass came from a humble background to rise fast through the antiquities service. The eldest son of a farmer, he was brought up in a village near the city of Damietta, in the north of Egypt. After studying Greco-Roman archaeology in Alexandria, he was hired as a young inspector with the antiquities service in 1968, just as Harrison was finalizing his plans to x-ray Tutankhamun, and Harris and Weeks were working their way through the royal mummies in Cairo. He later spent several years in Philadelphia, earning a PhD in Egyptology, and when he returned to the antiquities service in 1987, was appointed director of the area including the Great Pyramids at Giza.

This was the position that ended so disastrously for Carter after his men fought back against a group of French tourists. But Hawass thrived, masterminding the first formal site-management plan for the Giza plateau, including entrance gates, visitor centers, stables for tourist-carrying camels and horses, and conservation efforts. More controversially, he also starred in a series of TV documentaries about the pyramids and other sites, including live specials for Fox TV in which he pried open coffins live for the cameras and sent a robot to drill through a stone door at the end of a shaft in the Great Pyramid (revealing only a second stone slab).

Inevitably, he upset more than a few Egyptologists, who accused him of dumbing down the subject and chasing audiences at the expense of careful archaeology. But his force of energy and conviction captivated viewers around the world. On camera, he enthused wide-eyed about mummies and tombs and secret chambers as if they were the most precious jewels of the universe, and made a traditionally esoteric subject accessible, without a hint of snobbery. For the millions who watched, it was the first time that they had ever learned about ancient Egypt from an Egyptian. And according to some, such as Salima Ikram, an Egyptologist at the American University in Cairo who has worked in Egypt since the early 1990s, Hawass also made Egyptians themselves care about their heritage in a way that they hadn't before.[4]

Hawass was promoted to head of the antiquities service in March 2002. He set about modernizing the service, clamping down on bribery and corruption among local inspectors, and introducing site management plans at archaeological sites around the country. And he continued working with American film companies such as National Geographic and the Discovery Channel, appearing in a string of films with names like *Secrets of the Pyramids* and *Quest for the Lost Pharaoh*.

But this latest project was to be one of the most impressive yet. A few months earlier, in October 2004, National Geographic, together with the German electronics company Siemens, had donated to the antiquities service a computed tomography (CT) scanner, mounted in a trailer that could be driven wherever it was needed around the country. Worth millions of dollars, it was state-of-the-art technology that Egyptian scholars could previously only have dreamed of.

Hawass used the scanner to launch the Egyptian Mummy Project, a much-needed (and much-praised) effort to catalog and study all of the human mummies held in the many museums and storage houses owned by the antiquities service. Selected mummies would be CT scanned to collect data on topics such as the average age at death during different periods of Egyptian history, and the spread of ancient disease.

The scanner was tested out on a handful of not-so-important mummies in the Egyptian Museum. But then, instead of gradually working through the mummy collections as most observers had expected, Hawass announced that the scanner's first major project, beginning in January 2005, would be to scan the royal mummies, with National Geographic there to film the whole thing. They would be starting with the most precious mummy of all: Tutankhamun.

This is what seems to have got experts including Saleh Badeir, the orthopedics professor in charge of the scientific team charged with scanning the mummies, so upset.[*] He quit the project, complaining publicly that scanning Tutankhamun so soon was against the originally agreed plan, and that the team needed to gain more expertise before disturbing such a

---

[*] Although the details are murky—Hawass now claims that starting with Tutankhamun's mummy was actually Badeir's idea.

precious and fragile mummy. "All the attention suddenly turned to Tut-ankhamun's mummy without any previous intention," he told the news-paper *Al Ahram*.[5] "Why the rush?" Though he supported the idea of CT scanning in theory, Badeir evidently feared that the change in direction had more to do with attracting viewing figures than answering serious academic questions. "Instead of being a very important scientific event it only serves media addicts."

Several prominent archaeologists cited concerns too, largely over the transparency of Hawass's plans. Cairo University professor Abdel-Halim Nureddin complained that other experts hadn't been informed about the details of the project, and questioned whether Tutankhamun's mummy would be safe while removed from its tomb and scanned. Others, including Gaballa Ali Gaballa, former head of the antiquities service, were uneasy about the role of National Geographic, questioning who would ultimately own the information and images that came out of the project, and asking why the Egyptian media were excluded from witnessing the event.

No stranger to controversy, Hawass's response was robust as always. The mummy would be scanned by a professional team of Egyptian archae-ologists and scientists, and the plan had been approved by the antiquities service, who would own all of the data produced by the project. Egyptian journalists were excluded from the tomb only because having too many people present would risk contaminating the mummy.

Anyway, the film crew was booked. The CT trailer had been driven to the Valley of the Kings. The project was going ahead regardless of the cam-paign against it. But in light of the criticism, perhaps it's not surprising if even the publicity-loving Hawass turned off his phones.

At four thirty in the afternoon, Hawass met his team in the hotel lobby. They arrived at the Valley of the Kings in late afternoon after it had been closed to tourists for the day, under a sky that was, unusually, full of clouds. Buffeted by the wind, Hawass gave cheery interviews to the waiting jour-nalists from Egypt, the United States, France, and Japan. But he found the worsening weather unnerving. Rain, a rare occurrence in the Valley, would be a disaster—moisture in the air when they brought Tutankhamun out of his tomb risked damaging the mummy: "I heard people whispering about THE CURSE."[6]

As darkness fell, the team piled into the cramped burial chamber to rouse the mummy one more time. The room was a bustling sea of men, some dressed in shirts and jeans, others in traditional robes called galabiya, all hands reaching toward the open coffin. Then came a shout in Arabic: "In the name of Allah the merciful!"[7] Suddenly, the mummy was swaying and seasick as its wooden tray was lifted by two thin ropes and balanced on the sarcophagus wall.

Hawass dramatically threw back the mummy's cotton shroud, the moment captured in slow motion by the American film crew, who were squashed into a corner against a backdrop of mottled tomb paintings. It was a sorry sight for the cameras. As Harrison had found nearly four decades earlier, the mummy's skin was black, eye sockets empty, both ears rubbed away to dust. Its taut, stuffed belly looked almost comical next to broken stick-limbs and pigeon toes, the disarticulated pieces lying in the sand like stones. Egypt's immortal king had been reduced to a sad, charred puppet.

The mummy was swept out of the tomb and into the wind and swirling sand. The clouds denied it an exhilarating glimpse of the stars as it was hauled onto a hydraulic lift and hoisted into the nearby trailer. Inside, Hawass leaned forward over the mummy, smiling for the cameras, the two faces inches apart. Then the tray was pushed into the depths of the scanner.

Electromagnetic radiation swept through the mummy from every direction until barely an atom of privacy remained. Images of teeth and bone began to pop up on a nearby computer screen squeezed into a corner of the trailer, as the body was cut into black-and-white slices less than a millimeter thick. Harsh light bounced off every surface of the mummy, the decrepit figure drowning in the machine's clean white-and-blue curves. It was a strange conjunction of the ancient and the futuristic, as if this Egyptian pharaoh was being abducted by aliens.

Then the million-dollar scanner shuddered to a halt.

=====

CT SCANS (sometimes known as CAT scans) are routinely used in medicine for checking inside patients' bodies for problems such as brain tumors and internal injuries. The technique is now bringing a mini-revolution to archaeology and paleontology too, where it's also useful to look inside precious objects without cutting them open. Instead of producing a flat image like an old-style X-ray plate, a CT scanner sends X-rays through an object from hundreds of angles, then crunches the numbers by computer to produce a 3D virtual reconstruction of that object's insides. (Or as Hawass puts it, characteristically bending the English language to his will, "this machine can change the dead to be alive."[8]) Researchers can move the resulting reconstruction around on the computer screen to inspect it from any angle, zoom in to see tiny details, or even fly straight through to admire complex internal structures.

In the last decade or so, paleontologists have used CT as an alternative to breaking fossils open with a hammer and chisel—revealing for example previously unknown insect species hidden in opaque chunks of amber, the cleavage patterns inside billion-year-old worm embryos, and the spacing of vertebrae in a four-ton mummified dinosaur.[9] Archaeologists have used the method to study everything from the writing on ancient scrolls too delicate to unfurl, to the intricate gearing inside a two-thousand-year-old clockwork device called the Antikythera mechanism.[10]

Tutankhamun was getting the full medical treatment, in an advanced machine designed for living patients.* There was an hour of nervousness in the windswept valley as technicians tried to get the halted scanner working again. It turned out that the delicate machinery had overheated, because sand had blocked its cooler fan. Two plastic electric fans were obtained from a nearby office, and the scanning resumed. In less than half an hour, the machine's work was done. It had produced more than 1,700 images of the pharaoh's body.

Tutankhamun was returned to his coffin, while back in the trailer, the computer, operated by Siemens' specialist Hani Abdel Rahman, built up the X-ray slices into a three-dimensional model. As the king's fragile body was brought to life on the screen, Hawass finally sank back in his chair and smiled. But it was just the start of a busy night—the team had five more mummies to scan after Tutankhamun, including the three mummies—the Elder Lady, Younger Lady, and Boy—from the side room of KV35.

═══════

FRANK RÜHLI is a paleopathologist (an expert in the injuries and diseases of long-dead things, for those who prefer plain English) at the University of Zurich in Switzerland. In 2005, he was in his early thirties, but he was already one of the world's foremost mummy researchers. He had studied

---

* A Siemens SOMATOM Emotion 6, if you're interested in that kind of thing.

ancient Egyptian mummies held in collections around the world, in countries from Switzerland to Australia, but never in Egypt itself.

In late February 2005, Rühli received an email from National Geographic. Egyptian researchers analyzing the CT scans of Tutankhamun's mummy were having trouble agreeing on certain points. Time was short but could he fly to Cairo the next week to provide a second opinion? Rühli is passionate about his subject and despite its perhaps nonurgent nature, he doesn't like to hang around. He talks fast and fluently and sends staccato emails with the minimum number of words necessary to get his point across. He said yes immediately.

Hawass's Egyptian team, led after Badeir's departure by Mervat Shafik, a senior radiologist at Cairo University, had spent two months scrutinizing the CT scans, followed closely by the National Geographic film crew. A press conference to announce the researchers' results was already scheduled for the beginning of March. They would need to finalize their report before then.

Rühli was invited to study the scans along with two other foreign experts, Eduard Egarter-Vigl and Paul Gostner, a pathologist and radiologist, respectively, from Bolzano, Italy, who were known for their work on Ötzi the Iceman, a 5,300-year-old mummy found frozen in the Alps in 1991 (and now kept in Bolzano). The three of them had a week to plough through the hundreds of images, squeezed into the small CT trailer—now parked around the side of the Egyptian Museum—with the Egyptian team members squashed in behind. They weren't allowed to take images or data away from the trailer, but discussed their findings in the evenings over beer in the luxurious garden of the nearby Marriott hotel. For Rühli, getting a privileged view inside the body of such a famous historical figure was a dream come true. "It was one of the best weeks of my life," he told me.

But interpreting the clues inside a three-thousand-year-old body isn't easy, especially one that has been gutted by ancient embalmers, dismembered by modern archaeologists, and thrown about by looters. If you see some damage, how do you know if it reflects an injury or condition that affected the person during life, was caused by the mummification process, or was inflicted in modern times? The researchers couldn't all agree, so toward the end of the week, reinforcements were called in again, in the shape of Ashraf Selim. He wasn't experienced in studying mummies, but was a senior professor of radiology at Cairo University, and head of Egypt's largest private radiology institute.

Selim says he received a phone call out of the blue from Hawass himself: "At the time I didn't know him except on the news." Hawass asked him to judge between the two teams' findings and help to finalize a report. Because of the looming press conference, Selim would have only one day to look at the CT images. Selim refused, saying he was too busy, but Hawass wasn't about to take no for an answer, telling him: "It's very important to Egypt." Selim says he sat with the images until three o'clock in the morning before meeting with the Egyptian and foreign teams the next day. "I solved the conflict between both teams," he tells me. That's not quite how the others see it, however, and several disagreements were included in the final report, which all of the researchers duly signed.

The press conference was held on March 8, 2005, with the results— seen as a matter of national importance—announced to the world by President Mubarak's culture minister, Farouk Hosni.

Several of the findings matched what previous investigators had seen. Overall, the scans showed a slightly built young man, who was "well-fed and healthy and suffered no major childhood malnutrition or infectious diseases."[11] Tutankhamun's teeth were in excellent condition (apart from an impacted wisdom tooth), with large, front incisors and an overbite also seen in other kings from the same family line. As well as a slightly receding chin, Tutankhamun had a mild cleft palate, though he probably wasn't aware of it and there wouldn't have been any external signs. Like Harrison, the team noticed a slight curve in the king's back, but agreed that his spine looked normal and the body was probably just laid out this way by the embalmers.

The team noted at least five different types of embalming material in the body and skull, concluding that the priests had mummified Tutankhamun's body with great care. And, of course, they found the king's penis, to the delight of journalists around the world. "I don't know why the media got so excited," says Selim. "It's of no clinical importance for us. It's very dry. It just broke off and fell in the sand."

So what about the cause of death? After scrutinizing the skull, the researchers all agreed that there was no sign of a blow to the head. "This was one of the big mysteries that I solved personally," Selim told me. He says he determined that the bone fragments in the skull came from the top of the spine (as Grey, Boyer, and Rodin had previously suggested).

The team also concluded, like Harrison, that Tutankhamun's missing chest was a red herring with no relevance to the king's demise, arguing that with such a serious injury, you'd expect to see damage elsewhere on the body, perhaps on the vertebrae or arms. The ribs appeared to have been cut with a sharp instrument, suggesting that someone had removed them after death, but who? The team was divided as to whether this was done by the ancient embalmers for some unknown reason, or in modern times, by whoever stole the missing beaded bib. Playing to pro-Egyptian sentiment, Hawass blamed it squarely on the British archaeologist Carter—claiming that counter to the records the archaeologist left, he must have chiseled the bib from the mummy's chest, taking the ribs with it, before placing the body back in the tomb.

Several of the researchers saw a clue to the king's death elsewhere: Tutankhamun had a fractured left femur (thigh bone). Derry and Harrison had both noted this but didn't think it was important—the mummy's fragile bones are broken in countless places, due to their handling during and since the mummy's unwrapping. But this break looks a bit different from the others. It has ragged rather than sharp edges, and the scans hint at a dense material inside, perhaps embalming fluid that has seeped into the crack. A fracture in this location—right at the end of the bone just above the knee— is well known in young men in their late teens.

Some of the team, including Selim and Gostner, believe this is likely to be a fracture that Tutankhamun suffered during his life. Because embalming materials seem to have seeped in, they argue that the wound was still open when the body was embalmed, suggesting the injury happened just before Tutankhamun's death. A broken leg on its own wouldn't kill him but bleeding or infection that followed it might. The team came up with a new scenario for the king's death: he suffered an accident, perhaps while hunting, in which he badly broke his leg; then an infection set in that killed him a few days later.

Rühli, on the other hand, slows right down when it comes to drawing such conclusions, arguing that trying to tell the difference between damage that occurred before or after death is "a minefield." He argues that the evidence isn't strong enough to say that Tutankhamun broke his leg while he was alive. He points out that the mummy is damaged at the site of the fracture, leaving the bones exposed. Just by looking at the mummy, "you can clearly see the fracture and the material inside," he says. So the dense material inside the crack could easily have been inadvertently pushed there by Carter and Derry, for example when they painted the mummy with a protective coat of melted wax. He adds that the CT scans show no signs of a hemorrhage or bleed, which you would expect if the bone had been broken during life.*

The press release did a good job of acknowledging the disagreements within the team, although Hawass felt there was certainty enough. "These results will close the case of Tutankhamun," he said. "The king will not need to be examined again."[12]

≡≡≡

A COUPLE OF MONTHS LATER, the antiquities service put out another press release, this time on efforts to reconstruct from the CT scans what Tutankhamun would have looked like.[13] It wasn't the first time anyone had tried to re-create Tutankhamun's face. In the 1960s, the BBC commissioned a sculptor to produce a clay bust from Harrison's X-rays (he took on the time-consuming task for free, hoping that the publicity would boost his career, and was sorely disappointed when all mention of his masterpiece was cut from the final film). In 2001, the ex–FBI agents, Cooper and King, commissioned another bust based on the same X-rays, which was made by a physicist in London and delivered to them in a cardboard box.

This time, three separate faces were created by independent artist-scientist teams from the United States and France (both chosen and sponsored by National Geographic), as well as Egypt (selected by the antiquities service).

The French and Egyptian teams knew they were working on Tutankhamun and referred to ancient images to guide their reconstructions, which presumably allowed for a fair bit of subjectivity in the final result. The Egyptian team's version, perhaps not surprisingly, is kingly and handsome, with a broad, angular face, high cheekbones, and strong jaw. The American team worked blind, with no idea whom they were re-creating, so their bust is probably the most insightful. They identified the racial type as Caucasian, specifically North African. Their face is quite similar to the French

---

* In the National Geographic documentary about this study, *King Tut's Final Secrets*, much is made of apparent signs of healing within the break, which Egarter-Vigl and Gostner say prove that the injury happened while Tutankhamun was alive, probably between one and five days before his death. Rühli does not see any evidence that the break had begun to heal (though this wasn't mentioned in the film). When I interviewed Gostner by email in 2012, he had changed his mind too, saying that there are no signs of healing, although because of the apparent presence of embalming material in the wound, he still believes the break represents an injury that occurred at the end of the king's life.

version and shows a weaker-looking man than that produced by the Egyptian team, with a ski-jump nose and receding chin.

Hawass, ever the salesman, said the faces created by the teams were remarkably similar to a famous statue of Tutankhamun as a child, in which his perfectly round, wide-eyed head is shown rising out of a lotus blossom. I'm not sure I see it myself.

National Geographic's documentary on the CT project, called *King Tut's Final Secrets*, aired on May 15, 2005, accompanied by a cover story in the June issue of *National Geographic* magazine. In the film, the uncertainty over the cause of Tutankhamun's death has disappeared, with no mention of Rühli's doubts over the timing of the fractured femur. The conclusion—described by the film's narrator as "a turning point in the history of the boy king"—appears unequivocal: Tutankhamun died from complications following a broken leg.

But the CT project was about much more than just a documentary and magazine article. These were curtain raisers, which stoked excitement for the main event: a touring international exhibition that it was hoped would beat even the blockbuster tour of the 1970s.

After Hawass took charge of the antiquities service, Tutankhamun became the centerpiece of his strategy to bring in tourists—and money—to Egypt. In 2003, Hawass and the culture minister Hosni secured a law that allowed the Tutankhamun treasures to leave the country once more (such travel had been banned after a statue in the previous tour was damaged in Germany in 1981). This paved the way for two related exhibitions.

The first, called "Tutankhamen: The Golden Hereafter," visited Basel in Switzerland, and Bonn in Germany, in 2004. While the 1970s exhibition was intended to soften American attitudes toward Egypt during negotiations with Israel, this tour grew out of more modern political concerns, including the war on terror.

Egypt openly promoted it as a peace initiative. President Mubarak's wife, Suzanne, went to Basel for the grand opening, noting rather dubiously that the "magnificent Egyptian heritage is in itself evidence that since the dawn of history Egypt has embraced a culture of peace."[14] Mubarak himself attended the Bonn launch, accompanied by the German chancellor Gerhard Schröder. The Egyptian leader stressed the exhibition as a way to combat conflict between different cultures and religions, and used the occasion to push for international cooperation to combat the worsening crisis in Darfur, Sudan, and to address the root causes behind the growing phenomenon of terrorism.[15]

Some commentators say this shielded a slightly more self-interested motive. Egypt was heavily dependent on income from tourism, but visitor numbers had dropped sharply after a series of attacks by Islamist terrorist groups, the worst being a massacre at Hatshepsut's temple at Deir el-Bahri in 1997, in which gunmen brutally murdered sixty-two people before fleeing into the hills and committing suicide in a cave. Most of the victims were tourists from Switzerland and Germany. As Christopher Knight of the *Los Angeles Times* put it: "Tut was sent to invite them back."[16]

The show was a huge commercial success; in Basel, more than 600,000 people saw the show in six months. For Hawass, it was an early lesson in the power of Tutankhamun's popular appeal. "The people at that time did not know the value of what King Tut can do," he told *USA Today*.[17] "We know this now."

The second leg of the tour, revamped by National Geographic and re-named *Tutankhamun and the Golden Age of the Pharaohs*,* went to the United States, starting at the Los Angeles County Museum of Art (LACMA) in June 2005. It ended up making the 1970s tour look like a quaint educational effort, breaking the mold for museum exhibitions in that it was a completely commercial venture, aiming quite openly to make as much money up front as possible. It was sponsored not by a museum but by three commercial companies: National Geographic, AEI (Arts and Exhibitions International, a relatively new company formed to create profit-making extravaganzas for museums), and AEG (Anschutz Entertainment Group, which makes family movies, owns sports teams, and produces rock concerts).

Egypt too would take a hefty cut. In negotiating the deal, Hawass hoped to earn about $10 million from each U.S. city, to go toward antiquities as well as a hugely expensive Grand Egyptian Museum, planned to be built in Giza.[18]

The show was assembled and presented by the antiquities service and the sponsors, leaving the museums themselves with no say over the content or presentation of the exhibits they were hosting—or the cost of tickets. According to the *New York Times*, the exhibition did no less than redefine the role of museums, by outsourcing their traditional job—curating content—to commercial companies.[19] Or as one arts blog more succinctly put it: "LACMA curators have effectively left the building."[20]

---

* Before this exhibition, the alternative spelling, Tutankhamen, was more common, but *Tutankhamun and the Golden Age of the Pharaohs* cemented the spelling with a *u*.

Scientific studies on Tutankhamun's mummy were key to marketing the exhibition, providing fresh results that earned headlines around the world. The National Geographic–sponsored CT study was timed perfectly to promote the big U.S. opening. The tour ended up lasting another six years and visiting seven U.S. cities (as well as London, UK, and Melbourne, Australia).

The exhibition consisted of fifty objects from Tutankhamun's tomb. The gold mask and coffin were still not allowed to leave Egypt, but the show did include his golden crown, one of the gold coffinettes that had contained his internal organs, and a lifelike wooden torso, perhaps used as a dress model. These were joined by seventy objects from other royal tombs of the Eighteenth Dynasty, including a sensuous unguent spoon shaped like a swimming woman and a painted leather collar from a royal hunting dog. The last gallery of the exhibition proudly presented the big finale: the results of the CT scans.

This was Tutankhamun done up for Hollywood. LACMA rolled out the red carpet for its glamorous opening night gala, while inside, the museum was transformed as if for a movie set, with plywood pillars, flowing drapes, and scorpion-shaped wall lights. The galleries featured sand-colored carpets and walls, with enlarged photos of desert landscapes and slanting doorways reminiscent of stone gateways and tomb entrances. As visitors first entered the exhibition, a set of heavy black curtains opened to reveal a film featuring Zahi Hawass, with a voice-over by an old friend, Egyptian actor Omar Sharif.

To one reviewer, the mysterious lighting, curtains, and waiting invoked "the atmosphere of an amusement park where you know that things are fake, while trying hard to look real. [It] creates the expectation that the Tutankhamun torso will burst out in the ancient Egyptian rendering of 'It's a small world after all.'"[21]

The exhibition itself was well received by critics, who agreed that the objects on display were exquisite. But in general, media attention was quite negative—there was much criticism of the commercial organization of the event, while groups of protestors, upset by light-skinned depictions of the king, maintained that "Tut is back and he is black."[22] The final CT gallery was initially meant to house a bust showing Tutankhamun's reconstructed face, but after protests that it looked too "un-African," it was removed and replaced with a photo.

It didn't matter though. Just as in the 1970s, visitors came in droves—the exhibition was ultimately seen by nearly 8 million people worldwide—leaving marketers enthusing over Tutankhamun's "huge brand recognition."[23] Memorabilia on sale this time included a plastic Tut mask tissue dispenser and a Tut-themed olive oil gift set, while one industrious bar-owner invented the Tutini cocktail in the pharaoh's honor.

The exhibition also focused attention on Hawass himself, with publications around the world rushing to profile the charismatic king of archaeology. The *New York Times* described him as "part Indiana Jones, part P. T. Barnum,"[24] while the *Los Angeles Times* called him "the Arab equivalent of a first-class Irish yarn spinner."[25]

But these articles also highlighted his supposed darker side. Critics claimed that he regularly took credit for the work of others and was intolerant of dissenting views to the point of stifling academic debate, not hesitating to suspend antiquities service employees or evict foreign archaeologists who failed to toe the line. Hawass emphatically denies these accusations, as I was to find out when I later visited him, but he failed to convince Britain's *Sunday Times*. "He rules Egyptology with an iron fist and censorious tongue," its correspondent concluded. "Nobody crosses Zahi Hawass and gets away with it."[26]

Hawass's media-hungry style came in for more criticism too, including his handling of the CT study, which Thomas Hoving, the ex-director of New York's Metropolitan Museum of Art, who had coordinated the 1970s tour, dismissed as a media stunt rather than serious scholarship. Even one of Hawass's friends described him (in the nicest possible way) as "a media whore . . . who understands how to talk to people at the lowest possible level."[27]

"I'm not doing this for fame. I'm already famous," Hawass responded. "I'm not doing this for power. I don't need power. I'm doing this because I'm the only one who can do it. It's the first time that Egypt is being explained to the public."[28] And thanks to him, more people knew Tutankhamun's name than ever before.

═══════

HOW TO FOLLOW the commercial success of CT scanning the boy king? Hawass's next big documentary followed another dramatic storyline: the search for the lost queen Nefertiti. *Nefertiti and the Lost Dynasty*,[29] made by

National Geographic, first aired in July 2007. It focused on the CT scans of the two mysterious women from the side room of tomb KV35.

Both women had previously been considered as candidates for Nefertiti, Akhenaten's beautiful wife. An Egyptologist named Susan James suggested in 2001 that the Elder Lady has a pronounced physical resemblance to the famous Berlin bust of the ancient queen, including a square jaw, elongated neck, and pronounced filtrum (the little vertical groove underneath your nose).[30] Like Harris, who thought that she might be Hatshepsut before changing his mind to Queen Tiye, James noted the Elder Lady's bent left arm, a pose associated with female royalty.

Another Egyptologist, Joann Fletcher of the University of York, UK, subsequently suggested (in a 2003 documentary followed by a 2004 book[31]), that Nefertiti was instead the Younger Lady.* Her claim proved controversial among some Egyptologists, not least Hawass, who described her as "nuts" and "an amateur,"[32] and accused her of breaking rules by publicizing her work without running her results past the antiquities service first. Fletcher denies this, arguing that she did submit a report as required, although this didn't stop the antiquities service, led by Hawass, from temporarily banning her from working in Egypt. They even issued a report saying that the mummy was male, though this was conveniently forgotten by the time of the CT study.

In *Nefertiti and the Lost Dynasty*, Selim's CT scans are presented as ruling out both women as Nefertiti, but provide drama for the TV cameras by then suggesting them as other prominent members of Tutankhamun's family. Based on mild degeneration in the Elder Lady's spine and knees, Selim and Rahman decided that she was aged between forty and sixty when she died, just the right age for Queen Tiye, as Harris had suggested. Some Egyptologists have since pointed out that this evidence is hardly conclusive—after all, Nefertiti could have been that age too. In the film, Hawass chooses his words carefully. He pronounces merely that the mummy could be Tiye. But no alternatives are presented, and there's something so persuasive, almost hypnotic, about his delivery that the casual viewer is left in no doubt that the true identity of this enigmatic mummy has at last been found.

---

* This idea was first suggested by Marianne Luban in 1999, although Fletcher's claim was higher profile.

Meanwhile, scans of the Younger Lady showed that she died in her thirties, possibly a more likely age for Nefertiti. But Selim concluded that of two right arms found near the mummy, a straight one fit her best, rather than a bent one with clenched fist favored by Fletcher. (One of the problems with the royal tombs is that there are sometimes several dismembered body parts left lying around by the ancient looters, so it can be hard to know what belongs to whom.) Selim and Hawass decided that she wasn't an important royal after all, so she couldn't be Nefertiti.

According to Selim, this mummy's skull is asymmetrical at the back, and has an unusual extra fragment between the two plates at the rear of the skull. Of the royal mummies, only Tutankhamun has similar anomalies, Selim claims. In the film (none of this has been published in a formal academic paper), Hawass and Selim reach a surprise conclusion: the Younger Lady could be none other than Tutankhamun's mother.

Because the study hasn't been published, it's hard for other radiologists to give a second opinion. But some Egyptologists are skeptical about this too—after all, Tutankhamun's mother was probably a queen herself, so if a straight arm rules out Nefertiti, wouldn't it rule her out too? Several of them, such as Aidan Dodson of Bristol University, UK, argue that the rush to identify these women as key missing persons from Tutankhamun's time ignores the archaeological context of the tomb. As Loret noted back in 1898, the royal mummies found in Amenhotep II's tomb had all been carefully rewrapped and labeled, whereas the two women were found naked on the floor in another room. Dodson argues that however much we'd like to believe otherwise, these mummies probably aren't famous royals at all, but relatives of the tomb's owner, Amenhotep II.

═══

THE ELDER AND YOUNGER LADIES have since been moved from the KV35 tomb to the Egyptian Museum in Cairo, so I make a trip there to visit them. I'm keen to see for myself these two women who have prompted so much heated argument and speculation. The Valley of the Kings has yielded plenty of anonymous mummies, so what is it about this pair that causes so much fascination?

I try the Royal Mummy Rooms first, but it turns out they haven't made it into these specially designed chambers, or into the climate-controlled cases that the pharaohs enjoy. Instead I find them, alongside the bones of the unnamed king from KV55, in a deserted walkway just outside.

Like the other royal mummies, both are covered neck to toe with a sheet. The younger woman has a small frame and gray-black skin, with a shaved head, closed eyes, and a delicate, flattened nose. She'd look peaceful, pretty even, if it wasn't for the huge hole ripped out of her face (experts still argue over whether this wound killed her, or the damage was done later, by tomb robbers).

The elder woman is gray too. She must once have been beautiful, with high cheekbones, a delicate chin, and long, dark, wavy hair with a slight auburn tint. One eye is open, the other closed, and the top of her left hand is just visible above the top of the sheet, held over her throat with clenched knuckles and a thin thumb sticking out, as if she once held a scepter or staff.

She looks dignified but sad. I lean over the case to look down on her (something that isn't possible with the taller cases in the Royal Mummy Room, where you can only look in from the side). The pharaohs are fascinating to see but an anticlimax in a way, dried and dead and leaving me dispassionate. I'm not really the type to get too carried away by these things. Yet looking square into the face of the Elder Lady, I am suddenly confronted with the emotional power that Egyptian mummies can have. It's as though she's still there, her open eye staring straight at me with something between disdain and accusation, and quite unexpectedly I get that butterflies feeling of leaning over a cliff edge, when you scare yourself and have to step back.

Of all the royal mummies, the Elder Lady demands respect, making me feel as if I'm truly in the presence of someone who once ruled an empire at the height of Egypt's military might. It's all subjective, of course; my reaction has more to do with the emotional wiring of the human brain and the mummy's excellent state of preservation than anything relating to this woman's actual identity. And yet, staring into her open eye feels like gazing straight into a chasm that stretches three thousand years into the past. Suddenly, I'm not surprised that so many others have seen in her an ancient queen.

I'm jolted back to the present by the implausibly loud roar of low-flying planes passing directly overhead. It's October 6, and Egypt is once again celebrating Victory Day.

CHAPTER THIRTEEN

THE
THIRD DOOR

═══

THE MUSEUM OF EGYPTIAN ANTIQUITIES in Cairo, commonly known as the Egyptian Museum, is a huge pink-and-white neoclassical building adorned with arched windows and flags, which reminds me (a tiny bit) of a giant piece of Battenberg cake. Thousands of visitors each day pass through security at its main entrance, a huge doorway set between two lofty columns right in the center of the building's grand façade. They're greeted by high ceilings, giant statues, and century-old glass cases that house the most impressive collection of ancient Egyptian artifacts in the world.

Most of them probably don't notice a much plainer wooden door, all the way over to the right. This is the "backstage" entrance, used by staff and visiting archaeologists, and it takes you to the parts of the museum that the public doesn't get to see. There are no turnstiles here, just a sleepy guard at a desk who asks you to sign your name in an old notebook. Inside is a maze of dimly lit, dusty corridors with low vaulted ceilings, a hum of Arabic, and a large director's office furnished with sofas and ornate clocks. Stone stairs lead down to the museum's mysterious basement, off-limits to all but the most privileged, and stuffed to the brim with tens of thousands of forgotten objects that the curators don't have room to display.

If you ignore that entrance too, though, and turn the corner around the building to your left, you'll come to a third option. After the history-filled spaces beyond the first two doors, crossing this threshold is like entering another world, or at least jumping a century or two forward in time. A flight of stairs takes you down to a metal double door, secured with multiple layers of locks that admit only authorized personnel. On the other side, there are no ancient artifacts, nor even a speck of dust. Instead, you'll find a series of rooms with shiny floors, UV lights, and sterilized walls, filled with high-tech laboratory equipment and workers unrecognizable beneath hats, masks, gloves, and gowns.

This is Egypt's first ever ancient DNA lab. It's the site of the next (and last) phase of Zahi Hawass's investigations of Tutankhamun and the royal mummies: the most ambitious—and controversial—studies they have ever been subjected to. The lab was built in 2006, and its first project was another TV-friendly tale: the hunt for the mummy of the audacious Hatshepsut.

Toward the beginning of the Eighteenth Dynasty, 150 years or so before Tutankhamun's reign, lived a queen who dared to be king. Hatshepsut was the eldest daughter of a pharaoh, Thutmose I, but as power was inherited through the male line, she didn't take the throne when her father died; instead it went to her younger half-brother. He became Thutmose II, and Hatshepsut married him. When he died too, Hatshepsut—still just a teenager—became queen regent to his toddler son by another wife.

At first, Hatshepsut performed her role as expected, guiding and supporting her young stepson, Thutmose III. Before long, however, she started performing kingly functions, such as making offerings to the gods and raising obelisks, on her own behalf. Eventually, she went the whole hog and took the role of the pharaoh for herself, with her stepson relegated to second-in-command. As there was little precedent for a female ruler in Egyptian history, she depicted herself as a male king, with a royal headdress and false beard.

She ruled for seven years as regent and another fourteen as king, ably watching over a strong Egypt and commissioning hundreds of temples and monuments in her name, including the awesome mortuary temple built into the foot of the Deir el-Bahri cliffs. When she died, her stepson finally got his own stab at power and became one of Egypt's great pharaohs, with a string of wives and victorious military campaigns that extended Egypt's dominions to their greatest ever extent, stretching from northern Syria to the heart of the Sudan. Later in life, he set about wiping his stepmother's name from history, smashing her statues and chiseling away her image and name wherever they were found.

Hatshepsut is one of the few Eighteenth-Dynasty rulers for whom a mummy was never located—she didn't turn up in either of the royal mummy caches found at the end of the nineteenth century. Archaeologists have discovered two tombs bearing her name, prepared at different stages of her life, but neither contained her mummy.

It was possible that priests had hidden it for safekeeping, like the other pharaohs. So the idea of the Hatshepsut project was to CT scan and DNA test various anonymous individuals from around the Valley of the Kings that Hawass thought might be Hatshepsut, then compare them with identified royal mummies related to the missing queen. Of course, this assumed that her mummy had survived at all, which was a long shot, especially considering her stepson's campaign to erase all trace of her as king.

In charge of the DNA project was a mild-mannered Egyptian geneticist named Yehia Gad, who had dreamed of investigating the royal mummies for well over a decade. Based at the National Research Centre (NRC) in Cairo, Egypt's main government-funded research institute, he initially specialized in disorders of sex development. Then in the early 1990s, he traveled to the United States and learned about a recently invented technique called polymerase chain reaction (PCR)—also being used around this time by the Mormon ancient DNA researcher Scott Woodward—that can amplify tiny scraps of DNA into large enough amounts to be studied. One of its uses is in genetic fingerprinting, a method that can identify related individuals based on their DNA. After Gad returned home, his lab became one of the first in Egypt to offer DNA fingerprinting, for cases such as paternity and immigration disputes.

But he really wanted to be doing something else. Over the years, he saw growing numbers of studies from around the world, like Woodward's, that used PCR to extract DNA from ancient specimens, and he harbored a far-fetched desire: that he would one day open a lab in Egypt capable of extracting DNA from Egyptian mummies. Ancient DNA was (and still is) an extremely difficult field to work in, however. Researchers have to study tiny amounts of very degraded DNA, which are easily swamped by modern DNA molecules (from bacteria in the air, for example, or the investigators themselves). Keeping the two apart requires hugely stringent—and expensive—precautions against contamination, including working in a dedicated lab that has never been used for studying modern DNA.

Gad faced a catch-22. He couldn't build such an ambitious lab without generous funding, but he couldn't convince a funding agency to give him the money without a track record of scientific publications in the field—for which he needed a lab. To work on mummies, he would also need the support of the antiquities service, and this was not forthcoming. Gad watched the abortive attempts by foreigners to DNA test the royal mummies during the late 1990s and in 2000, and saw the bad press that this generated within Egypt. Perhaps an Egyptian-led DNA project would be different. But in 2002, when Hawass took charge of the antiquities service, the idea seemed further away than ever.

Hawass had previously rejected the idea of DNA testing the royal mummies, arguing that samples were too easily contaminated, which would lead to inaccurate results, and that it was better to concentrate on "more beneficial research," such as the cause of Tutankhamun's death.[1] As late as March 2005, after Tutankhamun was CT scanned, he insisted that the mummy would not be disturbed again.

But later that year, encouraged by Gad that research techniques had advanced, Hawass changed his mind. He followed his multimillion-dollar agreement with National Geographic with another huge deal, this time with the Discovery Channel, to DNA test the royal mummies in the basement of the Cairo museum. Hawass approached the head of the NRC: he wanted an ancient DNA lab and could pay whatever it would cost to build one.

As artifacts were cleared out of a large section of the museum's basement, it fell to Gad, and his colleague Somaia Ismail, to oversee construction of the lab itself. Despite Gad's long-standing interest in the topic, neither of them had worked with ancient DNA before. So Gad read up on the internationally agreed requirements, and worked with museum engineers to design the space he wanted.

The result was a network of underground rooms, like an ultramodern version of an Egyptian tomb. In a royal tomb, every chamber has a specific purpose, from the entranceway and storerooms to the burial chamber itself. In Gad's DNA lab, a small entrance corridor leads to a dressing room, where researchers must don disposable gowns, caps, gloves, and masks before proceeding any further. Then there's a sequence of other dedicated rooms, with one-way doors between like surgical theaters: a biopsy room for taking samples from the mummies, followed by spaces for extracting, amplifying, and sequencing their DNA.

To get any further, though, Gad and Ismail would need help. Hawass insisted that the research team had to be all Egyptian, but there wasn't anyone in the country with the expertise to carry out such challenging research. Someone would have to train the team—in how to take samples from the mummies, and how to analyze the DNA—and then melt into the background.

The Discovery Channel producer, Brando Quilici, called in a forensic anthropologist and Egyptologist named Angelique Corthals. She had experience in isolating DNA from Inca mummies—frozen bodies recovered in Argentina in the 1990s—as well as Egyptian ones, and was based at the KNH Centre for Biomedical Egyptology in Manchester, UK.

To find out more, I track down Corthals, who turns out to be a young, forthright woman with bouncy, curly hair. She chats cheerily to me on the phone from her lab in New York, where she now works at the American Museum of Natural History. Since the royal mummies project, she has returned to working on frozen South American bodies, and her main interest is the spread of infectious disease among ancient people, for example, whether they suffered the same kinds of infections as we do today, and how the spread of disease back then relates to what happens now. She tells me she was glad to get out of Egyptology, because of "petty politics," such as researchers being possessive over mummies, and not wanting to share.

"Not the Egyptians," she's quick to add. But her comments emphasize the smallness and strangeness of Egyptology as a field, especially when it comes to the scientific study of mummies. It's now illegal to remove any archaeological artifacts from Egypt. That leaves foreign researchers fighting over B-list mummies taken out of the country long ago. Meanwhile Egypt itself, which retains the most important individuals such as the royal mummies as well as all newly discovered finds, doesn't tend to have the budget, expertise, or equipment needed for high-tech studies—unless funded by foreign TV companies, whose desire for fast results and dramatic storylines does not sit easily with the interests of objective, meticulous science.

Corthals calls the Cairo DNA lab the "bat cave" and tells me that her involvement in the project entailed an exhausting regular commute between Manchester and Cairo. When she first arrived, in June 2006, the lab had been built, but it was empty. Before starting work, Corthals had to order the necessary scientific equipment and reagents from scratch.

"The budget was amazing," she says. "We could order whatever we wanted." As well as the money from Discovery, the biotech company Applied

Biosystems donated a sequencing machine worth half a million dollars, plus its latest forensic kit for extracting and amplifying DNA, including reagents that cost thousands of dollars for just a few thousandths of a liter.

Corthals taught Gad and his team how to take samples from mummies while minimizing contamination with modern DNA, and causing the least possible amount of damage to the mummy itself. She had previously worked with the Egyptologist Bob Brier, analyzing DNA from the "modern mummy" that he made in 1994.[2] Corthals found that even on this modern specimen, it was "futile" trying to isolate any DNA from the mummy's skin cells. "Embalming has damaged the cells tremendously," she says. She found that bone samples worked much better—ideally from the flat bones (for example the skull, pelvis, or sternum) or the long bones of the arms and legs. Bone cells are surrounded by a mineral capsule, which she says protects them—and the DNA inside—compared to other tissues.

But a mummy's bones aren't always so easy to get to. "You can't pierce a hole in the face of Tut, can you?" as Corthals puts it. She developed what she calls the "window technique," which involves cutting a square somewhere on the mummy that won't be seen by the public, then pulling out a plug of bandages, skin, and flesh—everything down to the bone. Then she uses a biopsy needle to collect the sample itself, the kind used by doctors on living patients for the painful procedure of taking bone marrow biopsies. It's kind of a cross between a thick needle (actually a hollow tube, two to three millimeters across) and a drill, which bores a hole, then pulls a sample of powdered bone back into the tube.

After collecting the bone sample using the biopsy needle, she replaces the square plug back into its hole, so the damage is barely visible. Corthals taught Gad to take four to five samples from different sites on each mummy, a procedure that could take several hours. The team practiced on a couple of anonymous mummies from the museum. Then they moved straight on to their first big project: the search for Hatshepsut.

Their two suspects came from a small, nonroyal tomb called KV60, located close to Hatshepsut's tomb in the Valley of the Kings. One of these mummies was found in a coffin labeled as belonging to a wet nurse. The other, nicknamed "the strong one" in the documentary,[3] lay naked on the floor in a mess of rags. She was obese, with "huge, pendulous breasts," but was mummified to a high standard with her left arm bent across her chest. Hawass wondered if the pair might be Hatshepsut and her wet nurse*—perhaps the

---

* The Egyptologist Elizabeth Thomas had tentatively suggested this back in the 1960s.

queen's body had been hidden in the tomb of her wet nurse to protect her from looters.

The mummy from the wet nurse's coffin was already in the Cairo museum, though it took staff several hours of searching to find her. Meanwhile the so-called strong one was still in the tomb where she had been found, so she was flown from Luxor to Cairo, getting her first taste of X-rays as she passed through airport security.

The plan was to DNA test the two KV60 mummies, as well as Thutmose I* (Hatshepsut's father) and Ahmose-Nefertari (thought to be Hatshepsut's great-grandmother), to see if there was a match. Corthals and Gad took samples from the mummies in the sterile biopsy room, with the Discovery camera crew and antiquities officials including Hawass watching anxiously through a window. Corthals describes as "muscle and grit" the procedure of drilling into the mummies' bones. "I remember we were both sweating, for two reasons," she says. "It's physically demanding, although you don't want to exert too much force or you'll break the bone. And we were boring holes into Egypt's most precious national treasure."

For the rest of the project, a cameraman sat in the lab eight hours a day, dressed up just like the researchers in a gown and mask, and filmed the team's every move. When Corthals attempted the first DNA extraction, he moved in for a close-up shot and his camera knocked her hand just as she was trying to pipette a minute amount of extremely expensive reagent. "I was very angry," she says. "That only happened once, I can tell you that."

It put the team under huge pressure, being filmed every step of the way during what was initially meant to be just a practice run while the lab was being established. Gad and his team were still learning, and Corthals says she never promised anything more than preliminary data. But Quilici and Hawass were in a hurry for results. "Yehia and I had to impress on both of them that for this kind of work, six months is a short deadline for preliminary results," says Corthals. "They wanted results in the first fifteen days." In the end, she says, the team was allowed two months. (Quilici didn't respond to my requests for an interview, but Hawass denies that he tried to hurry the team, saying he told them to "take your time.")

---

* If you've been paying attention, you'll remember that James Harris raised serious doubts over the identity of this mummy in the 1970s, which are shared by most experts today. The researchers don't appear to have taken this into account, though in the end it didn't matter too much for the Hatshepsut study as they didn't get any genealogical information from his DNA anyway.

Against all the odds, however, by the end of August, the team did manage to amplify some DNA sequences from the mummies. They were trying
to extract two different types of DNA from the mummies' bones. The first
was nuclear DNA. This is packed into the nuclei of cells, and makes up
the main part of the genome that we inherit from our mother and father.
The second type was mitochondrial DNA, a much smaller string of genes
carried inside tiny energy-producing factories called mitochondria, that are
present within each cell. These are inherited just from the mother.

The researchers extracted nuclear DNA from both KV60 mummies, but
weren't able to do the same for Ahmose-Nefertari or Thutmose I, so although
this was an impressive achievement—Corthals says she was "ecstatic" at the
result—it didn't tell the team anything about the mummies' identities.

Mitochondrial DNA is easier to detect, as there are thousands of copies
of it in every cell, compared to just one for nuclear DNA. Here, the team was
able to amplify a couple of short fragments from both the "strong" mummy
from the KV60 floor, and the mummy identified as Ahmose-Nefertari, for
the first time allowing a direct comparison. Here, the data was promising
but inconclusive.

According to Corthals, there was "some degree of similarity" between
the DNA of the two mummies, but the data are "not nearly enough scientifically to make any call as to their relationship." Added to that, we don't
know for sure that the mummy tested is definitely Ahmose-Nefertari,* and
we don't know that Ahmose-Nefertari was definitely Hatshepsut's great-
grandmother. And even if she was and the DNA matched perfectly, the
KV60 mummy could be any family member in the same maternal line, not
necessarily Hatshepsut.

Corthals and Gad had made a heroic achievement in getting the DNA
lab up and running so quickly, but their work did not ultimately reveal anything about the identity of Hatshepsut's mummy.

A second line of inquiry came from Ashraf Selim. He CT scanned the
two mummies from tomb KV60, as well as two further candidates from the
Deir el-Bahri cache, which it seems were added at this stage to make Discovery's coverage of the hunt more exciting. In the resulting film, these in-

---

* The mummy identified as Ahmose-Nefertari is one of two bodies found together in a coffin labeled
with this queen's name, rescued from the Deir el-Bahri cache in 1881. Gaston Maspero and Émile
Brugsch concluded that this mummy was Ahmose-Nefertari only after the other one—previously the
prime candidate because it was in much better condition—turned out to be male.

dividuals are dubbed the "screaming one," referring to a mummy with its face twisted into an eternal open-mouthed shriek, and the "serene one."

In November 2006, late at night after the museum had closed to the public, the mummies were removed from their cases and carried outside to the parked CT trailer, where Selim and his assistant Hani Abdel Rahman were waiting. First, Selim scanned the mummies identified as Thutmose I, II, and III. The researchers used the CT scans of their faces to create a "composite family portrait" of what they expected Hatshepsut to look like.

Then it was the turn of the four Hatshepsut suspects. Selim quickly ruled out the late-entry Deir el-Bahri mummies—the serene one because her straight arms suggested she wasn't an important royal, and the screaming one because she wasn't embalmed to a high standard and was aged over fifty, too old for Hatshepsut. He compared the two KV60 mummies against the composite family portrait and concluded that the strong one, from the floor, had the most similar face to Hatshepsut's relatives. But he couldn't rule either mummy out.

Later the same night, at around four in the morning, Selim scanned one last object: a carved wooden trinket box from the Deir el-Bahri cache. It had Hatshepsut's name on it, and contained what looked like well-preserved organs. Inside the scans revealed a liver and some intestines, but also a surprise—a broken tooth. A local dentist was called in who identified the tooth as a molar, with one surviving root and one root missing. The mummy found in the wet nurse's coffin didn't have any suitable space in her mouth where the tooth could have come from, ruling her out as its owner. But her companion from the tomb floor had very bad teeth, with several missing. For one of them, a molar from the upper right of the mummy's mouth, there was a root still embedded in the gum.

The CT scans showed that the left-behind root was roughly the right size to fit the Hatshepsut tooth—could the strong one be the tooth's owner, and therefore the missing queen? Further analysis of the CT scans showed that this mummy was middle-aged when she died and not in good shape, with arthritis, osteoporosis, and a tumor near her abdomen. She seems to have been killed by an infection that spread from an abscess in her mouth, which must have caused agonizing pain and left her unable to open her mouth or eat. It would have been an inglorious end for one of history's greatest female rulers.

Secrets of Egypt's Lost Queen was shown on the Discovery Channel in July 2007. In the film, the DNA results were portrayed correctly as being preliminary and inconclusive. The root and tooth, however, were described as "an exact match," clinching the mummy's identity. "This is Queen Hatshepsut," concludes Selim, albeit somewhat hesitantly. "It's the kind of proof that almost never happens in a cold case 3,500 years old," confirms the narrator. "Definitive proof—the kind that solves cases." The mummy was claimed as the first Egyptian ruler to be positively identified since Tutankhamun.

If the identification is correct, the study has important implications for the history of the period, suggesting that Hatshepsut died of natural causes, and wasn't bumped off by her stepson, as some Egyptologists have suspected. Unfortunately, despite the conviction expressed in the documentary, the evidence from the tooth seems pretty flimsy. First, it's not certain that the contents of the wooden box came from the body of Hatshepsut. Organs from a royal mummy were usually placed into a specific type of marble jar for burial. The wooden box might instead simply contain keepsakes that belonged to the queen while she was alive, perhaps from a relative or loved one.

What's more, the root and tooth seem unlikely to come from the same person. One U.S. dentist was quick to point out what he calls "glaring problems" with the Egyptian team's analysis, not least that upper molars have three roots, while the tooth in the box (from its shape, and the fact that it originally had only two roots) was almost certainly a lower molar, for which there was no gap in the KV60 mummy's mouth.[4] Erhard Graefe, an Egyptologist based at the University of Münster, Germany, has since reached a similar conclusion.[5] The CT team maintains, however, that the tooth could still be an upper molar.[*]

Most Egyptologists I've spoken to are very skeptical that this mummy has anything to do with Hatshepsut, and say they would like to study the team's evidence. Unfortunately, neither the CT scans nor the DNA results have yet been published in a scientific journal. (Gad and Corthals are quite open about the fact that their DNA results are far too preliminary to publish, and although Selim describes the CT identification of Hatshepsut as "one

---

[*] Although there does seem to be some confusion over this. When I asked Selim about the critics' concerns, he said that despite the impression given in the documentary that the tooth in the box originally had just two roots (one surviving and one missing), it actually has two remaining roots (making three in total), suggesting it is an upper molar after all. But Paul Gostner, a radiologist who advised the Egyptian team and has also studied the original CT scans, told me that the tooth does have just one remaining root, though he suggested that it might still be an upper molar if a third root has broken off and become lost.

of our greatest discoveries," he acknowledges that it has yet to be confirmed by DNA analysis.)

Despite such reservations, however, it soon became common knowledge around the world that Hatshepsut had been found. Even the highly tentative DNA results morphed into conclusive evidence, thanks largely to Corthals's institution, Manchester University, which issued a press release announcing: "When the DNA of the mystery mummy was compared with that of Hatshepsut's ancestors, we were able to scientifically confirm that the remains were those of the 18th Dynasty queen."[6]

Hatshepsut's discovery was subsequently named one of the top science advances of 2007 by *Discover* magazine[7] (which repeated the claim that the DNA analysis "confirmed" her identification), and featured on the cover of *National Geographic*.[8] Meanwhile, Hatshepsut took her place alongside the other pharaohs in the museum's Royal Mummy Rooms, with no hint on the accompanying label of any doubt that the mummy is actually hers.

The Hatshepsut and Nefertiti documentaries were shown in the United States within two days of each other in July 2007. Hawass was on a high. Results, viewing figures, and cash for the antiquities service were coming thick and fast. And the Tutankhamun museum tour was still breaking attendance records, so much so that a second traveling exhibition of the king's treasures—*Tutankhamun: The Golden King and the Great Pharaohs*—was planned by the same organizers to launch in 2008, "to feed America's rabid appetite for all things Tut."[9]

Meanwhile, Hawass was still working toward his ultimate aim, a grand project that he hoped would be even more successful than any of the previous mummy studies: DNA tests of Tutankhamun and his closest family. The project would push Gad and his team to their limits, and divide the scientific community. But first, there was another appointment in King Tut's diary. After more than 3,300 years in his coffin, the mummy was moving home.

═══

I'M SITTING in the back of a large car, being driven at speed through Luxor's dusty streets with no idea where we're going. But I've learned this is quite common when meeting Egyptian officials. It doesn't seem to be the done thing to arrange an interview time in advance, you just have to turn up and fit in your questions along with whatever seems to be going on at the time.

In the front of the car is Mansour Boraik—the genial head of the antiquities service in Luxor, an area that includes the Valley of the Kings and associated memorial temples on the Nile's west bank, plus the awesome ruins
of Luxor and Karnak temples on the east bank. Boraik is trim and full of energy, with close-to-perfect English and a neat moustache flecked with gray.

The car pulls up just outside the southwest corner of Karnak temple
and Boraik jumps out so I follow, as he walks along the top of what looks
like a harbor wall. Which it turns out is exactly what it is.

Excavations over the past few years have revolutionized archaeologists'
view of Karnak, a huge temple complex dedicated to Thebes's main god,
Amun. The digs have revealed a hefty embankment running in front of the
sacred site, as well as here, at the start of a sphinx-lined avenue that stretches
nearly three kilometers from the temple wall all the way toward the temple
at Luxor.

It's a vivid insight into what this place must have looked like in Tutankhamun's time. Water lapped up against the temple walls, enabling huge
ceremonial barges to carry visitors—kings and queens, or statues of the
gods—right up to the gates. You can still see the holes in the stone-block
embankment wall where the boatmen moored their vessels, and the wide
steps that allowed royal visitors to step elegantly out of their boats, no matter
what the level of the Nile, and walk up to the temple gates. "We think Karnak
was like Venice," says Boraik.

In fact, archaeologists are realizing that the whole area around Thebes,
on both sides of the river, was crisscrossed with man-made lakes and
canals.[10] This was far from dry, dusty desert living, even when the Nile was
at its lowest. The waterways played a central role in religious festivals and
processions, and were probably also crucial for moving supplies around,
including the huge stone blocks used for temples and colossi on both sides
of the river.

Much of this watery landscape was first engineered by Tutankhamun's
predecessor, Amenhotep III. He's famous for his enormous palace, Malkata,
which featured a nine-hundred-acre artificial lake as well as a large T-shaped
harbor that linked his residence to the Nile. Amenhotep also built the avenue
of sphinxes (though later pharaohs added to it), and the excavation Boraik
shows me reveals that the embankment wasn't just a feature of Karnak itself,
but ran alongside these sphinxes too.

He thinks an ancient waterway must have run right along the avenue
all the way to Luxor temple, but he's unlikely to get the chance to check

that any time soon. Since Egypt's revolution, when archaeological work here stopped, local people have been backfilling the excavations—using "Sphinx Alley as a rubbish dump" and a nearby Ptolemaic* settlement as a soccer field. When I ask why, Boraik just shrugs. "They don't need to see monuments," he says.

Back in his office, in a building tucked behind the Luxor Museum, I drink tea out of a tiny glass while Boraik chain-smokes, me trying to get a word in edgewise as his phone rings constantly and an endless procession of people comes in and out on various errands, their ripples of Arabic washing over me like a stream.

Finally, we get around to the reason I'm there—I want to hear about the day that Tutankhamun's mummy was moved from the coffin and sarcophagus in which he had lain for more than three thousand years, into a brand-new glass case.

The move was made in an effort to protect the mummy from deterioration. Although conditions inside Tutankhamun's tomb preserved its contents for thousands of years, once the tomb was open to the public, it became a much more damaging environment. The temperature inside varied considerably, and moisture breathed out by the hundreds of people who visited each day pushed relative humidity in the tomb to 95 percent—perfect for the growth of microbes and mold.

The antiquities service, under Hawass, decided that Tutankhamun urgently needed a climate-controlled home that would keep the mummy stable and sterile. His new case, built by German glassmakers Glasbau Hahn, would be filled with nitrogen (in which microbes can't grow) and keep humidity within strict limits. It would also, by putting the mummy on show for the first time, be a powerful magnet for visitors.

Tutankhamun made his move on November 5, 2007, overseen by Boraik, Hawass, and a handful of specialist Egyptian conservators, as well as workmen, representatives from Glasbau Hahn—and the obligatory National Geographic camera crew.[11]

The tomb was closed for the operation, Boraik tells me, and it took all day to prepare both the case and Tutankhamun himself. The mummy was

---

* A dynasty of Greek origin founded by Ptolemy, one of Alexander the Great's generals, in 305 BC, which ended abruptly in 30 BC when Queen Cleopatra famously killed herself rather than be captured by the Romans.

left lying in its wooden tray of sand, but covered from neck to ankles with a beige linen shroud "to preserve the king's dignity." According to Boraik, visitors aren't missing much: "the only good parts are the face and feet." The rediscovered penis does sound worth a look though—Boraik says it has a straw through it to keep it stiff, emulating the god of the underworld, Osiris, who played an important role in fertility and rebirth and was often portrayed with a permanent erection.

Boraik says that his encounter with Tutankhamun's mummy—his first view of one of the most precious items he is responsible for protecting— was a profoundly moving experience. "I just said hello," he says. "It was a strange feeling to see his face after three thousand years. It took me back to his time. I saw a young king, and the sadness in his family." Boraik says he stayed for two minutes in silence, kneeling next to the mummy's head. Then he went outside to smoke.

When the new case was ready, the mummy was walked over to it in a process that had been carefully choreographed the day before—just in time for a photo opportunity during which Hawass enthused to the watching press about Tutankhamun's "beautiful buck teeth."

The king's outer coffin still lies in its stone sarcophagus in the center of the painted burial chamber, its head pointing west toward the setting sun and its golden face staring up toward the sky. But Tutankhamun—until that day the last Egyptian pharaoh still in his original sacred burial position— is no longer inside. He is now tucked into a modest corner of the tomb's antechamber, at roughly waist level for convenient viewing, surrounded by glass and illuminated by a spotlight that springs like an alien antenna from the end of his case. The final step in his journey from divine pharaoh to museum exhibit is complete.

CHAPTER FOURTEEN

FINGERPRINTS, FORENSICS, AND A FAMILY TREE

===

I MEET YEHIA GAD at his suggestion in the leafy, sunlit garden of the Marriott hotel in Zamalek, Cairo, where we're served iced tea by scrupulously polite waiters. He's a small man, in his fifties, with courteous manners and a wry smile. Scholarly debate and success in Egypt is often highly dependent on authority, perhaps sometimes to the expense of talent, with prominent figures like Hawass and Selim not slow to advertise their considerable attributes and achievements. Gad is different. He's modest and thoughtful, and when he talks about what he's done, it feels as though his aim is not to impress you with his experiences but to share them with you.

Hidden beneath that mild exterior, though, is the spark of a revolutionary. After Friday prayers on January 28, 2011, Gad marched with his sons-in-law from his local mosque to join the crowds pouring into Tahrir Square, in protest against President Mubarak's repressive regime. He shows me videos of the clashes taken on his mobile phone, and proudly tells me about the birth of his grandson, Ali, who arrived into a newborn Egypt on February 11, just two hours after Mubarak finally stepped down. He calls 2011 "the year of hope."

But back to our story: I've met up with Gad to hear about his work on Tutankhamun. Following his lightning-fast training with Angelique Corthals,

Gad entered the king's tomb on February 24, 2008. It was his first day taking bone samples alone, and he faced the world's most famous mummy. His mentor was three hundred miles away in Cairo, watching via a live video link. Hawass needed home support for the project—from archaeologists, antiquities officials, and the press—so his team had to be seen to be all Egyptian. Corthals stayed away, and Gad was on his own.

Gad had flown to Luxor the day before. Late that night, he got a phone call. "Are you sure? Will you be able to take it?" said the voice at the end of the line. "Insha'Allah," replied Gad. With God's will.

The next morning, he first took samples from the Elder and Younger Ladies in tomb KV35. Then it was time to open Tutankhamun's glass case. He stood on one side of the mummy, with his colleague Somaia Ismail next to him, a watchful Hawass standing directly opposite, and Discovery's cameras zoomed in as close as they'd go. "You could feel the tension coming up, up, up from everybody," says Gad. If he applied too much pressure, one of Tutankhamun's fragile bones could easily snap. "But I put my faith in God, and we did it." His haul consisted of six tiny bone samples, three from each of the mummy's legs.

When he was done, Corthals asked for a close-up shot on the video link. The fragments looked charred, and not as clean as the samples that she and Gad had previously taken in the biopsy room. Tutankhamun was not going to be an easy mummy to deal with. She just had to hope Gad had taken enough samples that something was going to work.

With the Tutankhamun samples safely back in Cairo, Corthals left the royal mummy project. She says she wasn't able to spend enough time in Egypt on top of meeting her teaching responsibilities in the UK. To continue to guide the Egyptian team's work, she recommended Albert Zink, head of a specialist mummy research center at the EURAC Institute in Bolzano, Italy, and author of a string of papers identifying DNA from ancient mummies up to five thousand years old. Like Corthals, he was particularly interested in studying the infectious diseases people suffered thousands of years in the past.

He in turn recommended a second expert, Carsten Pusch of the University of Tübingen in Germany. Pusch had previously worked on mummies held in a collection in the Tübingen museum, testing out different methods to extract DNA from them. So Zink and Pusch each began the grueling commute between their day jobs in Europe and the Cairo museum. Although Gad and his Egyptian team would do the work of analyzing Tutankhamun's DNA, Zink and Pusch would design and oversee the study.

Unlike the Hatshepsut project, which had been a test run for the team, everyone was keen that the data from the Tutankhamun project should be rock solid, and capable of convincing experts around the world. A crucial part of the international guidelines for working on ancient DNA, particularly from humans, is that all results should be replicated in a second, independent lab. That way, if you get the same result in both places, you can be hopeful that it's a true result from the ancient DNA, and not due to modern contamination within the lab. So in June 2009, a second DNA lab was opened, also paid for by Discovery, at Cairo University's Faculty of Medicine. It was staffed by a second Egyptian team, headed by a young geneticist named Sally Wasef.

Eleven mummies were included in the project. The first nine are familiar: Tutankhamun, the mummy from KV55, Amenhotep III, Yuya, Tjuiu, the two fetuses from Tutankhamun's tomb, and the Elder and Younger Ladies from KV35. Added into the mix were two female mummies from a small nonroyal tomb called KV21. Pottery found in this tomb suggested that it dated from earlier in the Eighteenth Dynasty, and most Egyptologists assumed that the two unidentified women inside were noblewomen or courtiers. But they had bent left arms, so Hawass felt they could be relatives of Tutankhamun.

The plan was to compare the DNA of all these mummies to come up with a family tree. The researchers hoped that this would finally solve mysteries such as the identity of the KV55 mummy, Tutankhamun's parents, and the fetuses from his tomb. The team would also test the mummies for DNA from the microbes that cause plague, tuberculosis, malaria, leishmaniasis, and leprosy, to see if they suffered from any of these diseases.

Meanwhile, Selim and his team continued CT scanning all of the mummies, and reanalyzed the scans of Tutankhamun. They were looking for any inherited characteristics or disorders that might run in the family, and of course, clues to how the various individuals died.

Gad and his team were testing for several different types of DNA. They were trying to amplify fragments of mitochondrial DNA (which is passed down the maternal line), as well as DNA from the male-determining Y chromosome, which is inherited from father to son.

But the main plan was to do genetic fingerprinting on the DNA that is passed down from both parents. This is a good way to look at family relationships without having to sequence the whole genome. We share almost all of our DNA with every other person on the planet; it's what makes us human as opposed to chimps or grapes. But there are some small variations, which can be used to identify us.

DNA fingerprinting homes in on one specific type of variable region called microsatellites. If you look at enough different microsatellites, you end up with a "fingerprint" that's unique for that particular person. In the royal mummy study, Zink and the team looked at eight microsatellites across the genome, with unwelcoming names like D13S317 and CSF1PO (which always makes me think of C3PO, the camp robot in Star Wars). You can use the details of a fingerprint to draw conclusions about family relationships, because we inherit our microsatellites (as the rest of our DNA) from our parents—half from one and half from the other.

Working conditions in the ancient DNA lab were now quite different from the Hatshepsut project in several respects. This time, the cameras had to stay outside. Hawass banned them after complaints from the team that the film crew was contaminating the lab—much to the annoyance of the Discovery producers, who after all had paid for the entire setup so that they could film the work done inside. Zink and Pusch also insisted that the researchers were given enough time to do their work properly.

And they took months. One problem, particularly for Tutankhamun, was that black resins and other materials used in the embalming process had crept right into the mummy's bones. Normally, when you purify DNA from a sample, you end up with a clear solution. But to Zink and Pusch's dismay, in Tutankhamun's case, the samples turned out inky black. They couldn't get rid of the impurities, which clung tight to the king's DNA, blocking any subsequent reactions. According to Zink, it took six months of hard work to figure out how to remove the contaminants, but finally the precious DNA was ready for amplifying and sequencing.*

In Discovery's film about the project,[1] there's a scene in which Zink and Pusch scrutinize a row of colored peaks on a computer screen. There is a dramatic pause. "My God!" whispers Pusch, the muffled words just audible from behind his surgical mask. Then the two hug and shake hands,

---

* In case you're interested in the details, Zink says they used a method called gel electrophoresis. This involves injecting the sample into a slab of gelatin, then applying an electric current to pull the charged components (including DNA) through the gel. Smaller molecules travel faster through the matrix of the gel than larger ones, so this separates the different components in the sample by size. The researchers then cut out the piece of gel where they expected the DNA to end up, and washed and purified it from there.

accompanied by the laughter and applause of Gad and his Egyptian colleagues. The geneticists have just achieved their first successful result.

Except that they haven't. As cameras weren't allowed in the lab, the real
moment of discovery wasn't captured on film. The researchers were asked
to stage a reenactment, weeks later, for the cameras. But they insist that
their excitement in the dummy scene is real. The first DNA to show up from
the mummies was from the Y chromosome. It showed that Amenhotep III,
KV55, and Tutankhamun all belonged to the same male line, whereas an
unrelated male mummy,* included as a control, did not. It was an important
sign that the analysis was working well.

After that, the team moved on to the more challenging task of genetic
fingerprinting. According to Zink, they painstakingly repeated the test twenty
to thirty times on each mummy. Then they used a computer program to compare all of the fingerprints and come up with the all-important family tree.

Although popular with TV viewers, Hawass's previous mummy studies
had met with some skepticism among academics, partly because they weren't
first published in academic journals, meaning that other scientists had no
chance to scrutinize and check the results. He didn't want any such doubts
with this study: Discovery would have to wait until the results were properly
published. On February 17, 2010, the team published a ten-page paper in
the prestigious *Journal of the American Medical Association* (*JAMA*).[2] The
same day, Hawass held a triumphant press conference at the Cairo museum.
Gad, Selim, Hawass, and Pusch sat in a row to announce the results, their
heads just visible over a forest of microphones carrying logos from TV companies all over the world.

What they had to say was dramatic, and appeared to change our historical
understanding of the period. After decades of inconclusive results, the team
at last offered some certainty. The study answered questions about Tutankhamun and his ancestry that had foxed archaeologists for decades, identified several anonymous mummies as being famous figures from the Amarna
period, and completely changed our view of the boy king. The journalists
loved it. But scientists watching from around the world weren't so sure.

Impressively, the researchers said they had isolated DNA from every
single mummy they tested. Seven mummies yielded a complete fingerprint
across all eight microsatellites, while the two anonymous mummies from

---

* The mummy once thought to be Thutmose I, sampled during the Hatshepsut project.

tomb KV21, and the two fetuses, produced partial data sets. Zink and Pusch used these results to construct a five-generation family tree, with the elderly couple Yuya and Tjuiu at the top. The DNA appeared to confirm that the Elder Lady was indeed Yuya and Tjuiu's daughter Queen Tiye, as originally suggested by James Harris, and supported by Selim's CT scans. (I can't help wondering if perhaps Pusch was just a tiny bit influenced by the mummy's striking looks, when he told journalists that her genetic material was "the most beautiful DNA that I've ever seen from an ancient specimen."[3])

The team concluded that the troublesome KV55 mummy was the son of Amenhotep III and Tiye—most probably Akhenaten—and the father of Tutankhamun. The computer analysis seemed unarguable. The calculated probability that the KV55 mummy was Tutankhamun's father, for example, was a slam-dunk 99.99999981 percent.

The DNA analysis seemed to confirm Selim's controversial suggestion that the Younger Lady from tomb KV35 was Tutankhamun's mother. And to the great surprise of pretty much every Egyptologist with an interest in the period, she appeared to be another—previously unknown—child of Amenhotep III and Tiye. In other words, Tutankhamun's parents were brother and sister.

The incomplete data on the fetuses weren't enough for a definitive identification but supported the idea that they were indeed Tutankhamun's stillborn daughters. And there was another surprise: the partial DNA profile of one of the mummies found in tomb KV21 suggested that she could be their mother—presumably Tutankhamun's wife Ankhesenamun. If Egyptologists were surprised to find Tiye and Tutankhamun's mother in a side room of Amenhotep II's tomb, the idea that Ankhesenamun had been lying unnoticed in KV21 seemed even weirder, because there was nothing else in the tomb to hint that it had anything to do with Tutankhamun's reign. It seemed an incredible stroke of luck that Hawass had included these unpromising mummies in the study.

Most of the tests for disease DNA came out negative. But the researchers did detect DNA from *Plasmodium falciparum*, the parasite that causes the most virulent form of malaria, in Yuya, Tjuiu, and Tutankhamun.

Selim presented the latest results of the CT scans. Surprisingly, there was plenty new to say about Tutankhamun, even though this study had already been reported once. In fact, much of the updated analysis contradicted conclusions that the team had reached the first time around.

Rather than the well-fed, healthy youth suggested by the initial study, Selim now argued that the young king was riddled with minor ailments and weaknesses. For example, Selim diagnosed scoliosis of the spine in Tutankhamun—as well as in his mother, grandmother, and two stillborn children. What previous investigators had agreed was simply a result of how Tutankhamun's body was laid out by his embalmers was now an inherited disorder affecting almost every member of the family.

Selim also concluded that Tutankhamun had a badly deformed left foot. As well as a clubfoot, the accompanying *JAMA* paper reported, the king had been born with a missing toe bone, and one of his metatarsals was being eaten away by necrosis, a disease in which a lack of blood supply causes the bone tissue to die. The team diagnosed clubfoot in KV55 and the two KV21 mummies too, and reported (among other things) that Yuya, Tjuiu, and Tiye were affected by festering surgical wounds.

In summary, the royal family was a sickly bunch, with Tutankhamun in the worst shape of all—a frail, limping cripple who needed a stick to walk. He was hardly the type you might expect to have met his end falling from a speeding chariot, as had been suggested in 2005.

The one thing Tutankhamun didn't suffer from, apparently, was a gender disorder. This might sound a bit random, but Egyptologists and medics alike had been speculating about this for decades. The debate was triggered mostly by those bizarrely curvaceous statues of Akhenaten, but there are some rather feminine figures of Tutankhamun, too.

Some experts think this was just part of the Amarna art revolution, with Akhenaten determined to show himself (and perhaps his family members) as strikingly different from their predecessors, with attributes of both the father and mother of all creation. But many scholars have seen evidence of an inherited disorder, passed from father down to son.

Speculation about Akhenaten's medical condition started early, soon after his strange statues were discovered. In 1855, Auguste Mariette, founder of the antiquities service, suggested that the king had been taken prisoner in Sudan and castrated. Another French Egyptologist, Gustave Lefebvre, wondered in 1890 if he was a woman masquerading as a man.

In 1907, the anatomist Grafton Elliot Smith accredited the pharaoh's peculiar physique to Fröhlich syndrome: a rare childhood metabolic disorder characterized by obesity, retarded growth, and delayed development of genital organs. But the syndrome also causes infertility, and it was hard to reconcile this with the fact that Akhenaten had apparently fathered six daughters (and perhaps some sons too). The Egyptologist Cyril Aldred subsequently suggested in the 1960s that perhaps Akhenaten was born normal, allowing him to father children, but later suffered from a tumor affecting his pituitary gland, which caused his symptoms later in life.[4]

In the 1970s, British medics focused on Tutankhamun himself, after seeing gilded figures of the king in the British Museum's touring exhibition that showed him with a sagging tummy and pert breasts.[*] In a series of letters to top medical journal *The Lancet*, various experts diagnosed poor Tutankhamun with a dizzying range of conditions, including an adrenal tumor; Klinefelter's syndrome (in which men carry an extra X chromosome in their cells); Wilson's disease (in which there's too much copper in the body's tissues); or even a "Tutankhamun syndrome" new to medical science.[6] Eventually Ronald Harrison felt obliged to write in, pointing out that as the only expert who had actually studied Tutankhamun's mummy, as opposed to simply admiring statues in an exhibition, he could confirm that there was no evidence the king had any of the suggested disorders.[7]

That didn't stop the speculation though. In 1980, a doctor from Philadelphia named Bernadine Paulshock suggested that because certain statues of Amenhotep III, Akhenaten, Smenkhkare, and Tutankhamun all show signs of breasts, this could represent a genetic disorder running in the family.[8] She suggested pseudohermaphroditism, where males also exhibit female characteristics, a condition that she argued was common in families with a long history of inbreeding.

In the 1990s, Bob Brier suggested that Akhenaten, with his elongated head and spindly limbs, suffered from Marfan syndrome, a disorder of the connective tissue that holds muscles and bones together.[9] And in 2009, scientists from Yale University came up with yet another suspect: a hormonal disorder called Antley-Bixler syndrome, in which a single mutated gene causes an elongated skull as well as overproduction of the sex hormone estrogen.[10]

Selim and his colleagues looked for signs of some of these disorders, but like Harrison found no evidence that either Tutankhamun or the KV55

---

[*] According to Egyptologist Aidan Dodson of the University of Bristol, UK, author of *Amarna Sunset: Nefertiti, Tutankhamun, Ay, Horemheb, and the Egyptian Counter-Reformation*,[5] these statues are now recognized as actually representing the female king Neferneferuaten, a co-ruler and possible successor of Akhenaten. It seems likely that she was none other than Nefertiti, who disappears from view just as Neferneferuaten appears in the record.

mummy suffered any such problems. Their skulls, although very wide, weren't pathological. Tutankhamun's penis, albeit detached from his body, looked normal too. They concluded that the womanly appearance of the statues was probably "a royally decreed style," and that neither Tutankhamun nor Akhenaten actually had a significantly bizarre or feminine physique.

To summarize, then, Tutankhamun was a full-blown male, at least. But he was no longer an active youth who perhaps died in a hunting accident. Instead he was a weak, inbred cripple, afflicted by a series of congenital disorders. Oh, and he was infected with malaria.

As supporting evidence for the king's diseased state, the team pointed to various foodstuffs found in Tutankhamun's tomb, including fruits, seeds, and oils that had possible medicinal uses. For example, the tomb contained thirty-six baskets of date-like fruit from the *Zizyphus* or Christ's-thorn tree, which was primarily eaten as food, but also prescribed to treat stomach complaints, fever, and pain. Coriander seeds, found in eight baskets, could be used to treat gastrointestinal complaints, infected wounds, or "demonic" diseases of the head.

The researchers also pointed out that more than a hundred "walking sticks" were found in the tomb, and argued that the blemish on the mummy's left cheek might be an inflamed bite from the malaria-carrying mosquito. Finally, they cited images of Tutankhamun that showed him "performing activities such as hunting while seated." For example, an ornamented chest from his tomb shows him sitting on a stool with his queen at his feet while he shoots arrows from his bow.

In the *JAMA* paper, the team came up with a scenario for how he died that impressively managed to include all of these factors, as well as the broken leg reported in 2005 (which has now mysteriously transformed from a mere possibility into a confirmed fact): "The project believes that Tutankhamun's death was most likely a result of malaria coupled with his generally weak constitution. The CT scan of the pharaoh earlier confirmed the presence of an unhealed break in the king's left thigh bone; the team speculates that the king's weakened state may have led to a fall or that a fall weakened his already fragile physical condition."

Meanwhile Hawass focused on the revelation that Tutankhamun was the product of incest. The union between Akhenaten and his sister "planted the seed of their son's early death," he wrote in *National Geographic*.[11] "Tutankhamun's health was compromised from the moment he was conceived."

The resulting documentary, called *King Tut Unwrapped*, showed over four hours on the Discovery Channel a few days later. A *New York Times* reviewer described it as "CSI: Egypt,"[12] and while he wasn't captivated by repeated shots of scientists in lab coats peering at test tubes and computer screens, the film certainly got the attention of the world's press, for example *National Geographic* daily news, which announced "King Tut Mysteries Solved: Was Disabled, Malarial and Inbred,"[13] or the *Daily Mail's* rather less concise "Unmasked: The Real Faces of the Crippled King Tutankhamun (Who Walked with a Cane) and His Incestuous Parents."[14]

The success of the latest project was stunning, and its dramatic findings soon became, as one blogger put it, "accepted cocktail-party fact."[15] But it wasn't long before cracks started to appear. In June 2010, *JAMA* published five letters[16] from scientists in various fields, attacking the Tutankhamun paper on a series of fronts. Each seemingly clear conclusion was suddenly dragged into a mire of academic uncertainty.

One letter, from Brenda Baker, an expert in ancient human skeletons at Arizona State University, complained that the KV55 mummy couldn't be Akhenaten, as pretty much everyone who had studied it, from Elliot Smith to Derry to Harrison, as well as a more recent examination by a physical anthropologist named Joyce Filer, had concluded that this individual was in his early twenties at most when he died (based on fusion of the ends of his bones, and the state of his wisdom teeth), whereas Akhenaten was thought to be at least in his mid-thirties.[*]

Selim says his CT scans show that the mummy's age at death was considerably older than previously thought, supporting the identification of Akhenaten. Pinning him down on the details proves difficult, though. The reasoning behind this conclusion isn't given in the *JAMA* paper, and Selim has given various age ranges at different times. In the paper itself, he concludes that the mummy was aged thirty-five to forty-five, in the accompanying press release, he says, "between forty-five and fifty-five,"[17] and in a documentary that features the CT study he says, "forty-five to fifty-five, even sixty."[18]

When I asked him to clarify in an interview in November 2011, he couldn't remember exactly what age range he had concluded. He says that

---

[*] James Harris was the only exception, concluding in 1980 that the mysterious KV55 monarch died in his thirties. Frustratingly, he never published the reasoning behind this conclusion.

assessing the age of any fully grown skeleton is a "very subjective judgment," but argues that the age at death of the KV55 mummy must be significantly older than early twenties because of signs of age-related decline such as arthritis in the spine and joints.

Filer says she's confident from her examination that there is no sign of arthritis on the bones, and cautions that even if there were, arthritis on its own doesn't give an accurate indication of age. In line with Derry and Harrison, she believes that the individual is most likely to be the younger Smenkhkare. Selim is sticking with Akhenaten, arguing that CT scans show details that aren't necessarily clear in a visual or X-ray examination.

A second letter questioned the team's suggestion of malaria as the primary cause of Tutankhamun's early death. Christian Timmann and Christian Meyer, molecular biologists from Hamburg, Germany, pointed out that as adults, Tutankhamun, Yuya, and Tjuiu were very unlikely to have died of malaria. In areas where malaria is endemic, as it presumably was in ancient Egypt, malaria tends to kill young children; anyone surviving to adulthood would almost certainly be semi-immune to the disease.[*]

The third letter was from Irwin Braverman of Yale Medical School and his colleague Philip Mackowiak, the scientists behind the previous suggestion that Akhenaten suffered from a variant of Antley-Bixler syndrome. The Egyptian team had ruled this out, saying there was "no evidence" of female breasts in the KV55 mummy or Tutankhamun. Braverman and Mackowiak pointed out that as KV55 is just a skeleton and Tutankhamun's entire chest is missing, this is a pretty meaningless statement. In their view, the case for Antley-Bixler (in both individuals) is still open.

Then, there was skepticism over Tutankhamun's supposedly crippled left foot. James Gamble, an orthopedic surgeon at Stanford University, argued that although the foot is in a slightly twisted position, the individual bones each look perfectly normal, ruling out clubfoot. He thinks it's much

---

[*] Timmann and Meyer have an alternative theory for Tutankhamun's death—sickle-cell disease (SCD). In SCD, a mutation in the gene for hemoglobin causes red blood cells to become rigid and sickle-shaped. Sufferers have severe anemia and often die young. The disorder can also cause bone necrosis like that seen in Tutankhamun's mummy, when deformed blood cells get stuck in the tiny capillaries of the feet. Hawass's team initially responded that the idea was "an interesting and plausible addition to the palette of potential disease diagnoses in Ancient Egyptian royalty that we are currently investigating." Timmann and Meyer have developed a test for the SCD gene, so they offered to collaborate with the Egyptian team, but say they received a letter from Hawass that "somewhat roughly" declined any cooperation, and claimed to have ruled out SCD two years earlier.

more likely that the foot just got scrunched up when bandaged by the embalmers, while the missing toe bone has probably just fallen out of the mummy during its various trials since 1925. Meanwhile, other experts have questioned the diagnosis of necrosis, pointing out that embalming materials applied to the body after death could have eaten away at the bone over time.

Egyptologists too have poured cold water on the idea that Tutankhamun was crippled. For example, Marianne Eaton-Krauss, an independent scholar based in Germany, who has published extensively on Tutankhamun's burial, describes the *JAMA* paper as "aggravating" and complains that it shows little knowledge of relevant Egyptological discussions.[19] She rejects the idea that sticks found in the tomb suggest Tutankhamun needed help to walk, arguing that staffs and staves were a sign of prestige in ancient Egypt, and would be a key part of any pharaoh's tomb contents. Rather than being intended as crutches, she points out, many of them were used in hunting or hand-to-hand combat, or to handle snakes.

She isn't persuaded by the "seated while hunting" argument either. She points out that the scene on Tutankhamun's ivory chest shows him fishing from a folding stool, a situation in which it's perfectly reasonable to sit down.* Similar images are known for other pharaohs, for example, a depiction of the Fifth-Dynasty king Sahure from the causeway of his pyramid complex at Abusir, which shows him seated while fowling.

Selim stands by his conclusions, claiming that the abnormalities seen in Tutankhamun's foot "could never have happened after he died." If the damage had occurred after death, he argues, you would expect to see breaks or damage in the other toe bones too. The Italian radiologist Paul Gostner, who advised on the study, supports Selim's diagnosis, arguing that the foot matches the diagnostic criteria for "grade 1 clubfoot" and that the CT images the team has published "aren't sufficient for a conclusive evaluation when viewed on their own."

Overall, however, some scholars remain concerned that many of the abnormalities diagnosed again and again in these royal mummies, including scoliosis and clubfoot, are simply side effects of mummification. Selim and his team are talented radiologists, they argue, but aren't experienced in the particular challenges of studying ancient mummies (as of course very few

---

* Apparently, he's using a bow rather than fishing rod because of the special royal status that this weapon had in ancient Egypt.

researchers are). Interpreting damage to a three-thousand-year-old mummified body is very different from diagnosing a living patient, or carrying out an autopsy on a fresh corpse.

There was one more letter, and because of my background in genetics, this is the one that intrigued me the most. It seemed to tear apart the flagship part of the paper, the multimillion-dollar DNA analysis.

The authors of the letter, Eske Willerslev and Eline Lorenzen, come from the Centre for GeoGenetics at Denmark's Natural History Museum in Copenhagen, one of the world's most respected ancient DNA labs. They claim that "in most, if not all, ancient Egyptian remains, ancient DNA does not survive to a level that is currently retrievable," before concluding: "We question the reliability of the genetic data presented in this study and therefore the validity of the authors' conclusions."

For an academic publication, this is about as strongly worded as scientists will get. Roughly translated, it basically means, "We don't believe a word of it." Yet this seems to be a robust, careful study, with a huge budget, state-of-the-art equipment, and well-respected international consultants. It's published in an authoritative journal, and the team appears to have followed the internationally accepted list of guidelines for ancient DNA to the letter. How can it have upset these other experts so much? I call Lorenzen and Willerslev, and then a string of other ancient DNA experts around the world, to find out what's going on, and immediately feel a little like Alice going down the rabbit hole. It turns out that in the field of ancient DNA, particularly when it comes to Egyptian mummies, very little is as it seems.

CHAPTER FIFTEEN

DNA DOWN
THE RABBIT HOLE

═══

"**I**T'S SO FRUSTRATING," says Eline Lorenzen, which is barely necessary as I can hear frustration if not anger dripping from every word as she speaks to me on the phone from her lab in Copenhagen. "Now everyone will be taught in school that King Tut died of malaria."

Lorenzen works at the Centre for GeoGenetics, part of Denmark's Natural History Museum. Led by evolutionary biologist Eske Willerslev, it is a leading center for ancient DNA research, where researchers tease aging genetic material out of everything from killer whales to moas. Lorenzen herself studies the DNA of large prehistoric animals such as the mammoth and woolly rhino (extracted from remains found frozen in permafrost in places like Canada and Siberia), to investigate whether climate change or hunting by humans finished them off.[*]

Together with Willerslev, she wrote the letter to *JAMA* that criticized Zink, Pusch, and Gad's DNA analysis of the royal mummies.[1] She tells me

---

[*] See Lorenzen, E. D., et al., "Species-Specific Responses of Late Quaternary Megafauna to Climate and Humans," *Nature* 479, 2011, 359–365. Since our interview, Lorenzen has moved to UC Berkeley, and is studying how ancient polar bears responded to past climatic warming events, to help predict how they will be affected by modern global warming.

that she felt obliged to speak out about it after seeing the huge press coverage that their results gained. "This is not seen as a rigorous study," she says. "When working with samples that are so well-known, it is important to convince readers that you have the right data. I am not convinced."

To find out if other experts agree with her, I start calling around. Although no one comes out and says the data on Tutankhamun and his family are definitely wrong, I have trouble finding anyone who believes them. "I'm very skeptical," says Willerslev. The study "could do a much better job," complains Svante Pääbo of the Max Planck Institute for Evolutionary Biology in Leipzig, one of the founders of the ancient DNA field. "I would be extremely cautious in using these data," agrees Ian Barnes, an expert on the survival of ancient DNA, based at the Royal Holloway University of London. The DNA analysis of Tutankhamun and his family might have been a media sensation, but behind the headlines, many scientists seem to have written it off.

Despite Zink's track record in publishing DNA from Egyptian mummies going back five thousand years, the critics don't believe that his team could possibly have detected the DNA that they claimed. And it's not just Tutankhamun. Enter the world of ancient DNA and you are soon asked to choose between two alternate realities: one in which DNA analysis from Egyptian mummies is routine, and the other in which it is impossible. "The field is split absolutely in half," says Tom Gilbert, a young professor who heads two research groups at Willerslev's geogenetics center.

One camp—the scientific mainstream, including the biggest labs such as Willerslev's and Pääbo's—argues that DNA from most Egyptian mummies simply doesn't survive well enough to be studied. Meanwhile, the other camp has been happily publishing and building careers on this very DNA for years. Unable to resolve their differences, the two sides publish in different journals, attend different conferences, and refer to each other as "believers" and "skeptics"—when, that is, they're not simply ignoring each other.

To understand their feud, it helps to take a quick look at the history of the ancient DNA field. American biologist James Watson and English physicist Francis Crick famously worked out in the 1950s that DNA is made up of long strands twisted together in pairs to form a "double helix." Each strand consists of a sequence of different molecular groups called bases, which have long unwieldy names but are given the letters A, C, G, and T for short. The order of these bases forms the instruction manual for how to build each living being, like a book written using a four-letter alphabet.

Each base—in other words each letter in the sequence—is paired with a corresponding base in the opposite strand, forming what geneticists call a "base pair."

In the following decades, scientists worked out ways to manipulate DNA—cutting it into pieces, sticking it back together, reading its sequence, and so on. But it took until the 1980s before anyone managed to extract DNA from an organism that was long dead. This is because DNA degrades over time, with the long strands breaking up into smaller and smaller pieces, until eventually nothing readable remains. Studying DNA from ancient samples requires isolating and amplifying the tiny amounts of genetic material still left. The older the sample, the harder it is.

In 1984, scientists from California extracted DNA from the quagga, a recently extinct relative of the horse.[2] The DNA was from a museum specimen, just 140 years old. Most experts wrote off the idea of properly ancient DNA, but a young PhD student named Svante Pääbo, at the University of Uppsala in Sweden, was convinced it could be done. Behind his supervisor's back, he persuaded an Egyptology professor at the university to help him take samples from some Egyptian mummies at the local museum in Uppsala, and at another in Berlin. He used a scalpel to remove little pieces of tissue from more than twenty mummies, then worked nights and weekends to isolate their DNA.

This involved trying to purify DNA from the samples, then introducing it into bacteria. As the bacteria then divide and grow, so does the DNA, until there's enough to analyze. This is called cloning, but it's not to be confused with the procedure by which geneticists can clone entire organisms. All that is cloned in this case is a small piece of DNA.

Pääbo's mummies yielded no results—except for one. From a one-year-old boy who died more than two thousand years ago, he managed to clone several chunks of DNA. The student came clean to his supervisor, and was rewarded with a paper in *Nature*, one of the world's most prestigious science journals. It was the second ancient DNA paper ever published, and the first to show the potential for analyzing DNA thousands of years old.[3]

A few years later, the newly invented technique of PCR began to revolutionize the field. Because PCR can amplify any desired DNA sequence by copying it over and over again, ancient DNA researchers no longer had to worry about the tricky process of cloning. Even if their samples only contained a few molecules of DNA, they could use PCR to convert that into large amounts.

This led to a burst of excitement, with papers triumphantly reporting the DNA of everything from prehistoric plants to insects preserved in amber. Most impressive of all, in 1994, was DNA from an 80 million-year-old dinosaur,[4] published in the journal *Science* by Scott Woodward (the Mormon from Utah who shortly afterward missed out on DNA testing Tutankhamun's mummy). It seemed that ancient DNA was about to provide an incredible, almost magical, window into past life on this planet.

Then came the fall. Scientists started to realize that when applied to ancient remains, PCR comes with a huge downside. The method is susceptible to contamination with unwanted DNA at the best of times—it's so sensitive that it can latch onto and amplify stray molecules of DNA from the surrounding environment, instead of from the sample. Usually, it's fairly easy to control for this, but it turns out that the problem is magnified when you're trying to amplify tiny amounts of old, broken-up DNA. The reaction works much better on modern DNA, so any trace of contamination—say, from the skin cell of an archaeologist who handles a sample, or a speck of dust in the lab—can dwarf any ancient DNA present and wreck a result.

When researchers started looking more closely at the DNA they had isolated from their ancient samples, they knew they had a huge problem. In most cases, the DNA they had reported so proudly wasn't ancient at all. Woodward's "dinosaur" DNA belonged to a modern human,[5] as did Pääbo's pioneering clone[6] (in both cases the DNA probably came from the researchers themselves). In another study on monkey mummies, DNA assumed to be from the ancient monkeys turned out to belong to pigeons that nested in a storehouse where the mummies had once been kept.[7]

The field had to start again. After much soul-searching, researchers introduced hugely strict criteria to minimize the risk of contamination. These include only using workspaces where DNA hasn't been amplified before, reporting any contaminated results, sequencing amplified DNA to check its origin, and repeating all experiments in two independent labs.[8]

Even with these precautions, several top researchers in the field, including Pääbo—who is now ancient DNA's grand old man, helping to set the standards for everyone else—decided that it was still too risky to work on ancient human or microbial DNA. If a scientist manages to amplify and sequence mammoth or cave bear DNA, they can be fairly certain that it wasn't just floating around in their lab. But if they retrieve DNA from a human or bacterium, they can't be sure that it came from their ancient sample as opposed to from a modern person, or bacteria present in the environment.

And if they can't be sure, what is the point in doing the work? Labs such as Pääbo's and Willerslev's focused on other types of specimen, such as extinct prehistoric species for which there are no equivalents today.

This left all work on DNA from human mummies extremely contentious. Egyptian mummies, however, were the most controversial of all. In addition to the problems with contamination, there were heated arguments over whether they even contain any DNA in the first place.

As DNA degrades over time, it breaks into shorter and shorter pieces, and the rate at which this happens rises rapidly with temperature. To obtain a useful sequence using PCR, you need DNA fragments at least seventy base pairs long, and how long these survive in a sample depends largely on how hot it is. You can amplify DNA from a mammoth that has been frozen in permafrost for tens of thousands of years, whereas bones buried in the tropics for only a few centuries might yield nothing.

In Egypt's baking climate, the skeptics argue that the chance of amplifiable DNA surviving in three-thousand-year-old mummies like Tutankhamun and his family is vanishingly small. In 2005, Tom Gilbert and colleagues calculated that fragments a hundred base pairs long would survive only five hundred years or so at around 80° F, the estimated temperature of a sealed Egyptian tomb.[9]

Another ancient DNA researcher, Franco Rollo of the University of Camerino in Italy, put this to the test.[10] He checked pieces of papyrus of various ages, from modern samples to archaeological finds up to three thousand years old, preserved in similar conditions to mummies. He estimated that DNA fragments large enough to be amplified by PCR vanished after around six hundred years.

Accordingly, once ancient DNA researchers started using rigorous controls against contamination, they had little luck getting DNA from Egyptian mummies. Rollo, who is best known for his work on Ötzi the Iceman, the five-thousand-year-old mummy found frozen in the Alps, drew a blank with two-thousand-year-old mummies from Saqqara in Egypt. He and his colleagues concluded: "In laboratories where rigorous criteria for the control of contamination are applied, the analysis of human and animal remains from Egyptian archaeological sites most frequently ends with the indication that no authentic DNA is left."[11]

"Preservation in most Egyptian mummies is clearly bad," agrees Pääbo. In the past, he too has had little luck trying to get DNA from Egyptian mummies. In one study published in 1999, he tested 132 mummies but only

managed to get DNA from two of the youngest ones.[12] After such disap-
pointing results, many researchers lost interest in Egyptian samples, and
focused instead on remains that have been preserved in cold conditions.

But here's where the story gets weird. Throughout all of this, other scientists have been publishing papers on DNA extracted from Egyptian mummies up to five thousand years old, far older than Tutankhamun. These
researchers are just as convinced that the DNA does survive, as the other
experts are that it doesn't. For example, Zink and his colleagues have reported ancient DNA from a range of disease-causing bacteria in hundreds
of mummies, including the strains that cause tuberculosis (TB) and diph-
theria, as well as the parasites responsible for malaria and leishmaniasis.[13]
Zink's published work has led to insights into the past evolution of these
pathogens that he hopes will help us to understand and predict the spread
of these diseases, today and in the future.

And in a high-profile study published in 2010, microbiologist Helen
Donoghue of University College London reported tuberculosis DNA from
Dr. Granville's mummy (named after physician Augustus Bozzi Granville,
who carried out the first mummy autopsy on it in front of fellows of the
Royal Society in 1825).[14] Donoghue says the idea that DNA can't survive
in Egyptian mummies is "rubbish," and argues that theoretical and papyrus
studies are of little relevance to what actually happens in mummies. She is
studying early Christian mummies from Nubia, and says that around a third
of them are testing positive for tuberculosis.

Skeptics such as Ian Barnes and Tom Gilbert believe that the researchers
claiming DNA from Egyptian mummies often confuse modern contamination for ancient DNA, just as the field's pioneers did in the 1990s. Often
these are groups who have moved into ancient DNA more recently from
medical diagnostics, and critics feel they haven't learned the lessons of
those early mistakes. Barnes argues that some TB studies of ancient mummies report positive results "higher than if you contracted TB, turned up
in a clinic, and got tested." For malaria too, he points out that even for
blood tests on living patients with an active outbreak of the disease, a PCR
test only works about 75 percent of the time, so he finds it hard to believe
that it could possibly work on bone samples from ancient mummies. Gilbert
is slightly more blunt. "I've given up on the field a long time ago," he says.
"It's full of crap."

Donoghue acknowledges that you have to be "super-careful" when
studying ancient human DNA. But she insists that the studies on microbial

DNA prove that genetic material does survive in these mummies, and points out that in some cases, the DNA results have been confirmed by detecting signs of lipids (fat molecules) from the pathogens concerned. She argues that the big labs have gone over the top in trying to compensate for the field's difficult past, and counters that their criticisms have more to do with territorialism than valid scientific concerns. Zink agrees, adding that no matter how rigorous his studies, the skeptics refuse to believe his results. "It's like a religious thing," he says. "If our papers are reviewed by one of the other groups, you get revisions like, 'I don't believe it's possible.' It's hard to argue with that."

By 2010, the two sides had pretty much stopped talking to each other. "There's enough dead stuff around—you're not obliged to get into anyone else's area," says Barnes. That year, ancient DNA researchers held two rival conferences: the skeptics' International Symposium of Biomolecular Archaeology, in Copenhagen in September, and the believers' International Conference on Ancient DNA, in Munich the next month. Hardly anyone went to both.

This, then, is the tense atmosphere into which the royal mummy study dropped like a bomb. Zink and his team were studying by far the most controversial type of ancient DNA (human) on the most controversial possible subjects (Egyptian mummies). They also reported unprecedented success compared to even the most optimistic previous studies; not only did they retrieve DNA from every single mummy they tested, they were able to amplify relatively long fragments of DNA for their age, up to 250 base pairs, which even other believers describe as remarkable. And, of course, the study gained glowing media coverage, with its findings filtering down into living rooms and classrooms around the world. To say that it reignited tensions between the two camps would be something of an understatement.

So who is right? Well, whether or not you believe the team's results basically comes down to whether you think they have convincingly ruled out the possibility of contamination. Skeptics who have scrutinized the *JAMA* paper claim they haven't.

One concern is whether Gad took adequate precautions when he collected his bone samples from the royal mummies. "There is a complete lack of information about how this was done," says Lorenzen. "It rings alarm bells." With no details in the paper itself, DNA researchers worldwide were left in the surreal situation of trying to assess the quality of the work by watching the TV documentary. Lorenzen says that before writing her letter of complaint to *JAMA*, she emailed Zink and his colleagues several times asking for more details of their methods, but received no reply (a member of Zink's team says this may have been because of her "un-collegiate" tone).

Gad drilled deep inside the mummies' bones, where contaminating DNA is less likely to reach. This isn't a guarantee, however, and it's debatable how effective it would be on Tutankhamun's thin, fragmented skeleton, not to mention the tiny matchstick bones of the mummified fetuses. The team also tested the lab staff to rule out any contamination with their own DNA. But of course this doesn't exclude DNA from all the people to have handled the mummies previously, from early archaeologists such as Gaston Maspero and Howard Carter to the workmen who moved Tutankhamun into his new case just a few months before the DNA samples were taken. Unlike Gad, none of these men wore gloves or masks. "You see people on TV handling samples with their bare hands, their sweat dripping onto the mummy," notes Gilbert. "That's a classic route of contamination."

What concerns the critics most of all, though, is the type of DNA test that Zink and the team used. Ancient DNA researchers usually start a study by looking in a sample for mitochondrial DNA, which, if you remember, is much easier to find than nuclear DNA. Unusually, though, Zink's team only gives results for the more challenging nuclear DNA. What's more, rather than sequencing this DNA (which allows you to check, for example, that you're not picking up DNA from more than one individual at once), the researchers analyzed it using DNA fingerprinting. This technique is useful for determining family relationships, but it is rarely used for ancient DNA studies because it is ultra-susceptible to confusion from contamination.

Microsatellites, the variable regions of the genome that DNA fingerprinting targets, consist of a short sequence—for example "GATC"—repeated several times. The number of repeats varies in different people. By using PCR to amplify particular microsatellite regions, then looking at the length of the resulting pieces of DNA, you can calculate how many repeats each microsatellite is made up of—the more repeats, the longer the DNA.

It's a really cunning technique. The problem is that simply checking the size of PCR products offers no way to distinguish between ancient DNA and modern contamination. There's no sequence to analyze, just a colored band or peak on a computer screen, which could just as easily come from a modern workman as an ancient pharaoh. To make matters worse, the

PCR can slip on the sequence repeats, producing false "stutter bands" of varying sizes.

When working with modern, good-quality DNA, researchers can usually see which are the stutter bands and which are the real ones. But poor-quality samples of DNA are much trickier. For each microsatellite, the bands you're interested in may or may not be present, depending on whether the DNA has survived well enough to amplify. They may or may not be mixed with DNA from one or more other individuals. And on top of that, you may see stutter bands. Teasing out which bands are real and which aren't is fraught with difficulty. Get the answer wrong, and you'll end up with a completely different fingerprint.

Even when used in criminal investigations—where it has helped to imprison or even execute plenty of people—DNA fingerprinting doesn't necessarily give black-and-white results. Here, too, DNA from several people is often mixed together, and scientists are pushing the limits of the technique by chasing DNA profiles from smaller and smaller samples.

In an investigation carried out in 2010, for example, *New Scientist* magazine tested how objective the method really is.[15] Reporter Linda Geddes took a sample of DNA evidence from a real crime scene—a gang rape in the State of Georgia—that had helped to convict a man named Kerry Robinson. She sent it, along with Robinson's DNA profile, to seventeen analysts working in the same accredited U.S. government lab, and asked if they thought Robinson's DNA was in the sample. Only one of the seventeen agreed with the original judgment that Robinson "could not be excluded," while four said the evidence was inconclusive, and twelve ruled him out completely. As one attorney put it: "The difference between prison and freedom rests in the hands of the scientists assigned the case."

For ancient DNA, where tiny samples of degraded, fragmented DNA are mixed with modern DNA that amplifies much more easily, the problem can be even worse.

=====

IN OCTOBER 2010, a few months after the publication of Lorenzen and Willerslev's letter, I call Carsten Pusch for his reaction. He's clearly proud and excited about his role in the project, and is happy to talk me through the details.

As we chat, I check out Pusch's website. Prominently displayed is a photo of him sitting next to Egypt's antiquities chief Zahi Hawass at the press conference at which the DNA results were announced.* On the other side of Hawass are Ashraf Selim and Yehia Gad, the picture of respectability in ties and suits. The German geneticist makes a striking contrast against the three graying Egyptians, with long brown hair drawn back into a pony-tail, a gold chain around his neck, and two small hoops through his left ear.

Pusch argues that the study owes much of its success to the way in which the royal mummies were embalmed. He believes that the very em-balming materials that made the analysis of the royal mummies so difficult may actually have protected their DNA from degradation. "Nobody has thought about the components of the resin," he says.

Members of the royal family would have enjoyed a particularly elaborate embalming process, he points out, perhaps explaining why their DNA is better preserved than that of other Egyptian mummies. As yet there is no direct evidence for this idea, but Pusch says he is working with chemists at the University of Tübingen to try to identify the materials involved, and un-derstand how they might protect DNA.

Pusch's colleague Zink, the slightly disheveled director of Bolzano's mummy research center, is just as happy to discuss the project. He too argues that the mummification process, including the rapid desiccation with natron salt, probably helped to preserve the DNA beyond what would nor-mally be expected. "The Egyptians really knew how to preserve a body," he says.

Zink, a veteran of the field, was ready for the backlash against the study. In fact, "the skepticism we received was not as much as I had expected," he says. But Pusch seems genuinely surprised and hurt by the reaction from critics such as Lorenzen and Barnes. "I don't understand people's harshness," he says, after detailing the months of painstaking experimentation it took to coax DNA from the mummies' bones. "These people have never worked with royal mummies. This is pioneering work."

When I ask about contamination, both researchers say that they did pick up some contaminating DNA in their tests. They tested every micro-satellite lots of times for each mummy, and got different results on different runs. According to Zink, they never got a complete profile with one run,

---

* When I checked in August 2012, this photo was no longer displayed.

so they built up each mummy's fingerprint by looking at which bands came up most often across the different runs, using a "majority rule." For example, when repeating a test thirty times, if they saw a particular band more than fifteen times, they'd judge that to be an authentic result.

Despite the messiness of the data, Zink and Pusch say they are convinced that the bands the team selected are authentic because they came up in different experimental runs, in biopsies from different sites on each mummy, and in two different labs.* They also point out that none of the female mummies tested positive for the male Y chromosome—suggesting they were not contaminated with DNA from male archaeologists—and that the mummies tested all had different (but related) profiles, so the results could not have come from the same source of contamination.

The concern is that the team must have been under huge pressure to find something big in those unpromising samples: from Discovery, who built a million-dollar lab in return for permission to film the research; from the domineering Hawass, whose reputation rested on the success of the project; and from the world's waiting press. And in such circumstances, the use of DNA fingerprinting might make it all too easy for scientists trying to make sense of confused and ambiguous data to pick—in all good faith—the bands that made most sense for the family tree they were trying to construct.

The fact that all of the resulting DNA profiles made sense might therefore reveal more about the ability of the human brain to see patterns in random noise than it does about the family relationships of Tutankhamun and his kin. If so, that could explain, for example, why almost every anonymous mummy included in the study, even ones with no obvious archaeological link to Tutankhamun, ended up being identified as important members of his close family, and why several of Hawass's hunches about the mummy's relationships were found to be correct.

With so much room for interpretation, critics argue that the DNA tests should have been conducted "blind," so that the researchers doing the analysis and working out the relationships between the mummies didn't know which sample was which. They also want to see the raw data—those colored bands on the computer screen—to judge its quality for themselves (the

---

* Other experts have raised concerns over how useful the second lab really was. Sally Wasef and her team started work toward the end of the project, only repeated a small subset of the tests, and didn't take their own samples from the mummies—they were dependent on testing DNA supplied to them by Gad's team.

JAMA paper only gives the final profiles that were eventually derived for each mummy). There doesn't seem much chance of this, however. Zink says he's happy to discuss the team's methods and results with other researchers, but is reluctant to share the raw data, because the use of the majority rule means "there could be a lot of arguing."

Something else the critics are keen to see is sequence data, particularly from the mummies' mitochondrial DNA and Y chromosomes, as this would provide a valuable check on the family relationships revealed by the DNA fingerprinting. Zink and Pusch say that they do have some of this data, but chose not to include it in the *JAMA* paper as they are still working on it.[*] They insist that when they're ready, they will publish this in a separate paper that investigates the genetic origin of the pharaohs.

"People are asking so many questions," says Pusch. "We are able to do it. I just wish everyone would give us more time."

Of course, none of the criticisms mean that the team's results are definitely wrong. Gad, Zink, and Pusch appear to me to be talented and tenacious researchers working in very difficult circumstances. Maybe they really have pulled off the genetic feat of a lifetime. But unless they can provide the methodological details and raw data that will allow other experts to judge the validity of their work, there is, frustratingly, no way to know whether their results are real or not. A new history may have been written for TV audiences, but neither geneticists nor Egyptologists are ready to throw out their textbooks just yet.

There are some glimmers of hope for the future, however. Some recently published studies on animal mummies from Egypt hint that DNA does sometimes survive after all. The lack of convincing animal studies has been one reason why critics such as Gilbert are so skeptical that the DNA being claimed from Egyptian mummies is authentic. "It only ever 'works' on sam-

---

[*] These results do not appear in the *JAMA* paper, but the documentary *King Tut Unwrapped* includes a shot showing Y chromosome data for Tutankhamun on a computer screen. In August 2011, a Swiss genealogy company called IGENEA analyzed this screen shot and issued a press release concluding that Tutankhamun belonged to an ancestral line (or "haplogroup") called R1B1a2. This line is rare in modern Egypt but common in Western Europe, where it is found in up to 70 percent of British men. This was immediately cited as proof that the DNA represented contamination from a European archaeologist such as Derry or Carter. This is possible, but it's worth remembering that this scene in the documentary was reenacted later, so there's no guarantee that the computer screen is actually showing the correct data. I asked Gad if the DNA really does show Tutankhamun's haplogroup to be R1B1a2, but he refused to say. "This is not how science should be conveyed," he says. "All the haplotype information will be published hopefully soon." As of February 2013, however, no such paper has appeared.

ples like humans that are really easy to contaminate," he points out. But in a paper published in 2011, using rigorous methods and controls that even Gilbert approves of, a team amplified and sequenced short DNA sequences from a couple of mummified crocodile hatchlings, around two thousand years old.[16] Another preliminary study reports using PCR to amplify DNA from mummified ibises.[17]

But the real breakthroughs may come from a series of new techniques collectively known as next-generation sequencing. These reduce reliance on the troublesome PCR amplification step, or even skip it altogether. Instead they sequence DNA in a sample directly, reading thousands of tiny fragments at once, then use a computer to stitch them all together into a longer sequence.

So far, next-generation sequencing has required access to sophisticated (and very expensive) equipment. But it is fast becoming more routine, and within a few years, probably all ancient DNA will be done this way. Because it avoids amplification by PCR, it is easier to estimate the amount of modern contamination in your sample, and you don't have to worry so much about the contamination drowning out the ancient DNA you're interested in. You sequence all of the DNA you've got in a sample, so you can see exactly what's in there, including what species it is from, whether there is DNA from more than one individual or species, and whether it shows patterns of degradation that you'd expect from ancient DNA. Another big advantage is that you can look at much shorter fragments—down to about thirty base pairs long—which means being able to retrieve results from much older samples than before.

Using these techniques, the big labs such as Willerslev's and Pääbo's are looking again at ancient human samples, and they're managing to read entire genomes for samples where this previously wouldn't have been thought possible.

In 2010, Willerslev, Gilbert, Lorenzen, and colleagues used next-generation sequencing to read the full genome sequence of a four-thousand-year-old paleo-Eskimo from Greenland.[18] Willerslev had spent two months digging in Greenland's most remote northern tundra in 2006, looking for human remains, but with no success. Then, two years later, he found just the sample he was seeking—four tufts of hair from an extinct Eskimo group known as the Saqqaq, dug from the permafrost at Qeqertasussuk, on Greenland's west coast. The whole time the hairs had been sitting in a plastic bag in the National Museum of Denmark, just minutes from his Copenhagen lab.

The resulting genome sequence showed that the closest living relatives of the Saqqaq are the Chukchis, who now live at the easternmost tip of Siberia. The researchers also deduced that the owner of the hair was a man with brown eyes, thick hair, and dry earwax, at risk of baldness later in life. It was the first whole genome of an ancient human (and at the time just the ninth human genome ever sequenced)—"an absolutely amazing piece of work," according to Barnes.

It didn't stand on its own for long, though. Within a few months, teams led by Pääbo published the genome sequences of a 38,000-year-old Neanderthal[*] recovered from Croatia[19]—proving once and for all that modern humans did interbreed with their Neanderthal cousins, leaving their trace in our genome today—and a girl belonging to a previously unknown human species of about the same age, whose tiny finger bone was found in a cave in the Altai mountains in Siberia.[20]

And in 2012, a team led by Zink published the genome of Ötzi the Iceman, showing that he had brown eyes, type-O blood, was lactose intolerant, and that his closest modern-day relatives now live in Sardinia and Corsica.[21]

So far, no one has successfully used these techniques on Egyptian mummies. But there's every chance they could produce equally dramatic results. Going from 100-bp fragments down to 30 base pairs should make a huge difference to DNA survival time. Whereas 100-bp fragments are expected to survive only five hundred years in a hot Egyptian tomb, 30-bp fragments are predicted to last two thousand years or even longer.

"Everything becomes open again," says Willerslev. As the techniques are still new, researchers don't know yet exactly what will work and what won't. Most of the genomes published so far have involved samples preserved in the cold, but Willerslev is now using next-generation techniques to extract DNA from various South American mummies, some of which have been preserved in warmer environments (as well as the hair of the famous Native American chief Sitting Bull, which he was presented by the family in a basement ceremony in Dakota, involving singers, drummers, and a medicine man). "Some [of the samples] are definitely working," he says.

The hope—on both sides—is that by providing robust, detailed data that everyone can agree on, these new techniques will help to banish un-

---

[*] Actually DNA compiled from three different Neanderthal individuals.

certainty and mend the split in the field. They might even give us full genome sequences for the pharaohs. Hair (for those mummies that still have it) seems to be a particularly promising source, because the DNA is locked inside the shaft, protecting it from degradation and contamination.

Zink, after his success with Ötzi the Iceman, tells me that he would love to try next-generation sequencing on the royal mummies. But the Egyptian authorities are cautious about permitting such a project, he says, as the resulting data might provide politically sensitive information about the genetic origin of the pharaohs, and whether any royal blood persists in the modern population: "This goes right to their history."

Cost is also an issue—Willerslev reckons for example that the Greenlander genome alone cost several hundred thousand pounds. If the work were to be done in Egypt, this would be the kind of money that only a huge TV company could afford. In a field swamped with uncertainty, then, at least one thing is for sure. If this study ever happens, it will undoubtedly be captured on film.

CHAPTER SIXTEEN

SPARE RIBS
AND HAND KEBABS

══

KING TUTANKHAMUN looks invincible in his horse-drawn chariot as he leads his troops to battle. He stares straight ahead, bow and arrow poised for a killer shot, as his enemies fall in trampled piles beneath his wheels. Later, after sailing triumphantly home up the Nile, he sits in state to receive a gory memento of the defeated dead: their severed hands, strung onto spears like kebabs.

While Zahi Hawass's scientists were redefining Tutankhamun as a frail, inbred cripple, scholars elsewhere painted a picture of a very different kind of king. One of them was Ray Johnson of the University of Chicago's Oriental Institute, based in Luxor. For the last twenty years, Johnson has worked in Luxor Temple, painstakingly copying and publishing the reliefs inscribed on its walls.

In 2010, he published a dramatic new finding relating to Tutankhamun.[1,2] He had been studying hundreds of broken wall fragments that were later reused in nearby medieval buildings. He found sandstone blocks from Tutankhamun's additions to Luxor Temple, but he also found blocks—recognizable as Tutankhamun's from the carving style and the presence of his name—from a different temple. The images he found on them revealed an unprecedented insight into Tutankhamun's reign, including scenes of offerings, barge processions, rituals, and war.

The fragments were made up of small blocks called talatat, originally used by Akhenaten for constructing buildings quickly. After some investigation, Johnson was able to reconstruct their long and checkered history. Akhenaten had originally used them in a building at nearby Karnak dedicated to his god, the Aten, before Tutankhamun dismantled it and reused the blocks for his own mortuary temple, which was completed after his death by his successor, Ay. Later, the next pharaoh, Horemheb, dismantled the mortuary temple and reused the blocks for himself, to fill in a gateway at Karnak. In medieval times, the blocks were quarried yet again and used for buildings in front of Luxor Temple. Through it all, the reliefs originally carved by Tutankhamun had survived.

Fitting the scenes back together from these scattered blocks was like attempting the ultimate jigsaw. Johnson and his colleagues copied the markings from individual blocks then used a computer to fit them together. Particularly surprising were two sets of battle scenes. One shows a Nubian campaign in the south, while the other shows Tutankhamun in a chariot leading Egyptian forces in Syria. The images include a royal flotilla returning triumphantly up the Nile, with a manacled Syrian prisoner hanging in a cage from the sail yard of the king's barge. Other blocks show Tutankhamun receiving prisoners, booty, and the gory hand kebabs—a detail that hasn't been seen anywhere else in Egyptian art.

Battle scenes were already known on some items from Tutankhamun's tomb, for example a painted wooden casket that shows him fighting against the Syrians. These had been interpreted as symbolic, stylized images that would be used to show any king triumphing over his enemies. Experts assumed that Tutankhamun was too young to have actually led his troops in battle. But Johnson thinks the reliefs on the temple blocks are more than that: "The originality of such scenes strongly suggests that they could only have been observed and recorded on the battlefield," he wrote,[3] so Tutankhamun's presence in the images could mean that he was actually there after all. He points out that Egyptian art at this time stressed truthfulness, and argues that the wear on objects from Tutankhamun's tomb, such as armor, weapons, and chariots, proves the king was strong and active: "He was certainly old enough to participate in the manly art of war by ancient standards of maturity."

So, far from being a crippled, inbred weakling, Tutankhamun may have been a military leader who went into battle at least twice. If he did break his leg, Johnson thinks that rather than falling over on his cane, he could have fallen from his chariot while on a military campaign: "It is clear from [the battle scenes] that the young king was considerably more active than has been assumed, and it is also possible that this cost him his life."[4]

Unfortunately for Johnson, his reinterpretation of Tutankhamun was published just as the *JAMA* paper[5] appeared, supposedly showing exactly the opposite. The CT scans seemed to prove that there was no way this king would have made it into a chariot, in battle or otherwise. But the doubts subsequently cast on the idea of Tutankhamun's crippled foot have effectively reopened the case. What's more, recent reinterpretations of both Harrison's X-rays and Selim's CT scans support the idea of a strong, active king—as well as introducing a new, completely unexpected cause of death.

After CT scanning the royal mummies, the Egyptians guarded their raw data very closely. Independent experts were frustrated by not being able to verify the conclusions reached by Hawass's team, and even the foreign consultants, such as Rühli, were only allowed to take a few selected images home with them. But there's one man who did manage to get access to the scans: a retired obstetrician from Seattle.

Benson Harer is one of those people who questions everything and doesn't take no for an answer. Intellectual energy spills out in all directions—he's a philanthropist, the author of the awesome Law of Social Physics (which states that "the emotional intensity in the expression of an opinion is inversely related to the validity of the data supporting it"), and alongside a successful career in medicine is also a respected amateur Egyptologist, not to mention creator of one of the most extensive collections of ancient Egyptian artifacts west of the Mississippi.

Harer started excavating in Egypt in 1978—working with Kent Weeks as he set up the Theban Mapping Project—and has been back nearly every year since. As a physician, Harer is particularly interested in the medical aspects of Egyptology, and when he heard about the CT study of Tutankhamun, he was desperate to get a look at the scans. He started nagging Hawass, whom he says he has known since 1978, "when he was at the bottom of the pyramid."

It took Harer two years to persuade Hawass to let him see the data—"he kept promising and then falling through," but he finally got his wish in

2008. The data were only kept in one place—the computer in the CT trailer, parked in the Egyptian Museum courtyard, so he had to look at them there. He spent several hours going through the scans—like the previous foreign consultants, he wasn't allowed to take the information away, so he took as many photos as he could of the screen with his digital camera.

His conclusions were quite different from those of the original CT team. He didn't attach much significance to the supposed fractured leg or deformed foot. But he did notice several things that were weird about the way that Tutankhamun was treated by his embalmers—oddities not shared by any of the other royal mummies of the New Kingdom—which he felt provided a string of clues to the circumstances of the king's death. Several of the details had been noted before, but no one had brought them together or commented on what they might mean.

First was the position of Tutankhamun's embalming incision. This is the cut that the embalmers made in a corpse's tummy, so they could pull out the intestines. It's usually quite a long cut, positioned on the left, from the groin up past the hip toward the waist. But in Tutankhamun, it's shorter and higher, running from the navel almost to the left hip. Derry had noted this, but didn't comment on it particularly.

Secondly, Tutankhamun's diaphragm was intact. Normally when the embalmers reach in through the embalming incision, they have to cut through the diaphragm to reach the lungs, but in this case, they didn't bother.

Third, and strangest of all, Tutankhamun had no heart. Some of the other details could perhaps be put down to differences between embalming schools, but a missing heart is a fundamental omission. Whereas the Egyptian embalmers tended to discard the brain, they saw the heart as the center of a person's intellect and personality. Other organs were removed and mummified separately, but the heart was deliberately left in the body. Its owner was going to need it at the weighing-of-the-heart ceremony, held to determine whether the person was worthy of eternal life.

Mummies are sometimes found without their hearts, and in these cases, perhaps the embalmers messed up and pulled it out by accident. After all, you can find mummies in pretty much any condition—with missing body parts, or extra body parts (not necessarily human); one unfortunate man was even found wrapped up facing the ground, with his mask on the back of his head. But the ancient priests generally took more care with royalty. According to Harer, the CT scans of the royal mummies show that Tutankhamun is the only one of them known to have been mummified without his heart.

The heart couldn't have been lost or stolen in modern times, he says, because Tutankhamun's chest is packed full with resin-soaked—now rock hard—linen. Anyone who wanted to remove the heart would have to dig into this solidified packing, and even if they managed to put it back afterward, there would still be a gap where the heart once was. There's no hole in the packing, suggesting that the heart was never there.

The list of anomalies goes on. Tutankhamun's arms were found folded over his lower abdomen, not crossed over his chest, as is traditional for pharaohs. His skull is weird too, with those two layers of solidified resin—one settled in the back of the skull, and one at the top. It seems most likely that the resin was applied twice—once through the nose with the body lying on its back, and once through the base of the skull (an opening called the foramen magnum) with the body on its front, with the head end tipped upside down over the end of a table.* This is unusual—in almost all other royals, the nasal passage is the only route opened into the skull. In Ahmose, the embalmers used the foramen magnum instead. Tutankhamun is the only mummy in which they seem to have used both.

And, of course, there is that missing chest. The front part of Tutankhamun's ribs are gone, as is his sternum, and the left side of his pelvis is badly damaged too. Derry (without the benefit of X-rays) didn't notice this, while Harrison and the CT team both concluded that this damage was done in modern times, by Carter, or subsequent looters.

Rather than make any assumptions, Harer zoomed in on the ends of the ribs left behind, to look for clues. He noticed three things. First, although some of the ribs were clearly broken, others were cut smoothly. Second, they weren't cut in a straight line—all the ribs were slightly different lengths. Third, the rock-hard linen packing immediately beneath the cut or broken ends of the ribs was undisturbed.

Harer argues that these three details prove the ribs were removed in ancient times, not modern. First, he says, the ribs can't have been cut through

---

* Robert Connolly points out that in the 1968 X-ray images, Tutankhamun's nasal passage appears intact, suggesting that the brain was removed only through the foramen magnum. However, experts who have studied the 2005 CT images, including Richard Boyer, Paul Gostner, and Benson Harer, all agree that a hole has been broken through the right-hand side of Tutankhamun's nasal passage, "about the right size to admit a good-sized trocar" according to Boyer. He says that the defect is in an area "with lots of overlapping shadows" so he isn't surprised that it doesn't show up on the flat X-ray images. It is possible, of course, that this damage has been sustained since 1968, but it seems most likely that the Egyptian embalmers did indeed enter the brain twice, once through the nose and once through the foramen magnum.

with a horizontally held blade, say a hacksaw, because then they would have been cut in a straight line. Instead each individual rib is severed in a slightly different place, suggesting the use of a narrow, vertically held blade, such as a saber-type saw. But such a blade can't have been used in modern times because it would have dug into the packing beneath the ribs, leaving telltale marks.

Second, he argues, it would be pretty much impossible to cut through Tutankhamun's ancient bones today and leave a smooth edge. The bones are now so brittle and fragile, they would snap before you could cut all the way through, leaving a partly broken surface. He tested this idea using some leftover pork ribs (after leaving them for a few months to dry out). No matter how carefully he tried to saw through them, he always ended up with a spike where the last bit of the bone snapped. To create the clean edge seen on Tutankhamun's ribs, they must have been cut through when the body was still fresh, says Harer.

Because some of the ribs are broken and some are cut, Harer concludes that the king suffered a devastating injury that smashed the front part of his chest. The body presumably arrived at the embalming house with much of the chest already missing, so all the embalmers could do was to trim some of the ribs around the injured area to try to tidy it up.[6, 7]

This scenario nicely explains the other anomalies in how Tutankhamun was embalmed. The priests couldn't leave his heart in place because it was already missing or seriously damaged before they received the body. And they didn't need to cut through the diaphragm to reach the lungs because they could lift them straight out of the gaping hole in Tutankhamun's chest. That meant they positioned the embalming incision slightly differently because they only needed to access organs and intestines from the lower abdomen. The arms were placed low, below the injury, rather than folded across the damaged area.

When it comes to the skull, Harer thinks the embalmers must have tried to extract the brain through the nose as usual, but that this proved unsatisfactory—perhaps because the caved-in chest made it difficult to position the body on its front as necessary to drain the contents of the skull through the nose. So after pouring in some molten resin through the nose (with the body on its back, so the resin would settle in the back of the skull), they turned the body back over onto its front, and made a second large hole into the skull cavity through the foramen magnum. After the brain was completely removed, they poured in a second layer of resin with the head hanging upside down.

Once the chest was packed with resin-soaked linen, Harer thinks the priests placed the blue-and-gold-glass-beaded bib directly over the opening, perhaps to protect it. This might explain why Carter was unable to remove it, because the beads were stuck directly to the resin, rather than being laid on top of bandages or skin.* The surface of the packing on the mummy today is ragged and bumpy, where whoever removed the bib literally had to chisel it off. Harer also thinks the injury might explain why the embalmers piled so many layers of protective amulets and jewelry over Tutankhamun's chest area. As there are no other equivalent royal burials to compare him to, however, we don't know if this was normal practice.

Harer's scenario of a fatal chest injury has support from another source too. Robert Connolly, the anatomist in Liverpool, has been looking again at Harrison's 1968 X-ray images, and independently sees a similar picture.

Connolly worked with radiographers in Liverpool to digitize and enhance Harrison's old X-ray plates, before reanalyzing them.[8] He agrees that the best explanation for the king's absent heart is that it was already missing or destroyed before the embalmers got hold of the body. He also noticed the combination of broken and cut ribs and concludes that some were broken in an accident, with the embalmers later trimming away the rest for fast access to Tutankhamun's internal organs. "I think Tutankhamun died in an accident, some distance from home," he told me. "After a few days transporting the body at that temperature, putrefaction would have started. They would have wanted to get the odiferous gut out as quickly as they could."

So what could have ravaged the king's chest and pelvis in such a strange way? Apart from the possible broken leg (Harer says he's skeptical that this happened before death: "The embalming material inside the alleged fracture is very subtle if it's there at all"), Tutankhamun doesn't have any other major injuries, for example to his arms, skull, or spine. So something smashed up his front, but only his front.

---

* In his diary entry for November 15, 1925, Howard Carter states that the beaded bib was located "at the lowest level before reaching the skin." However in his later account of the discovery, *The Tomb of Tutankhamun*, he says that the bib was "next to the flesh, though not in actual contact with it; for there were several thicknesses of linen underneath, charred almost to powder." Harer believes that the first account is correct.

In an article published in June 2012,[9] Harer goes through some of the possibilities, mostly wild animal related. He discounts a lion attack, arguing that the king would never have traveled or hunted without an entourage. So even if he were set upon by a lion, the animal wouldn't have time to claw open and devour his chest before Tutankhamun's men intervened.

The now-extinct aurochs—a larger ancestor of today's domestic cows, with fearsome horns—is another contender. An aurochs bull could easily kill a man, but to be gored in the chest, the king must have stood facing the charging bull like a matador, which seems unlikely. It's also thought that the aurochs may have been extinct in Egypt at the time of Tutankhamun's death—no hunts in Egypt are recorded after the reign of Amenhotep III.

There's the old chestnut of Tutankhamun falling from (or being struck by) a chariot, but this would have caused multiple injuries from tumbling, perhaps breaking his arms, legs, neck, or back. Or he could have been kicked in the chest by a horse, but that would presumably result in a much more localized injury.

If the king was fowling in the marshes and lost his balance, he might have fallen in the water and been attacked by a crocodile. But a biting croc, with rows of razor sharp teeth on its upper and lower jaws, would cause equal damage to both sides of the body. There is another watery predator, however, that Harer claims could cause just the sort of injury seen in Tutankhamun: the hippo.

Although it seems lumbering, and perhaps even cute (in a big-boned kind of way), the hippo is often cited as Africa's most deadly animal—not counting the malaria-carrying mosquito. They can grow up to three tons, are surprisingly fast in water and on land, and although vegetarian, have huge saber-like teeth in their bottom jaw, which they're quick to use if they feel threatened.

Harer argues that when an angry hippo attacks, it typically catches its fleeing victim and clamps them in its mouth, with one or both saber teeth impaling the unfortunate person from the front. A twist of the hippo's head disembowels the victim, or rips out their chest, depending on the positioning of the teeth.

Connolly also favors the idea of a hunting accident, though he doesn't think there's enough evidence to speculate on the exact culprit. Other experts have expressed caution about the hippo idea, skeptical that the pharaoh would ever have been exposed to such a danger, and that such a huge animal could have destroyed Tutankhamun's chest and pelvis without leaving a series of injuries elsewhere on his body.

But when I asked hippo specialists, they were cautiously positive that Harer's scenario is at least possible. Erustus Kanga of the Kenya Wildlife Service confirms that hippo bites can cause clean-cut piercing or stab wounds, while David Durrheim, a public health expert who has reviewed hippo fatalities in South Africa, says that although most of the human deaths he came across were due to people getting trampled, hippo bites do also cause more localized injuries. "A well-placed hippo foot could certainly crush a human chest and a penetrating lower incisor could disembowel an unfortunate victim," he says.

Pharaohs from the Old Kingdom at least are known to have hunted hippos. Legend has it that King Menes, the first king of a unified Egypt, was killed by one. Hunting these animals was seen as an act of religious significance, as the hippo, associated with the god Seth, epitomized the forces of chaos—which it was the pharaoh's role to quell. Perhaps the eighteen-year-old Tutankhamun would have relished such an adventure, suggests Harer, particularly during a period when he was keen to restore order to the land after the disruption of Akhenaten's Aten heresy.

Alternatively, Tutankhamun could simply have been fishing or hunting birds in the marshes (there are statuettes of him doing this, standing on a little wooden skiff) when a hippo attacked his boat. Hippos are known to attack and topple boats without warning, then bite the unfortunate occupant when he or she falls into the water.

There is evidence that hippos did live in Egypt in Tutankhamun's time. One papyrus from the Eighteenth Dynasty includes a prescription for treating a hippo bite. And Ay, Tutankhamun's successor, has a rare scene of a hippo hunt in his tomb—could he have been asserting his dominance over the animal that killed his predecessor?

Although Harer thinks that a hippo is the most likely cause of Tutankhamun's death, he does have one other possible explanation for the king's missing chest. If he was killed in battle, perhaps by an arrow that struck his heart, his enemies might have cut open his chest and retrieved the arrow and heart before his body was recovered by his own troops. It's a scene that presumably isn't included in the triumphant battle reliefs that Ray Johnson is deciphering on those temple blocks.

Harer and Connolly's work adds yet another twist to the arguments over Tutankhamun's death. The king has gone from a tragic child who succumbed to tuberculosis, to a murder victim, daredevil chariot racer, malaria-infected cripple, brave soldier, and even a hippo's last meal. You can pick whichever story you like. We might not be any closer to a definitive answer over the pharaoh's demise, but the sheer range of explanations is surely a testament to human ingenuity and imagination.

Unfortunately, we're unlikely to get any more data to help solve the mystery any time soon. Dramatic events unfolding in Egypt were about to bring all scientific work on the mummies—not to mention Hawass's glittering career—to an abrupt halt.

CHAPTER SEVENTEEN

REVOLUTION

===

IN THE LAST WEEK of January 2011, Yehia Gad watched from his lab at the National Research Centre in Cairo as the protests outside grew. He was itching to take part in the marches, but worried about jeopardizing his job. If there was a revolution, he figured he'd be needed in a position of influence, to help build a new, democratic Egypt.

What started as a lone street trader burning himself alive in protest at police corruption in Tunisia was fast becoming a wave of mass defiance against repressive regimes around the Arab world. In Egypt, huge crowds were turning out to call for the fall of President Mubarak, whose thirty-year rule since Sadat's assassination was characterized by corruption, press censorship, and imprisonment without trial of thousands of political activists.

By the morning of Friday, January 28, Gad could stand by no more. He knew this would be the biggest demonstration yet, as Friday prayers would provide a natural starting point for marches afterward. Gad went to pray with his two sons-in-law at a mosque in the Cairo suburb of Nasr City, then walked with the other protestors the five miles or so to Tahrir Square.

Events that day exploded beyond everyone's expectations. Hundreds of thousands of people from all walks of life demonstrated for a democratic Egypt, enduring violent attacks from pro-government groups as military tanks looked on. The tense scenes were flashed to TV screens around the world, and suddenly, the country the rest of us had associated mostly with pyramids, mummies, and perhaps holidays by the Red Sea, took on a new dimension. We noticed that this was actually a police state. And its people were finally doing something about it. We looked on those Egyptian crowds with a newfound understanding, and respect.

That night, the Cairo museum was broken into and looted. The galleries containing items from Tutankhamun's tomb and the Amarna period were worst hit, with glass cases smashed and their contents thrown broken onto the floor. A statue of Tutankhamun astride a panther was ripped from its base then cast aside. A model boat from his tomb was destroyed. Two mummy heads were found on the floor—sparking rumors that Yuya and Tjuiu had been decapitated.[*]

It wasn't clear (and still isn't) whether the rampage was carried out by opportunistic looters as officially claimed. The intruders supposedly entered through a glass skylight in the ten-meter-high ceiling, triggering questions over who would just happen to be carrying that much rope with them, and stories circulated that it was an inside job, set up by government supporters to make the demonstrators look bad. If so, it backfired. Once the break-in became apparent, young protesters formed a human chain around the museum to protect it from further attacks.

Hawass did not march with the demonstrators. On January 31, his status as a key part of Mubarak's regime was cemented, when the president promoted him to Minister of State for Antiquities. Hawass issued repeated statements insisting that reports of looting at antiquities sites around the country were exaggerated, and that nothing was missing either from these sites or from the Egyptian Museum. "All of the Egyptian monuments are safe," he said. "I want everyone to relax."[1]

What was needed, he insisted, was a return to order. He appeared on foreign television, for example the BBC, expressing strong support for Mubarak on behalf of the Egyptian people.[2]

From that point on, Hawass's position as Egypt's antiquities chief, which had previously seemed so unassailable, began to unravel. Just a few days later, on February 11, Mubarak stepped down as president. Almost immediately, Hawass reported that several objects were in fact missing from the museum—including two gilded statues of Tutankhamun, one of his trum-

---

[*] Fortunately, this wasn't the case—the heads turned out to be from anonymous mummies, seen as unimportant, which were used to calibrate the CT scanner.

pets, statuettes of Akhenaten and Nefertiti, and Yuya's heart scarab—and that archaeological sites and storehouses in some parts of Egypt were indeed being emptied by looters. Hawass insists that at all times he accurately passed on the information he received from museum staff, but the turnaround inevitably led to claims that he initially suppressed knowledge of the losses to protect Mubarak's fading regime.

Foreign archaeologists across the country had been ordered by the police to put down their tools and take the first flights they could out of the country for their own safety, leaving the sites—particularly those close to Cairo—open to attack. Further south, though, it was quieter. In the Valley of the Kings, Kent Weeks kept working. And while Tutankhamun's treasures were looted in Cairo, his mummy was safe in its tomb. The only change in its circumstances was that the valley became eerily quiet, as the usual stream of tourists came to an abrupt standstill.

Hawass's critics within Egypt seized their opportunity to attack him with a battery of wild-sounding claims, for example, that he covered up the thefts at the Egyptian museum, oversaw corruption at the antiquities service, and smuggled antiquities on behalf of the Mubarak family. He was also under fire for his Tutankhamun projects, reflecting simmering resentment in some quarters at least for allowing foreigners to become so intimately involved with the Egyptian king. Allegations reported in the Egyptian press included that he illegally signed a contract with National Geographic to exhibit artifacts from Tutankhamun's tomb abroad without any guarantee of their return and even that he threatened national security by allowing foreign researchers to study the royal mummies.[3] Hawass has described these allegations on his blog as "false" and "ridiculous."[4]

After briefly resigning and being reinstated in March, Hawass was fired in July by the interim prime minister, Essam Sharaf, in a move apparently intended to ease pressure from protestors wanting to purge remnants of Mubarak's regime. A few days later, Hawass's replacement submitted a budget showing that the antiquities service was in huge debt, owing hundreds of millions of dollars to various banks.[5] The money that had poured in from the Tutankhamun exhibitions was all gone.

The next few months saw a succession of heads of the antiquities service, each apparently unable to deal with the dire financial concerns and appease the thousands of employees protesting for permanent jobs and better pay. With nobody clearly in charge, all work came to a standstill, from archaeological digs and conservation work to the DNA analysis and CT scans of the royal mummies. When I visited the antiquities service headquarters in Zamalek, Cairo, in October 2011, its corridors were full of bored employees watching the clock until it was time to go home. "We've been sat here for months," says one woman, a bright, young museum guide in a mauve head-scarf, now installed next to the plastic flowers in the visitors' waiting room.

With chaos at the antiquities service, I go to see Hawass. As the man who has controlled all recent studies on Tutankhamun's mummy and ef-fectively defined the king's image for the past decade, I'm interested to know what he thinks about the scientific arguments over his teams' work, and the prospects for the future research on the royal mummies.

When I first request an interview, I don't hear anything back. Since losing his position at the antiquities service, Hawass has barely been seen in public and his usually busy blog has been silent, sparking discussions of his possible whereabouts. Is he in hiding? Plotting a comeback? Secretly running the an-tiquities service from a private office? Then I get an email with just one line, "Yes you can come to see me tuesday at 11am," and an address.

After considerable searching, I find the building—an apartment block set off the main road in the bustling Mohandessin district of Cairo. Like many buildings in the city it's big, ugly, and caked in dirt, with an air con-ditioning unit hanging out of every window. When I step inside, I realize that it too has fallen from greater things. Loose wires now trail from the elaborate light fittings in its huge entrance hall, while marble floors and or-nate banisters are barely visible beneath decades-worth of dirt and dust.

The elevator is a clunky metal cage that looks like it hasn't been reno-vated since the 1950s. But it rises somehow and I emerge on the ninth floor. Facing me at the end of the corridor is a large wooden door, behind which is Zahi Hawass.

As I walk up to it, I have to admit I'm nervous. Hawass might be the darling of National Geographic, loved by TV audiences across the world for discovering ancient treasures and jumping around in his Indiana Jones hat. But Egyptologists seem actually quite scared of him. He has been described as "the Mubarak of antiquities,"[6] with critics painting a picture of a bully who is quick to punish anyone who crosses him—accusing respected schol-ars of smuggling antiquities for example, or banning them (and sometimes their colleagues) from excavating in Egypt. It's tough to get anyone to discuss their concerns on the record, but in a rare published comment, the inde-pendent Egyptologist Marianne Eaton-Krauss said of Pusch and Zink's DNA study, "The team members have my sympathy. Anyone who contradicts

[Hawass] risks losing not only their opportunity of working in Egypt but also that of the institution with whom the person is affiliated."*, 7

In my own experience, plenty of respected Egyptologists are keen to praise Hawass—his efforts to stamp out corruption in the antiquities service, for example, or his tireless energy and enthusiasm in promoting the cause of antiquities. But he does seem to make some Egyptologists jumpy. One researcher who promised to meet me to discuss work on the royal mummies abruptly cut off contact, while another phoned me repeatedly in London late one night, begging me to change a quote in a story I'd written that could be construed as not being completely favorable to the antiquities chief. Several researchers declined to talk to me on the record about research on the royal mummies or Hawass himself—even after he stepped down—saying that they feared damage to their careers. Justified or not, their perceived fears seem to be damaging a proper scientific discussion about the studies of Tutankhamun and his family.

In Egypt, of course, career damage is not all that critics of those in authority have to fear. Despite the revolution, this is still a police state, run by the same military regime that has been in charge for decades, with its reputation for corruption and human rights abuses. Antiquities, as a key part of Egypt's economy and image, are intertwined with that regime. And while there is nothing to connect this with Hawass himself, I recall that in March 2011, several weeks after Mubarak stepped down, the army is alleged to have used the Egyptian Museum—from its manicured gardens to its grand entrance hall—as a convenient base to interrogate and torture protestors.9

As I reach Hawass's office, I text my boyfriend back in London to let him know where I am, and knock at the door.

It's opened by a slim Egyptian woman who smiles and shyly beckons me into a cozy, carpeted set of rooms, its shelves lined with books. Then Hawass himself, beaming, smaller than I imagined, bounces up from behind his desk to shake my hand.

---

* University of Cambridge scholar Megan Rowland paints a similar picture in a 2011 report8 on the political sigificance of Egyptian antiquities. "Egyptological research . . . is subject to heavy censorship," she concludes. "Many Egyptologists have been victims of smear campaigns at the hands of SCA [antiquities service] officials when their research findings and theories have clashed with the 'authorised' discourse of the Egyptian officials—and the approval of these authorities is imperative if one hopes to obtain excavation permits in Egypt. Thus, in recent years the Egyptological community has become withdrawn and conservative in terms of its openness to publish findings that are critical of the shortcomings of Egyptian heritage management."

Suddenly, my fears and imaginings seem rather ridiculous. Whatever sides there are to Hawass, today I'm meeting the loveable, media-friendly ambassador for Egyptology. Despite his recent low profile, he is keen to talk and to impress upon me his considerable achievements. His office supports him in this endeavor—we're surrounded by a dizzying array of trophies, medals, and photos of Hawass with celebrities such as Barack Obama and Celine Dion.

The archaeologist is charming and full of energy despite his situation. He talks nonstop and jumps up every few minutes to locate objects that will better illustrate his latest point: his sweat-stained hat, his handwritten manuscripts (he's writing a book about the revolution, and another one about Tutankhamun[10])—"Look at this! Look! Look how many I wrote!"—and a tall pile of stuffed-full A4 envelopes that he says will soon prove his innocence in the investigations against him.

He rejects the idea that he was close to Mubarak or that he supported the dictator's regime. "I have never been a politician," he says. "I was wearing my jeans and my hat, working." He points out that he became a minister only after the revolution and says he regularly fought with members of the government over causes related to antiquities. As for torture in the museum, it's simply not true, he insists.

When it comes to archaeology, Hawass issues a blanket denial of pretty much everything negative that has ever been said about him. He denounces his critics as "corrupt" and "crooks who came out of their holes to hurt me"—all directed at me in a shout so loud that I fear I've made him angry, until I realize it's his normal speaking voice. His high profile in the media was necessary "to Egyptianize Egyptian antiquities," he says. "Everything I did was for Egypt." And he denies stifling debate or taking credit for others' discoveries, arguing that by law he had to scrutinize all results before they were announced to the media to prevent unscrupulous archaeologists from making false claims for personal gain. The strict rules were imposed by the antiquities service to protect everyone involved, he adds, explaining that as long as archaeologists obeyed the rules, they had no cause for concern. "But if anyone made a mistake, I punished him."

Hawass insists that his tenure was good for science, and says he's proud of how he extracted millions of dollars from U.S. media companies to ensure that research on the royal mummies was carried out for the first time in Egypt, by Egyptian teams. Taking control of such research after decades of studies carried out by foreigners is surely a major achievement by anyone's standards. But the criticisms of the work seem to have washed over him. "I'm very proud of the results," he says. "All of our results have been approved by archaeology." I get the impression that Hawass doesn't spend too much time worrying about what anyone else thinks. At this point in our interview, he walks out abruptly. I'm left sitting mystified, until I hear a toilet flush in the next room and he returns to continue exactly where he left off.

He seems honestly baffled at the suggestion that his research teams might share any further data or that it might be helpful to hold an international symposium—as some scholars have called for—at which experts from different backgrounds could come together to discuss the results. "What would a symposium achieve?" he asks. "I find it hard to imagine what other questions people might have."* For example, he seems incredulous that any scientist might wish to check the details of the CT scans that caused Selim to revise the age of the KV55 mummy—a controversial conclusion that was crucial to identifying this individual as Akhenaten: "Ashraf Selim is the best archaeologist in the world!" Similarly, he describes the finding that Tutankhamun was ill, disabled, and killed by a broken leg as "the final word on the subject."

Research on the royal mummies is "taking a rest," he tells me, but says he hopes to stay involved with the project in the future. With further analysis of the DNA results, he predicts, "the two fetuses now can lead us to the mummies of Ankhesenamun and Nefertiti." The team's published data (if correct) already suggest that one of the two female mummies found in tomb KV21 could be the fetuses' mother, presumably Tutankhamun's wife, Ankhesenamun. Hawass has a hunch that her companion is Ankhesenamun's mother, Nefertiti. "We can prove it later," he says breezily.

I think that's when I get it. Whether Hawass's motivation is money or glory or power (for him or for Egypt), he seems to care passionately about ancient Egypt and its antiquities and sharing that with the world. Though some critics scoff that he's not an intellectual, he understands people, and knows that the new results and discoveries created by science projects are key to getting them excited. But I'm not convinced that finding the dry, objective "truth" about the mummies has a great deal of meaning for him.

---

* The quotes in this paragraph are from additional interviews conducted by phone and e-mail in January 2011 and January 2013. All other quotes in this chapter are from our meeting in Cairo in October 2011.

Despite his research credentials, he is at heart a storyteller; the science is a means to an end, not an end in itself. It creates a story that others want to buy—something he is a genius at. Whatever the real facts are about these mummies, his narratives are what become true, in his own mind and in the minds of millions, through sheer force of belief and repetition.

Hawass's approach reminds me of the senior adviser* to President George W. Bush who scoffed at the "reality-based community" in 2004. U.S. journalist Ron Suskind wrote in the *New York Times* magazine that the aide defined this community to him as people who "believe that solutions emerge from your judicious study of discernible reality."[11] Suskind took this as a compliment until the aide continued: "That's not the way the world really works anymore. We're an empire now, and when we act, we create our own reality."

Suskind argued that Bush and his closest circle acted according to a "faith-based" reality, based on gut instinct and moral or religious positions, in which factual data or evidence are all but irrelevant. "Open dialogue, based on facts, is not seen as something of inherent value," he said. "It may in fact create doubt, which undercuts faith. It could result in a loss of confidence in the decision-maker and, just as important, by the decision-maker."

Similarly, when Hawass pronounces on camera that a particular mummy is Queen Hatshepsut, or Tiye, or Akhenaten, or that Tutankhamun was a cripple who died of a broken leg, he is creating that most precious commodity: certainty. The actual truth—generally the doubt—that underlies the headlines is seen as irrelevant, even counterproductive. The royal mummy studies have fulfilled their purpose—created the dramatic narrative needed to sell the TV documentaries and museum exhibitions. Where would be the point in undermining that? At least until the next study, which will create a new story and a new wave of interest.

Of course, it's not just Hawass. This is pretty much the history of Tutankhamun's mummy since its discovery, with precious few studies carried out without a film crew in tow. His identity has flipped from one extreme to another, with stories created by journalists, Egyptologists with books to sell, filmmakers, politicians, and scientists. Because that's what we—the audience—all like to read and watch. When something moves from dusty academia into popular culture, it's rare that you'll hear someone make the one true statement: "Actually, we just don't know."

---

* Since claimed to be Karl Rove.

CHAPTER EIGHTEEN

AUDIENCE
WITH THE KING

===

I DON'T RECOGNIZE IT UNTIL I SEE THE SIGN. The entrance to
Tutankhamun's tomb today looks nothing like the steep, stone passage-
way shown in Harry Burton's black-and-white photos from the 1920s. Instead, just beneath the grand square doorway to the tomb of Rameses VI
is a brick wall, neat and low, with a cream-painted grill gate. It leads to a
room with some dated information boards, cubbyholes for cameras, and
a bored-looking guard.

The original entrance tunnel, the one excavated by Carter, slopes down
from the back right corner of this room. Modern visitors are helped down by
sturdy banisters and metal steps that lead onto a wooden ramp. But the passage is still steep, narrow, and claustrophobic, giving a sense of how tough
it must have been for Carter and his team to maneuver Tutankhamun's
thousands of fragile possessions up and out of the tomb.

I emerge into a small, bare box with roughly cut walls and ceiling and
a wooden platform for a floor. This is the antechamber that gave Carter his
first candlelit glimpse of those wonderful things. Now it feels cramped and
scruffy, totally ordinary, with no sense of the glamor and history conveyed
in Burton's pictures. Straight ahead is a low opening that leads down to the
annex, where an excited Carter and Carnarvon once crawled underneath a

golden monster-headed couch to peep through to the jumble of treasures beyond. Mohammed, the tomb's *gaffir* (guardian), helpfully points his flashlight inside for me, but there's nothing to see, just a bare stone space.

To the right, the wall has been knocked down and replaced by a wooden banister that overlooks the burial chamber. This is the loftiest room in the tomb because its floor is lower than the antechamber, while its ceiling is just as high. It's also the only decorated space. There on the yellow-painted walls are Tutankhamun's mummy in procession to the tomb; Ay in his leopard-skin cloak; twelve crouching baboons representing the twelve hours of the night—all pockmarked with reddish-black spots of long-dead fungus. The far right corner of the burial chamber holds a metal grill gate: the entrance to the treasury, where the great jackal Anubis once stood guard.

From this standpoint, you can look down onto Tutankhamun's sarcophagus and coffin. They're not exactly shown off to best advantage, surrounded by a raised chipboard platform draped with trailing wires and lights mounted on metal rigs, and some scruffy workmen's bags and tools. Yet they manage to transcend this mundane backdrop, forming a golden island that at last gives me some sense of Carter's awesome discovery.

The sarcophagus is often described as pink granite but to me the color looks closer to terracotta. It's nearly five feet high and nine feet long, but only when seeing it for real do I realize how enormous that actually is. The chest's huge size emphasizes the delicacy of the lovely goddesses carved onto each corner, wingtips just touching in the whisper of a kiss. Inside, the king's gold-covered coffin stares up at the rough ceiling. Black unguents still cover its toes, you can see a few drips trailing down toward its ankles—if you can pull your gaze for long enough from the magnetic attraction of those huge, godlike eyes.

It's February 2012. Tourist numbers have yet to rebound since the revolutionary events of last January, and so far I've had the tomb to myself (and Mohammed). But now a small group joins me on the balcony to admire the view. They're not quite as impressed as I am. "It's all fake," a tall man in a baseball hat announces to his companions, who nod appreciatively. "His real sarcophagus is in Cairo."

Tutankhamun's mummy, in contrast to the glittering contents of the burial chamber, is barely noticeable. I find its glass case tucked in a corner, against the left wall of the antechamber as you enter the tomb, protected by a wooden rail. A linen cloth covers the body from neck to ankles, leaving a floating black face that's cracked like parched earth.

The figure is desperately underwhelming: an almost-absence that draws you in like a vacuum. It has no ears. Its eyes are sunken pits. Its nose is flattened. There's hardly any bulk under the sheet, just a shallow mound for the tummy and the barest hint of stick legs. Peeking out of the bottom are his black feet. They glisten like ash, with splayed, bony toes that look like they could crumble to dust any second.

The mummy is modestly lit, so it's hard to make out details in the blackness of its skin. There are no answers here, just an enigmatic hole in linen-colored space.

I ask Mohammed, who is clearly wondering why I'm still in the tomb after half an hour when most tourists are in and out in less than five minutes, what he thinks of the king. After all, he spends more time with him than most. He shrugs. "He's just a boy." That's the feeling I get too. I'm struck more than ever by the surreal, almost cruel, juxtaposition between the hugely powerful international persona of "King Tut"—Hollywood star, master of marketing and brand recognition, key player in international politics—and this frail twig.

Here, taking my own audience with the ancient king, I've reached the end of my archaeological adventure. I've followed the twists and turns in this mummy's story from its dramatic awakening in 1925 through a battery of X-rays and CT scans and DNA tests to this fragile vigil in a museum case. So does it leave us any closer to understanding the truth about Tutankhamun?

After unpeeling the layers of claim and counterclaim over the last ninety years, it's possible to understand where the different myths and stories come from, and to assess the strength of evidence for the various different versions of Tutankhamun with which we've been presented.

To take the surest ground first, the conclusions that Douglas Derry reached during his 1925 autopsy still stand. Tutankhamun was male, of slight build, around five foot six inches tall, with buck teeth and a particularly large head just like that of the king found in tomb KV55. And I haven't found anyone who doubts Derry's estimate of the king's age of death at around eighteen.

Derry also found no obvious sign of any illness or deformity—which is clearly at odds with the most recent CT analysis, and the conclusion that Tutankhamun had a mangled left foot. I would argue that Derry was right on this one too.

CT team members Ashraf Selim and Paul Gostner are convinced that the damage they see—a twisted club-like foot, missing toe bone, and bone damage that resembles necrosis—all affected Tutankhamun during his life. Other experts are skeptical, arguing that these signs could easily be damage sustained by the mummy after death. Selim and his colleagues argue that unpublished scans prove their case, but unless they make these available, it's impossible for anyone else to verify their conclusion.

There might be another way out of this impasse, however. If Tutankhamun's foot really shows such serious deformities, they should show up in the X-rays taken by Ronald Harrison in 1968. Perhaps Harrison can help to solve the mystery.

Anatomy professor Robert Connolly, who now holds all of Harrison's Tutankhamun data, is convinced that in Harrison's X-ray plate, the left foot was perfectly normal, suggesting that the damage picked up in the CT scans has occurred since 1968. Frustratingly, Harrison never published this X-ray image,* and the relevant plate is now missing from Connolly's collection.

I checked Harrison's archives at Liverpool University, but there's no X-ray plate of the left foot there either. On page 215 of his never-published book manuscript, however, Harrison briefly describes what his X-rays of the feet showed: "There is no evidence of major deformity such as hallux valgus (bunion), as the metatarsal and proximal phalanx of the big toe are in a perfectly straight line."

Harrison was an experienced anatomist, and it seems unlikely to me that in ruling out any "major deformity" in the feet, he would have missed such significant problems as clubfoot or a missing bone. This suggests that either this damage has indeed occurred since 1968, or that Harrison saw it but believed it was postmortem. Then I found another telling detail on page 164.

"The recent investigating team noticed that the toes of the left foot are free of resin and consist of little more than their skeletal framework," Harrison wrote. "One of the guides in the Valley of the Tombs of the Kings remarked that he had been present at the earlier opening of the tomb and recalled one of Howard Carter's team using a blow lamp to remove some resin from the foot of the mummy, in order that it could be analyzed chemically!"

It makes you wonder what else Carter and his team did that isn't noted in their official reports. Anyway, if the left foot was manhandled in this way, it seems to me that this could easily account for the damage seen by Selim

---

* A 1978 book chapter[1] about the BBC film of Harrison's work includes an X-ray image from the project that appears to show a normal left foot. Unfortunately, it turns out this is actually an image of the king's right foot, flipped and mislabeled.

and Gostner. The heat from the blow lamp could damage the surface of the bones in a way that might give the appearance of necrosis. Melting and scraping off the resin could help to twist the foot (if the mummy's tight bandaging hadn't already done this job). And once the delicate toe bones were exposed, it wouldn't be that difficult for one of them to fall out.

The idea of a healthy, active young man fits better with items found in Tutankhamun's tomb, from the slingshots and fire-starter kit of the boy, to the weapons, armor, and chariots of the grown man. And there's one other hint of supporting evidence. André Veldmeijer, an expert in ancient Egyptian leather based at the Netherlands-Flemish Institute in Cairo, has studied the extensive footwear from Tutankhamun's tomb. He tells me that the king's shoes and sandals (including those worn during life) show no obvious difference between the left and right sides, which is perhaps not what you'd expect for someone with a clubfoot.

In the absence of convincing data otherwise, therefore, I think it's safest to assume that Tutankhamun's feet were just fine. I can't see any strong reason to conclude that he was lame or walked with a stick.

When it comes to the DNA evidence and what it tells us about Tutankhamun's family relationships, I think we have to treat this with caution too, at least until more evidence comes to light or the team publish further details. That goes especially for findings that go against the archaeological clues—for example, that Tutankhamun's mother was Akhenaten's sister, or one of the mummies from tomb KV35—or medical ones, for example, that the king survived malaria as a child only to be struck down as an adult. In the meantime, all we can really say is that Tutankhamun was almost certainly of royal birth, and closely related to the KV55 mummy, which from its age seems perhaps more likely to be Smenkhkare than Akhenaten (although working out the age of such ancient mummies is fraught with difficulty, so we can't rule out either of them). Regarding the fetuses, it does seem most likely that they were Tutankhamun's children, but there isn't actually any direct evidence for this.[*]

---

[*] The fetuses don't seem to have suffered any obvious deformity either. They were CT scanned at Cairo University in July 2008 by the radiologist Sahar Saleem. In a paper[2] published with Hawass in November 2011, she reports no evidence of major congenital abnormality in either child, with previously diagnosed problems (including the deformed shoulder seen by Harrison, and mild scoliosis reported by Selim) down to postmortem damage. The scans also suggest that the larger fetus had packing stuffed under the skin to bulk out its shape. This is interesting because this technique isn't otherwise seen until the Twenty-First Dynasty, except in the mummy of Amenhotep III. This has previously been used to argue that this mummy isn't Amenhotep III at all but a later king, but finding such packing in the fetus too (which is definitely from Tutankhamun's time) proves that it was used in the Eighteenth Dynasty after all.

So what killed Tutankhamun? With no compelling evidence that he was in fact ill, crippled, or inbred, I don't think Hawass's conclusion that a fall struck down an already weakened king has much going for it. That he broke his leg shortly before death is possible at least, but by no means certain—any death scenario based on it is fun speculation but not much more.

One of the few things experts do agree on is that there's no physical evidence of murder—though this doesn't mean Tutankhamun wasn't subjected to poisoning or strangling or some other method that doesn't leave a mark on a three-thousand-year-old body. There's also some archaeological evidence suggesting that although Tutankhamun may have died suddenly, he wasn't murdered, at least not in any kind of planned attack on the throne. Ironically, it's the very evidence that investigators such as Bob Brier have previously used to build the case for foul play.

Brier based his conclusions heavily on the Hittite letters, in which an Egyptian queen, probably Ankhesenamun, wrote to the Hittite king after the death of her husband, begging him to send a son for her to marry. Brier argued that Ankhesenamun's words show she was under threat from someone close to home as she struggled to find a successor for Tutankhamun, and, as we've seen, concluded that her chief adviser Ay murdered the king so he could seize power himself. But another Egyptologist named Robert Hanawalt has since argued precisely the opposite.[3]

First, points out Hanawalt, the Hittite king didn't initially believe Ankhesenamun, sending his envoy to check if she was telling the truth about having no successor to the throne. In other words, Tutankhamun's death caught the Hittites by surprise. This suggests he was healthy, and his death unexpected. If the Egyptians' king was ailing—ill or crippled—their mortal enemies the Hittites would presumably have known about it.

Second, the very fact that there wasn't immediately a successor in place suggests that Tutankhamun's death was not part of a premeditated attempt to seize the throne. Hanawalt points out that if you're going to mastermind a coup, the number one thing you need to have is a plan for a swift takeover of power—that's the whole point, after all. Yet the Hittite letters suggest that no candidate came forward for months, until Ankhesenamun's desperate plan to marry a Hittite prince failed, and the elderly Ay finally stepped into the breach.

I find Hanawalt's argument quite persuasive. But it's still speculation, and I feel obliged to point out here that although Tutankhamun's widow,

Ankhesenamun, is seen as the most likely candidate for the author of the Hittite letters, not all experts agree that it was definitely her.

If not murder, one possible cause of death might be the plague, which is known to have been rife in Egypt at this time. When the Hittite king learned that the son he had sent to Egypt to marry Ankhesenamun was killed on the way, he got his revenge by attacking Egyptian territory in Canaan and northern Syria. Unfortunately for him, the prisoners his army brought home carried with them a plague that ravaged the Hittite land and eventually killed both the king and his successor. Scholars believe that this plague was a problem across Egypt at this time, and may have affected the royal family there. Plenty of Tutankhamun's family members certainly seem to have been dying off at this time—he is thought to have had at least two short-lived predecessors in just a few years after Akhenaten's death. And whoever the KV55 mummy is, something killed him as a young man too.

Alternatively, a violent accident remains a realistic possibility. Accidents (including car crashes) are by far the most common cause of death in young men today, and if Tutankhamun enjoyed activities such as hunting and charioteering, as suggested by the objects in his tomb, he must have confronted some physical risks. In line with this idea, Benson Harer's conclusion that Tutankhamun's chest was crushed before his body even arrived at the embalmers is for me among the most thoughtful and persuasive theories out there, and neatly ties up several oddities regarding the mummy that have been ignored by most other investigators. Whether it was a hippo that caused the injury is of course a very speculative suggestion. But I'd love to believe it. And to be honest, it's as good as anything else we've got.

With so little to go on, we all inevitably bring our own assumptions and inclinations to the table. My favorite interpretation of the king, based on everything I've seen and discovered over the past couple of years plus a dose of gut feeling and personal preference, is that he was a fit, boisterous young man who loved sports and hunting and escaping his entourage until one day he took one risk too many. But that's just me. You're welcome to choose your own.

Of course, as you've probably worked out by now, this book isn't really about Tutankhamun. Not the ancient king, anyway. I hope I've burst a few bubbles, but I shouldn't think we will ever really know the truth of what happened to him 3,300 years ago. Instead, after tracing the mummy's turbulent afterlife over the past ninety years, here's the tale I think it really tells.

It's the story of the people who have studied Tutankhamun and the other royal mummies—who these scientists were, where they came from, and most importantly, what they were trying to find. But more than that, it's about all of us—why we are so fascinated with Tut, why we love these stories so much, and why we care so intimately about the fate of a boy who lived millennia ago. In other words, what studying this mummy really illuminates is not Tutankhamun himself but us today: what makes us human and the different things we're searching for. The more we probe this sorry pile of bones, the more we shine a light deep into our own souls.

In 1927, after studying Tutankhamun's mummy and the contents of the tomb, Howard Carter concluded: "The mystery of his life still eludes us—the shadows move but the dark is never quite uplifted."[4]

That's still true today. The more we find out about him, the further away the real man seems to be. And I think this is what fascinates us so much about Tutankhamun, because it means that we can see anything we like in him. He's a mirror that reflects back to us our desires, motivations, and weaknesses. Depending on who you are, he can be a source of treasure, perhaps, or a murder mystery, a route to ancient knowledge, or proof of the superiority of your nation. Some of the themes stay the same, while others change over the decades. In the 1920s, he was a link to the spirit world, or a way to prove the truth of the Bible. Today, he's a marketing tool, used to sell anything from museum tickets to budget flights.

There's a well-known quote about Stonehenge, the five-thousand-year-old circle of stones in Wiltshire, England, which has inspired a range of interpretations from religious temple to healing center to astronomical observatory. In 1967, the archaeologist Jacquetta Hawkes wrote that "every age gets the Stonehenge it deserves—and desires,"[5] arguing that the various theories were more a product of the culture of their time than any insight into the prehistoric psyche.

I reckon Stonehenge has nothing on the world's most famous pharaoh. As I stand in his tomb, I look again at the mummy and see not an ancient king but a set of stones packed full to bursting with human obsessions and desires: a gateway to God, riches, fame, knowledge, peace. The origins of civilization. The economic success of a country. The pride and identity of a race.

For me at least, this bundle of human needs and imaginings is the real Tutankhamun.

I say goodbye and walk back up the steps into the dazzling sun. On the valley floor, small huddles of tourists listen intently to their guides. Kent Weeks sits in his dust-colored caravan. And the mountains rise creamy brown on all sides, rugged and pebbly, dotted with outcrops of cliffs. Behind the entrance to Tutankhamun's tomb, the pyramid-shaped peak of El-Qurn stands tallest of all, protective, watchful, unchanged since the ancient Egyptians came here to lay down their most precious dead.

A BRIEF WINDOW

===

A S I WRITE THIS IN SEPTEMBER 2012, the ancient DNA lab at Cairo's Egyptian Museum lies empty, and its CT scanner is unused. Since last year's political upheavals and the departure of Zahi Hawass, research on the royal mummies has come to a standstill.

Egyptian scientists Yehia Gad and Ashraf Selim say they are still analyzing data from their studies on the mummies, and that they hope to publish more on them in the future. But without the energy and international connections of Hawass, not to mention that the antiquities service now appears to be millions of dollars in debt, it seems that the driving force behind these studies has ebbed away.

Hawass's current successor is an archaeologist and ex–antiquities inspector called Mohamed Ibrahim. Appointed in December 2011, he kept his seat as antiquities minister when Mohamed Morsi of the Muslim Brotherhood's Freedom and Justice Party was elected prime minister in Egypt's first free elections, held in June 2012.

So far, Ibrahim says he has been busy appeasing thousands of poorly paid antiquities service employees, restarting essential conservation work and trying to stem the looting that still afflicts archaeological sites across the country.[1] Royal mummy research is not a high priority in such circumstances, and Ibrahim shows no signs of chasing a media profile like that of

Hawass. For the time being at least, the era of big-budget mummy documentaries may be over.

The political changes are still fresh, however, and archaeologists across the country are waiting to see how the new regime will affect their work. How Egypt moves forward will determine not just the fate of Tutankhamun, but archaeology here as a whole. The field has been largely defined, perhaps understandably, by reaction against the colonial abuses of the past, including a reluctance to allow archaeological samples to leave the country and a desire for high-profile research to be carried out by all-Egyptian teams. But by rejecting the funding and expertise that foreign collaborations might provide, this approach has arguably taken research on the mummies out of Egyptian hands, because it has ended up being paid for and controlled by U.S. media desires and pressures.

What many researchers dream of now is a new beginning for Egyptology, a chance for the field to become more open, more egalitarian, and more scientific, in spite of the extreme journalistic, political, and commercial pressures focused upon it. "It should be about the ancient Egyptians instead of everyone's egos," says Salima Ikram, a mummy expert at the American University in Cairo who has worked in Egypt for the past two decades.

On the other hand, under a Muslim-led government, it is perhaps easy to imagine the antiquities service instead becoming more nationalistic—with Egyptian archaeologists more focused on what they can do with their own talents, even if this means missing out on some of the expertise or technology that's available in the West. However, there are few signs so far of any hardening toward foreign scientists. Panicky reports (mostly on right-wing blogs) of prominent Muslim clerics pressuring President Morsi to destroy "symbols of paganism" such as the Great Pyramids appear to have been exaggerated. And his Freedom and Justice Party does not share the views of the more hard-line Islamist Salafi party (which gained 25 percent of the vote in the recent parliamentary polls), which advocates covering the faces of ancient Egyptian statues with wax.

There's a third possibility. Some commentators suggest that if Hawass is the only person who can make more big-money deals happen—and bring in tourists, the revenue from whom Egypt so desperately needs—then maybe even his old links to the Mubarak regime won't be enough to dissuade the government from reappointing him. Hawass himself certainly seems keen on the idea. He told me in 2011, "I'm the only one who can bring the tourists back," and in July 2012, insisted to the Huffington Post that "because I am clean and honest, I will return."[2]

It's up to Egyptians where they go now, and it is their heritage—but actually it's more important than that. Not withstanding those sociologists who criticize Westerners for trying to co-opt Egypt's heritage as our own, this isn't just about the history of Egypt but of all of us. The archaeological heritage in Egypt is unique. With an estimated one third of the world's antiquities, a dry climate that preserves even organic materials beautifully, and thousands of years of unbroken history, it is the most important repository we have of information about humanity's past.

———

IN THE MEANTIME, the flow of theories regarding Tutankhamun and his family continues. In a paper published in September 2012, London-based surgeon Hutan Ashrafian suggests that Tutankhamun and several of his predecessors—Akhenaten, Smenkhkare, Amenhotep III, and Thutmose IV—suffered from an inherited form of epilepsy, affecting the temporal lobe of the brain.[3] Such a condition has been known to alter levels of sex hormones, which Ashrafian says might explain the feminized appearance of statues of kings such as Akhenaten and Tutankhamun.

Ashrafian says that epileptic seizures could have caused the early deaths of Smenkhkare, Akhenaten, and Tutankhamun (and even explain Tutankhamun's broken leg, if he injured himself during a fit), and might have caused religious visions supposedly experienced by these kings, including a religious experience that Thutmose IV recorded on a stone slab known as the Dream Stele, and of course Akhenaten's dramatic conversion to the sun disc Aten. In fact, the surgeon goes as far as to suggest that his epilepsy inspired monotheism. (The British tabloid newspaper The Sun has a slightly different take on the study, announcing in its headline, "Tutankhamun's Death 'Could be Linked to His Man-Boobs.'"[4])

It's an imaginative addition to the long line of Tut theories, but yet again, there's no direct evidence for it. As we've seen, the strange depictions of Akhenaten may be the result of a royally decreed artistic style, while the curvy statues previously thought to represent Tutankhamun may actually show a female predecessor (perhaps Nefertiti, ruling alongside her husband, Akhenaten). And one neurologist has commented that if you're looking for a medical explanation for religious visions, you could just as well pick bipolar disorder, schizophrenia, or even intoxication from eating the wrong kind of mushrooms.[5]

Meanwhile, the German Egyptologist Hermann Schlögl has invited two independent geneticists to reanalyze the DNA results published by Albert Zink and his colleagues in *JAMA*. In a book about Nefertiti published to coincide with the centenary of the discovery of her famous bust in 1912, he presents an alternative royal family tree. Schlögl argues that the mummy of Amenhotep III—identified by the Zink team as the father of the Younger Lady from KV35 and the grandfather of Tutankhamun—has been misidentified.[6] Schlögl concludes that this mummy is actually Tutankhamun's elderly successor, Ay.[*] This allows him to identify the Younger Lady, Tutankhamun's mother, as Nefertiti (who has previously been suggested as Ay's daughter).

Again, it's a nice idea, but as with the original family tree, this depends on the DNA data being accurate, which is open to dispute. I can't help thinking that it's just one more example of our determination to enforce certainty on these mysterious mummies. And it goes to show that the debate caused by the *JAMA* paper is far from over.

===

WHAT OF TUTANKHAMUN HIMSELF? How long is his desiccated figure likely to survive? Despite recent conservation efforts, it seems inevitable that before long, the mummy will return to the earth. That fate was sealed when Carter first opened the tomb. The ancient Egyptians came up with the perfect time capsule, which kept its contents fresh for thousands of years—through floods, war, famine, the rise and fall of civilizations—and probably would have done so through thousands more. A glass case, well maintained or not, seems scant protection against such ravages of history.

The risks from war and instability in the region are all too real, as shown by the looting of Tutankhamun's mummy, presumably during the Second World War, and of the Cairo museum and other archaeological sites during the recent uprising. But perhaps an even bigger danger is from the flash floods that periodically sweep the valley. When torrential rain does occasionally fall on this desert landscape, floodwater flows down the mountain-

---

[*] As discussed in chapter 9, James Harris also raised concern over the identity of this battered, odd-looking mummy, suggesting that it might be Akhenaten instead.

side in ever growing rivulets that meet and stop in the central valley floor, depositing tons of rubble. Howard Carter said he witnessed four such downpours during his thirty-five years in the area: "It will fill up valleys and turn them into seething rivers. In a few moments a ravine may be foaming with innumerable cascades carrying rocks down to its boulder-strewn bed."[7]

Rocks deposited by such floods are what kept Tutankhamun's sealed tomb hidden for so long. But as soon as any tomb is opened, the flooding becomes potentially devastating. For tombs that have stood open for any period of time, the floods have destroyed contents and wall paintings, and left them full of rubble.

With everything that the mummy has been through in just ninety years, I find it hard to see how it will survive many more decades or centuries, let alone millennia. We're living in a privileged time window during which it is possible to meet our shadow king. For Tutankhamun, this bizarre and eventful afterlife is a mere flash of existence between two types of oblivion, past and future: three thousand years erased from human memory, and the eternal end of physical destruction.

This time round, though, the one thing we really know for sure about Tutankhamun—his name—seems certain to live on.

CHRONOLOGY OF ANCIENT EGYPT

Dates of reigns given for the kings (or high priests) mentioned in the text.

LE = Lower Egypt only; UE = Upper Egypt

All dates are more or less uncertain prior to 690 BC. Parentheses around a name and date indicate a coruler or rival ruler.

PREDYNASTIC PERIOD	
Badarian Culture	5000–4000 BC
Naqada I (Amratian) Culture	4000–3500
Naqada II (Gerzian) Culture	3500–3150
Naqada III Culture	3150–3000
EARLY DYNASTIC PERIOD	
Dynasty 1	2900–2720
Dynasty 2	2720–2580
OLD KINGDOM	
Dynasty 3	2580–2515
Djoser	2650–2630
Dynasty 4	2515–2405
Dynasty 5	2405–2275
Dynasty 6	2275–2120
Merenre I	2300–2290
FIRST INTERMEDIATE PERIOD	
Dynasties 7, 8	2120–2100
Dynasties 9, 10 (LE)	2100–2000
Dynasty 11a (UE)	2080–2010
MIDDLE KINGDOM	
Dynasty 11b	2010–1940
Dynasty 12	1940–1760
Dynasty 13	1760–1660

SECOND INTERMEDIATE PERIOD	
Dynasty 14 (LE)	1700–1650
Dynasty 15 (LE—Hyksos)	1650–1535
Dynasty 16 (UE)	1660–1590
Dynasty 17 (UE)	1585–1540
Seqenenre Tao	1550–1545
NEW KINGDOM	
Dynasty 18	1540–1278
Ahmose I	1540–1516
Amenhotep I	1516–1496
Thutmose I	1496–1481
Thutmose II	1481–1468
Thutmose III	1468–1414
(Hatshepsut)	*(1462–1447)*
Amenhotep II	1415–1386
Thutmose IV	1386–1377
Amenhotep III	1377–1337
Akhenaten	1337–1321
(Smenkhkare)	*(1326–1325)*
(Neferneferuaten)	*(1326–1319)*
Tutankhamun	1321–1312
Ay	1311–1308
Horemheb	1308–1278
Dynasty 19	1278–1176
Rameses I	1278–1276
Seti I	1276–1265
Rameses II	1265–1200
Merenptah	1200–1190
Seti II	1190–1185
Siptah	1186–1178

NEW KINGDOM (continued)	
Dynasty 20	1176–1078
Rameses III	1173–1142
Rameses IV	1142–1136
Rameses VI	1132–1125
Rameses XI	1110–1095 (LE) + 1095–1078
THIRD INTERMEDIATE PERIOD	
Dynasty 21	1078–943
Pinedjem I	1063–1041 (UE)
Pinedjem II	997–974 (UE)
Dynasty 22	943–736
Shoshenq I	943–922
Dynasty 23 (LE)	736–666
Dynasty 24 (LE)	734–721
Dynasty 25	722–664
LATE PERIOD	
Dynasty 26	664–525
Dynasty 27 (Persians)	525–404
Dynasty 28	404–398
Dynasty 29	398–379
Dynasty 30	379–340
Dynasty 31 (Persians)	340–332
HELLENISTIC PERIOD	
Dynasty of Macedonia	332–310
Dynasty of Ptolemy	310–30
ROMAN PERIOD	BC 30–395 AD
BYZANTINE PERIOD	395–640
ARAB PERIOD	640–1517
OTTOMAN PERIOD	1517–1805
KHEDEVAL PERIOD	1805–1914
BRITISH PROTECTORATE SULTANATE	1914–1922
MONARCHY	1922–1953
REPUBLIC	1953–

List kindly provided by Aidan Dodson, an Egyptologist at the University of Bristol, UK, who specializes in Egyptian dynastic history and funerary archaeology.

ACKNOWLEDGMENTS

AS I DESCRIBED IN THE PROLOGUE OF THIS BOOK, writing *The Shadow King* has taken me on a journey from London archives to the Egyptian desert, and I'm greatly indebted to all of the people who have helped me along every step of the way.

To begin the list with some of the archivists and librarians who were kind enough to offer their assistance, I am grateful to Jaromir Malek, Elizabeth Fleming, and all at the Griffith Institute in Oxford. Thank you so much for introducing me to the fascinating world of Howard Carter and his Tutankhamun. Thanks also to archivists at University College London, the University of Liverpool, and all at the British Library, one of my favorite places in the world.

A large number of scientists, historians, and Egyptologists shared their time and expertise when I was researching *The Shadow King*, as well as various other news and feature articles that also informed the book. In Egypt, they include Salima Ikram, Zahi Hawass, Ashraf Selim, Yehia Gad, and Tarek El Awady in Cairo; Kent Weeks, Mansour Boraik, and Raymond Johnson in Luxor; and Barry Kemp at Amarna. I am especially grateful to André Veldmeijer, Marcia Peters, and all at the Netherlands-Flemish Institute for their help and hospitality during my visit to Cairo in October 2011.

Elsewhere, I'm indebted to Dylan Bickerstaffe, Chris Naunton, Peter Clayton, Joyce Filer, Stephen Buckley, Rosalie David and all at the KNH Centre for Biomedical Egyptology in Manchester, Angus Graham, David Jeffreys, Megan Rowland, Sylvie Weens, Ben Harer, Irwin Braverman, James Gamble, Ian Barnes, Tom Gilbert, Svante Pääbo, Eske Willerslev, Eline Lorenzen, Helen Donoghue, David Lambert, Matthew Collins, Marianne Eaton-Krauss, Frank Rühli, Paul Gostner, Carsten Pusch, Albert Zink, Angelique Corthals, Christian Timmann, Christian Meyer, Ernst Rodin, Allan Dallas, David Durrheim, Erustus Kanga, Shin Maekawa, Martha Demas, Neville Agnew, Janet Shepherd, and Donald Reid. I am especially grateful to Robert Connolly, whom it was a pleasure to meet and get to know. Extra thanks also to Aidan Dodson for offering invaluable advice and comments on the entire manuscript (though any errors are of course mine).

I was touched by the help and support offered by the families and descendants of some of the people whose work I describe in this book, including Ramsay Derry, Douglas Derry, Jo Laurie-Pile, Audrey Carter, Lesley Easterman, and Justine Harrison. I hope I've done justice to your loved ones' stories.

I would like to thank my agents, Peter Tallack, without whose enthusiasm and support this book would not have happened, and Karolina Sutton at Curtis Brown, for being generally brilliant. Thanks also to my editors: Bob Pigeon, Carolyn Sobczak, and my lovely copy editor Sarah Van Bonn.

And finally, thank you to my family for your ongoing support and encouragement: to my parents, my Grandma, my partner Ian (your comments on my early drafts were so, so appreciated), my beautiful Poppy, and of course baby Rufus, whose arrival in October 2012 gave me the deadline I needed to finish this book on time.

ILLUSTRATION CREDITS

Valley of the Kings from the air. *Jo Marchant.*

Hatshepsut Temple. *Jo Marchant.*

Village of Gurna. *Jo Marchant.*

Elder Lady mummy. *G. Elliot Smith*

Valley of the Kings. *Vaughan Sam.*

Opening of Tutankhamun's tomb, February 16, 1923.
Griffith Institute, University of Oxford.

Tutankhamun autopsy, November 1925. *Griffith Institute,*
University of Oxford.

Douglas Derry, ca.1909. *Ramsay Derry.*

Douglas Derry, ca.1930. *Ramsay Derry.*

Tutankhamun mummy. *Griffith Institute, University of Oxford.*

Head of Tutankhamun. *Griffith Institute, University of Oxford.*

Fetus from Tutankhamun tomb. *Griffith Institute, University of Oxford.*

Tutankhamun coffin opening, 1968. *Pilkington Brothers Ltd.*

R. G. Harrison and team. *Linton Reeve.*

X-ray of Tutankhamun's skull. *Linton Reeve.*

Small samples from royal mummies. *Jo Marchant.*

Kent Weeks. *Jo Marchant.*

Museum of Egyptian Antiquities. *Jo Marchant.*

Statue of Akhenaten. *seamon53/Shutterstock.*

Bust of Nefertiti. *Vladimir Warangel/Shutterstock.*

Egyptian postage stamp. *rook76/Shutterstock.*

Tutankhamun exhibit wall. *Frank Trapper/Corbis.*

Zahi Hawass in front of Tutankhamun mummy. *Zahi Hawass.*

Zahi Hawass at press conference. *Getty Images.*

Pharaonic graffiti. *Jo Marchant.*

Tank by Egyptian Museum. *K. Desouki/AFP/Getty Images.*

Soldier guarding Tutankhamun's mask. *Pedro Ugarte/AFP/Getty Images.*

Zahi Hawass in his office. *Jo Marchant.*

Entrance to Tutankhamun's tomb. *macro_tb/Shutterstock.*

NOTES

Chapter 1: Tunnel of Legends

1. Quoted in Mayes, S., *The Great Belzoni: The Circus Strongman Who Discovered Egypt's Treasures.* London: Putnam, 1959 (reprinted by Tauris Parke in 2003), 161.

2. Quoted in Romer, J., *Valley of the Kings.* London: Michael O'Mara, 1981 (reprinted by Phoenix in 2001), 166.

3. Quoted, e.g., in Romer, J., *Valley of the Kings*, 214.

4. Maspero, G., and É. Brugsch, *La trouvaille de Deir-el-Bahari.* Cairo: F. Mourès & Cie, 1881.

5. Maspero, G., *Les Momies royales de Deir-el-Bahari.* Paris: Ernest Leroux, 1889.

6. Wilson, E., "Finding Pharaoh," *The Century Magazine*, May 1887, 3–10.

7. Quoted in Wilson, E., "Finding Pharaoh."

8. For example, in Romer, J., *Valley of the Kings.* However, other scholars believe this story refers to a different mummy found by Brugsch at Saqqara, or to the mummy of Amenhotep II when taken to Cairo years later—see Ridley, R. T., "The Discovery of the Pyramid Texts," *Zeitschrift für Ägyptische Sprache und Altertumskunde* 110, 1983, 74–80.

Chapter 2: Clues by Candlelight

1. Maspero, G., *Les Momies royales de Deir-el-Bahari.* Paris: Ernest Leroux, 1889.

2. Quoted in Romer, J., *Valley of the Kings.* London: Michael O'Mara, 1981 (reprinted by Phoenix in 2001), 187.

3. Maspero, G., *Les Momies royales de Deir-el-Bahari.*

4. Quoted in Romer, J., *Valley of the Kings*, 201.

5. "Carter, Here, Tells of King 'Tut's' Tomb," *The New York Times.* April 20, 1924.

6. Quoted in Tyldesley, J. A., *Tutankhamen: The Search for an Egyptian King.* New York: Basic Books, 2012, 39.

7. Davis, T. M., *The Tomb of Queen Tîyi.* London: Constable & Co., 1910, 2.

8. Romer, J., *Valley of the Kings*, 267.

9. Mackowiak, P. A., *Post-Mortem: Solving History's Great Medical Mysteries.* Philadelphia: American College of Physicians, 2007.

10. Lady Burghclere, "Biographical Sketch of the Late Lord Carnarvon," introduction to *The Tomb of Tut.Ankh.Amen Volume 1* by Howard Carter and A. C. Mace. London: Cassell, 1923.

11. James, T. G. H., *Howard Carter: The Path to Tutankhamun.* New York: Kegan Paul, 1992 (reprinted by Tauris Parke in 2008).

12. James, T. G. H., *Howard Carter: The Path to Tutankhamun.*

13. Romer, J., *Valley of the Kings*, 293.

14. Ibid., 296.

Chapter 3: Opera of a Vanished Civilization

1. Carter, H., and A. C. Mace, *The Tomb of Tut.Ankh.Amen Volume 1*. London: Cassell, 1923.

2. Discussed in Romer, J., *Valley of the Kings*. London: Michael O'Mara, 1981 (reprinted by Phoenix in 2001).

3. Carter, H., "Pharaohs Hid Tombs from Evil Spirits," reprinted by *The New York Times*. May 31, 1923.

4. Quoted in Frayling, C., *The Face of Tutankhamun*. London: Faber and Faber, 1992, 2.

5. Quoted in James, T. G. H., *Howard Carter: The Path to Tutankhamun*. New York: Kegan Paul, 1992 (reprinted by Tauris Parke in 2008), 253.

6. Carter, H., and A. C. Mace, *The Tomb of Tut.Ankh.Amen Volume 1*, 96.

7. Hoving, T., *Tutankhamun: The Untold Story*. New York: Simon and Schuster, 1978.

8. Carter, H., and A. C. Mace, *The Tomb of Tut.Ankh.Amen Volume 1*.

9. "Gem-Studded Relics in Egyptian Tomb Amaze Explorers," reprinted by *The New York Times*. December 1, 1922.

10. See: http://dlib.etc.ucla.edu/projects/Karnak/resource/ObjectCatalog/1858.

11. Carter, H., and A. C. Mace, *The Tomb of Tut.Ankh.Amen Volume 1*, 123.

12. Gilberg, M., "Alfred Lucas: Egypt's Sherlock Holmes," *Journal of the American Institute for Conservation* 36(1), 1997, 31–48.

13. "They Have an Eye for Profits," *The New York Times*. January 27, 1923.

14. Untitled article in *The New York Times*. January 26, 1922.

15. "Would Put Mummy in Great Pyramid," *The New York Times*. February 15, 1923.

16. Ibid.

17. "Commons Debates Pharaoh," *The New York Times*. February 22, 1923.

18. "Wants Body Treated with Reverence," reprinted by *The New York Times*. February 24, 1923.

19. Quoted in Frayling, C. *The Face of Tutankhamun*, 44.

20. Wallis, E., "A Kind Word for Mummies," *The New York Times*. December 31, 1922.

21. Frayling, C., *The Face of Tutankhamun*, 46.

22. Quoted in James, T. G. H., *Howard Carter: The Path to Tutankhamun*. New York: Kegan Paul, 1992 (reprinted by Tauris Parke in 2008), 260.

23. Ibid., 261.

24. Lucas, A., "Notes on Some of the Objects from the Tomb of Tutankhamun." *Annales du Service des Antiquités de l'Égypte* 41, 1942, 135–147.

25. Ibid.

26. "Only Five Entered the Tomb," *The New York Times*. February 17, 1923.

27. Carter, H., and A. C. Mace, *The Tomb of Tut.Ankh.Amen Volume 1*, 183.

28. Ibid., 184.

29. Ibid., 186.

30. "Royalty Inspects Pharaoh Treasures," reprinted by *The New York Times*. February 19, 1923.

31. "Splendor of Tomb of Tut-Ankh-Amen Astounds Experts," reprinted by *The New York Times*. February 20, 1923.

Other sources include:

> Howard Carter's private journals and diaries, Harry Burton's photographs, as well as eyewitness accounts of the opening of the burial chamber, written by A. C. Mace and A. H. Gardiner. All held at the Griffith Institute in Oxford, UK. They are also available online at http://www .griffith.ox.ac.uk/tutankhamundiscovery.html.
>
> Other articles in *The New York Times* from December 1922 to February 1923.
>
> Dodson, A., *Amarna Sunset: Nefertiti, Tutankhamun, Ay, Horemheb, and the Egyptian Counter-Reformation*. Cairo: The American University in Cairo Press. 2009.

Chapter 4: Death on Swift Wings

1. "Carnarvon Is Dead of an Insect's Bite at Pharaoh's Tomb," *The New York Times*. April 5, 1923.

2. Quoted in Frayling, C., *The Face of Tutankhamun*. London: Faber and Faber, 1992, 44.

3. Quoted, e.g., in Frayling, C., *The Face of Tutankhamun*, 50.

4. "Carnarvon's Death Spreads Theories about Vengeance," *The New York Times*. April 6, 1923.

5. Quoted in Frayling, C., *The Face of Tutankhamun*, 47.

6. "Death by Evil Spirit Possible, Says Doyle," *The New York Times*. April 6, 1923.

7. Quoted in Frayling, C., *The Face of Tutankhamun*, 47.

8. Noted in Tyldesley, J. A., *Tutankhamen: The Search for an Egyptian King*. New York: Basic Books, 2012.

9. Battle, G. G., "Carnarvon and Wells," *The New York Times*. April 15, 1923.

10. "Carter Goes to Luxor to Reopen the Tomb," *The New York Times*. October 4, 1923.

11. Quoted in Frayling, C., *The Face of Tutankhamun*, 52.

12. "Nerves Are Taut in Pharaoh's Tomb," *The New York Times*. December 9, 1923.

13. Carter, H., *The Tomb of Tut.Ankh.Amen Volume 2*. London: Cassell, 1927, 27.

14. Ibid., 51.

15. Quoted in James, T. G. H., *Howard Carter: The Path to Tutankhamun*. New York: Kegan Paul, 1992 (reprinted by Tauris Parke in 2008), 337.

16. "Carter, Here, Tells of King 'Tut's' Tomb," *The New York Times*. April 20, 1924.

17. Taylor, J. H., *Egyptian Mummies*. London: British Museum Press, 2010.

Other sources include:

> Howard Carter's private journals and diaries, held at the Griffith Institute in Oxford, UK. They are also available online at http://www.griffith .ox.ac.uk/tutankhamundiscovery.html.

Articles in *The New York Times* from April 1923 to April 1924.

Pinch, G., *Handbook of Egyptian Mythology*. Santa Barbara: ABC-CLIO, 2002.

Chapter 5: A Brutal Postmortem

1. Derry, D. E., "Report upon the Examination of Tut-Ankh-Amen's Mummy," in *The Tomb of Tut.Ankh.Amen Volume* 2 by H. Carter. London: Cassell, 1927.

2. Smith, G. E., *The Royal Mummies*. London: Constable, 1912.

3. Private correspondence between Douglas Derry and Grafton Elliot Smith, now held in the archive of University College London.

4. Carter, H., *The Tomb of Tut.Ankh.Amen Volume 2*. London: Cassell, 1927, 135.

5. Ibid., 119.

6. Ibid., 113.

7. Letter from Douglas Derry to his son Hugh, written in 1925, kindly made available to me by Derry's grandson, Ramsay Derry.

8. Carter, H., *The Tomb of Tut.Ankh.Amen Volume 2*.

9. Howard Carter journal entry, November 27–December 14, 1925 (held in the Griffith Institute, Oxford, UK).

10. Ibid., October 23, 1926.

Other sources include:

Howard Carter's private journals and diaries, and photographs of the initial examination of Tutankhamun's mummy, taken by Harry Burton in November 1925. All now held in the Griffith Institute in Oxford, UK, and available online at http://www.griffith.ox.ac.uk/tutankhamun discovery.html.

Douglas Derry's private notebooks from the examination of Tutankhamun's mummy, held in the archive of University College London.

Private notes and correspondence kindly made available to me by Douglas Derry's grandson, Ramsay Derry.

Taylor, J. H. *Journey Through the Afterlife: The Ancient Egyptian Book of the Dead*. London: British Museum Press, 2010.

Waldron, H. A., "The Study of the Human Remains from Nubia: The Contribution of Grafton Elliot Smith and His Colleagues to Palaeopathology," *Medical History* 44(3), 2000, 363–388.

Chapter 6: Palm Wine, Spices, and Myrrh

1. Carter, H., *The Tomb of Tut.Ankh.Amen Volume 3*. London: Cassell, 1933, 28.

2. Ibid., 121.

3. "Howard Carter Seeks Tomb of Alexander," *The New York Times*. September 6, 1931.

4. James, T. G. H., *Howard Carter: The Path to Tutankhamun*. New York: Kegan Paul, 1992 (reprinted by Tauris Parke in 2008), 454.

5. Marchant, J., "Tutankhamun: The Tomb Is Opened to All," *The Observer*. July 18, 2010.

6. Herodotus, *The Histories*, Book II, Chapters 86–89, c. 430 BC. Translated by George Rawlinson in 1858.

7. Quoted in a letter from anatomist R. Harrison to pathologist E. G. Evans, dated June 9, 1960, now held in the archive of the University of Liverpool, UK.

8. Lucas, A., "The Question of the Use of Bitumen or Pitch by the Ancient Egyptians in Mummification," *Journal of Egyptian Archaeology* 1(4), 1914, 241–245.

9. Lucas, A., "'Cedar'-Tree Products Employed in Mummification." *Journal of Egyptian Archaeology* 17, 1931, 13–21.

10. Harris, J. E., and K. R. Weeks, *X-raying the Pharaohs*. London: Macdonald, 1973, 92.

11. Lucas, A., "The Use of Natron by the Ancient Egyptians in Mummification," *Journal of Egyptian Archaeology* 1, 1914, 119–123.

12. Brier, B., "A Thoroughly Modern Mummy," *Archaeology*, Jan./Feb. 2001.

13. *Mummifying Alan: Egypt's Last Secret*, first broadcast on Channel 4 (Britain) on October 24, 2011.

14. Derry, D. E., "Note on the Skeleton Hitherto Believed to Be That of King Akhenaten," *Annales du Service des Antiquités de l'Égypte* 31, 1931, 115–119.

15. Engelbach, R., "The So-Called Coffin of Akhenaten," *Annales du Service des Antiquités de l'Égypte* 31, 1931, 98–114.

16. Finn, C., "Recreating the Sound of Tutankhamun's Trumpets," *BBC News*. November 7, 2011, http://www.bbc.co.uk/news/world-middle-east-13092827.

17. Haines, W. R., "D. E. Derry," *British Medical Journal* 1(5228), 1961, 832–833.

18. Letter from Douglas Derry to Dora Mansfield, dated June 5, 1950 (kindly made available to me by Derry's grandson, Ramsay Derry), in which he describes the incident.

19. Haines, "D. E. Derry."

20. Pollak, E., "When They Dug Up King Tut!" *The Milwaukee Journal*. October 28, 1952.

Other sources include:

Engelbach, R., "Mummification I: Introduction: Herodotus, with Notes on his Text." *Annales du Service des Antiquités de l'Égypte* 41, 1942, 235–239.

Gilberg, M., "Alfred Lucas: Egypt's Sherlock Holmes," *Journal of the American Institute for Conservation* 36(1), 1997, 31–48.

Ikram, S., and A. Dodson, *The Mummy in Ancient Egypt: Equipping the Dead for Eternity*. London: Thames & Hudson, 1998.

Rivas, B., and A. Bullen, *John Derry: The Story of Britain's First Supersonic Pilot*. Sparkford: Haynes, 2008.

Taylor, J. H., *Egyptian Mummies*. London: British Museum Press, 2010.

Thompson, J., *A History of Egypt: From Earliest Times to the Present*. London: Haus, 2009.

Chapter 7: Letters from Liverpool

1. Letter from anatomist R. Harrison to pathologist E. G. Evans, dated June 9, 1960, held in the archive of the University of Liverpool, UK.

2. Harris, R., and R. G. Harrison, "The Effect of Low Temperature on the Guinea Pig Testis," *Proceedings of the Society for the Study of Fertility*, 1955, 23–34.

3. Fairman, H. W., "Once Again the So-Called Coffin of Akhenaten," *Journal of Egyptian Archaeology* 47, 1961, 25–40.

4. Smith, G. E., *The Royal Mummies*. London: Constable, 1912.

5. Derry, D. E., "An X-ray Examination of the Mummy of King Amenophis I," *Annales du Service des Antiquités de l'Égypte* 34, 1934, 47–48.

6. Harrison, R. G., "An Anatomical Examination of the Pharaonic Remains Purported to Be Akhenaten," *The Journal of Egyptian Archaeology* 52, 1966, 95–119.

7. Correspondence between Harrison and Ali Abdalla, held in the archive of the University of Liverpool, UK.

8. Letter from Harrison to Johnstone dated May 25, 1967, held in the archive of the University of Liverpool, UK.

9. Photograph no. 256-p1566, taken by Harry Burton, held in the archive of the Griffith Institute in Oxford, UK. Available online at: http://www.griffith.ox.ac.uk /tutankhamundiscovery.html.

10. El-Aref, N., "Mummy Scan Furore," *Al Ahram Weekly*. January 20–26, 2005.

11. "Tutankhamen Postmortem," part of the BBC's *Chronicle* series. Directed by P. Johnstone; first broadcast on BBC2, October 25, 1969.

12. Correspondence between Frank Leek and John Harris, held in the archive of the Griffith Institute, Oxford, UK.

13. Forbes, D., ". . . And (2) Carter Not Guilty? (Editor's Reply)." *Kmt* 5(2), 1994, 3.

14. As of September 2012, these photographs are available online here: https: //picasaweb.google.com/115265054906687312356/Luxor1943, and described in a Luxor News blog post here: http://luxor-news.blogspot.co.uk/2010/11/1943 -photos-from-all-over-egypt.html.

15. "Tutankhamun CT Scan," press release issued by the SCA, Cairo, March 8, 2005.

Other sources include:

"Tutankhamun CT Scan," press release issued by the SCA, Cairo, March 8, 2005.

"A Mummy in the Closet," *Time*. October 31, 1960.

Thomas, H., *Harry Thomas' Memory Lane Volume 1*. Rhyl, UK: Gwasg Helygain, 2003.

Correspondence between Harrison and Madeleine Smith of the British Museum, held in the archive of the University of Liverpool, UK.

Dawson, W., Foreword in *Diseases in Antiquity*, ed. D. S. Brothwell and A. T. Sandison. Illinois: Thomas, 1967.

UK press clippings from summer 1960.

Correspondence between Ronald Harrison and others, including Ali Abdalla and Paul Johnstone, held in the archive of the University of Liverpool, UK.

"Sir Archibald Douglas Reid," *British Medical Journal*, 1924, 174.

Chapter 8: Secrets from Blood and Bone

1. Harrison, R. G., and A. B. Abdalla, "The Remains of Tutankhamun," *Antiquity* 46, 1972, 8–14.

2. Leek, F. F., "Observations on the Dental Pathology Seen in Ancient Egyptian Skulls," *Journal of Egyptian Archaeology* 52, 1966, 59–64.

3. Leek, F. F., "Teeth and Bread in Ancient Egypt," *Journal of Egyptian Archaeology* 58, 1972, 126–130.

4. Leek, F. F., "The Human Remains from the Tomb of Tut'ankhamūn," *Tut'ankhamūn's Tomb Series Part V.* Oxford: Griffith Institute, 1972.

5. Leek, F. F., "A Technique for Oral Examination of a Mummy," *Journal of Egyptian Archaeology* 57, 1971, 105–109.

6. Leek, F. F., "How Old Was Tutankhamun?" *Journal of Egyptian Archaeology* 63, 1977, 112–115.

7. Harrison, R. G., "The Tutankhamun Post-Mortem," in *Chronicle: Essays from Ten Years of Television Archaeology*, ed. R. Sutcliffe. London: BBC, 1978, 52.

8. Connolly, R. C., "Kinship of Smenkhkare and Tutankhamen Affirmed by Serological Micromethod," *Nature* 224, 1969, 325.

9. Harrison, R. G., unpublished book manuscript, held in the archive of the University of Liverpool, UK.

10. Harrison, R. G., Connolly, R. C., and A. B. Abdalla, "Kinship of Smenkhkare and Tutankhamen Demonstrated Serologically," *Nature* 224, 1969, 325–326.

11. Letter from Ronald Harrison to Ali Abdalla dated January 19, 1970, held in the archive of the University of Liverpool, UK.

12. Connolly, R. C., Harrison, R. G., and S. Ahmed, "Serological Evidence for the Parentage of Tut'ankhamūn and Smenkhkare," *The Journal of Egyptian Archaeology* 62, 1976, 184–186.

Other sources include:

> Correspondence between Ronald Harrison and others, including Soheir Ahmed, Ali Abdalla, and Paul Johnstone, held in the archive of the University of Liverpool, UK.

Chapter 9: X-raying the Pharaohs

1. Harris, J. E., and K. R. Weeks, *X-raying the Pharaohs.* London: Macdonald, 1973, 126.

2. Ibid, 70.

3. Wente, E. F., "Who Was Who Among the Royal Mummies," *The Oriental Institute News and Notes* 144, 1995.

4. Smith, G. E., *The Royal Mummies.* London: Constable, 1912.

5. Harris, J. E., et al., "Mummy of the 'Elder Lady' in the Tomb of Amenhotep II: Egyptian Museum Catalog Number 61070," *Science* 200, 1978, 1149–1151.

6. Letter from Soheir Ahmed to Ronald Harrison, dated December 5, 1974, held in the archive of the University of Liverpool, UK.

7. Harrison, R. G., et al., "A Mummified Foetus from the Tomb of Tutankhamun," *Antiquity* 53, 1979, 19–21.

8. Letter from Ronald Harrison to Ali Abdalla, dated May 1, 1972, held in the archive of the University of Liverpool, UK.

9. Harris, J. E., and K. R. Weeks, *X-raying the Pharaohs*.

10. Harris, J. E., and E. F. Wente, eds. *An X-ray Atlas of the Royal Mummies*. Chicago: University of Chicago Press, 1980.

11. Connolly, R. C., et al., "An Analysis of the Interrelationships Between Pharaohs of the 18th Dynasty," *Masca Journal* 1(6), 1980, 178–181.

12. Germer, R., "Die Angelbliche Mumie de Teje: Probleme Interdisziplinaren Arbeten," *Altaegyptischen Kulture* 11, 1984, 85–90.

13. Letter from Ronald Harrison to Soheir Ahmed, dated March 19, 1982, held in the archive of the University of Liverpool, UK.

14. Steve Martin first performed his homage to King Tut on *Saturday Night Live*, April 22, 1978. It was subsequently released as a single, reaching no. 17 in the U.S. charts.

15. Chase, M., "Museum Show Inspires Tutmania," *The New York Times*. March 8, 1978.

16. Hoving, T., *Making the Mummies Dance: Inside the Metropolitan Museum of Art*. New York: Simon and Schuster, 1993, 402.

17. Kron, J., "Egyptian Fever: A Rise of the Nile Style," *The New York Times*. June 23, 1977.

18. Chase, M., "Museum Show Inspires Tutmania."

19. McAlister, M., *Epic Encounters: Culture, Media, and U.S. Interests in the Middle East Since 1945*. Berkeley: University of California Press, 2005, 126.

20. Chase, M., "Museum Show Inspires Tutmania."

21. Thompson, J., *A History of Egypt: From Earliest Times to the Present*. London: Haus, 2009.

Other sources include:

> For more on the identities of the royal mummies, see: Bickerstaffe, D., *Refugees for Eternity: The Royal Mummies of Thebes. Book Four: Identifying the Royal Mummies*. Chippenham, UK: Canopus Press, 2009.

Chapter 10: Living Image of the Lord

1. "Tells of Opening Pharaoh's Tomb," *The New York Times*. October 13, 1923.

2. Bucaille, M., *The Bible, the Qur'an and Science: The Holy Scriptures Examined in the Light of Modern Knowledge*. New York: Tahrike Tarsile Qur'an, 2003 (first published in 1976).

3. Selin, H., ed., *Encyclopaedia of the History of Science, Technology, and Medicine in Non-Western Cultures*. Dordrecht: Kluwer Academic Publishers, 1997.

4. Bucaille, M., *Mummies of the Pharaohs: Modern Medical Investigations*. New York: St. Martin's Press, 1990.

5. Ibid., 43.

6. Ibid., 49.

7. Ibid., 26–27.

8. Freud, S., *Moses and Monotheism*. New York: Vintage, 1996 (first published in 1939).

9. Osman, A., *Moses and Akhenaten: The Secret History of Egypt at the Time of the Exodus*. Rochester, VT: Bear, 2002 (first published in 1990).

10. Osman, A., *Jesus in the House of the Pharaohs: The Essene Revelations on the Historical Jesus*. Rochester, VT: Bear, 2004 (first published in 1992).

11. Redford, D., "The Monotheism of the Heretic Pharaoh: Precursor of Mosaic Monotheism or Egyptian Anomaly?" *Biblical Archaeology Review* 13(3), 1987, http://members.bib-arch.org/publication.asp?PubID=BSBA&Volume=13&Issue=3&ArticleID=1.

12. Nkrumah, G., "Ahmed Osman: Akhenaten as Moses, and Jesus, Tutankhamun. A Case of Double Identities," *Al Ahram*, January 2004, 8–14.

13. Gadalla, M., *Tutankhamun: The Living Image of the Lord*. Greensboro, NC: Tehuti Research Foundation, 1997.

14. "A Special Letter to Prof. Zahi Hawass: Is Tut-ankh-amun the Biblical Jesus?!" Editorial in *The Ambassadors* online magazine, January 2008, http://ambassadors.net/archives/issue23/editorial.htm.

15. Woodward, S., et al., "DNA Sequence from Cretaceous Period Bone Fragments," *Science* 266, 1994, 1229–1232.

16. Griggs, C. W., et al., "Evidences of a Christian Population in the Egyptian Fayum and Genetic and Textile Studies of the Akhmim Noble Mummies," *BYU Studies* 33(2), 1993, 215–243.

17. Greenfield, J., "Secrets of the Ancient World Revealed Through DNA," *Ostracon* 12(1), 2001, 21–23.

18. Lobdell, W., "Bedrock of a Faith Is Jolted," *The Los Angeles Times*. February 16, 2006.

19. El-Jesri, M., "Drop the Mummy, and Nobody Gets Hurt: Recent Controversy over Moving King Tut Puts Egyptologists in the Spotlight," *Egypt Today*. January 2005.

20. http://www.smgf.org/faqs.jspx.

21. Greenfield, J., "Secrets of the Ancient World Revealed Through DNA."

22. "Researchers to Test DNA of King Tut," *The Japan Times*. November 8, 2000.

23. "Delay in DNA Probe of Egypt's Legendary Pharaoh Tutankhamun," *Al Bawaba News*. December 11, 2000.

24. "DNA Tests Halted on King Tut's Mummy," *ABC News*. December 13, 2000.

25. Hirano, S., "Team Told Not to Probe Tutankhamen's DNA," *Yomiuri Shimbun/Daily Yomiuri*. February 21, 2001.

26. El-Aref, N., "Mummy Scan Furore," *Al Ahram Weekly*. January 20–26, 2005.

27. Rose, M., "Who's in Tomb 55?" *Archaeology*. March/April 2002.

28. McAlister, M., *Epic Encounters: Culture, Media, and U.S. Interests in the Middle East Since 1945*. Berkeley: University of California Press, 2005.

29. For example, see "Blood Types and Ancient Egypt: Debunking Neo-Nazi Appropriation of Ancient Egyptian Heritage" (http://www.africanamericancultural centerpalmcoast.org/historyafrican/bloodtype.htm) and "The BEST Evidence of White Egypt: Death Blow to Afrocentricism" (http://www.egyptsearch.com/forums /ultimatebb.cgi?ubb=print_topic;f=15;t=002315).

30. "Outraged Black Activists Protest That King Tut Has Been Whitewashed," *American Renaissance*. June 16, 2005.

31. For example, see "Obama Akhenaton" (www.youtube.com/watch?v=vHr HBJD8PKo) and "Is Obama the Clone of Akhenaten?" (www.youtube.com /watch?v=5fhTkpv9OYo).

32. Freeman, "Barackhenaten and Renaissance Tiye," in Freeman's Blog: Explore the Sorcery of Your Government (http://thefreemanperspective.blogspot.co.uk /2009/02/barackhnaten-and-renaissance-tiye.html).

Chapter 11: Evil Pyramids and Murderous Mold

1. Däniken, E. V., *Chariots of the Gods?* New York: Souvenir Press, 1969 (reprinted by Berkley in 1980).

2. Vandenberg, P., *The Curse of the Pharaohs*. London: J. B. Lippincott, 1975 (reprinted by Hodder and Stoughton in 1976).

3. See http://us.macmillan.com/author/philippvandenberg.

4. Gruber, E., Salama, E., and W. Ruhm, "Real-time Measurement of Individual Occupational Radon Exposures in Tombs of the Valley of the Kings, Egypt," *Radiation Protection Dosimetry* 144, 2011, 620–626.

5. Dean, G., "The Curse of the Pharaohs," *World Medicine*, June 1975, 17–21. Also discussed in correspondence between Ronald Harrison and Soheir Ahmed, held in the archive of the University of Liverpool, UK.

6. Dean, G., "The Curse of the Pharaohs."

7. Di Paolo, N., et al., "Acute Renal Failure from Inhalation of Mycotoxins," *Nephron* 64(4), 1993, 621–625.

8. Bucaille, M., *Mummies of the Pharaohs: Modern Medical Investigations*. New York: St Martin's Press, 1990.

9. Russell, K., et al., "Gardening Can Seriously Damage Your Health," *The Lancet* 371(9629), 2008, 2056.

10. Janinska, B., "Historic Buildings and Mould Fungi: Not Only Vaults Are Menacing with 'Tutankhamen's Curse,'" *Foundations of Civil and Environmental Engineering* 2, 2002, 43–54.

11. Cox, A. M., "The Death of Lord Carnarvon," *The Lancet* 361(9373), 2003, 1994; El-Tawil, S., and T. El-Tawil, "Lord Carnarvon's Death: The Curse of Aspergillosis?" *The Lancet* 362(9386), 2003, 836.

12. Carter, H., *The Tomb of Tut.Ankh.Amen Volume 2*. London: Cassell, 1927.

13. "Curse of Pharaoh Denied by Winlock," *The New York Times*. January 26, 1934.

14. Nelson, M. R., "The Mummy's Curse: Historical Cohort Study," *British Medical Journal* 325(7378), 2002, 1482–1484.

15. Brier, B., *The Murder of Tutankhamen: A True Story*. New York: G. P. Putnam's Sons, 1998 (reprinted by Berkley in 2005).

16. Ibid., 2.

17. Introduction to *The Murder of Tutankhamen: A True Story*. New York: Berkley, 2005, xv.

18. Ibid., xix.

19. *The Assassination of King Tut*, 120 min., first aired on the Discovery Channel on October 6, 2002.

20. Boyer, R. S., et al., "The Skull and Cervical Spine Radiographs of Tutankhamen: A Critical Appraisal," *American Journal of Neuroradiology* 24, 2003, 1142–1147.

Chapter 12: Sliced, Diced, Brought Back to Life

1. Hawass, Z., "Facing Tutankhamun," *Sharm Time* 3–4, July 2008, 4–6.

2. El-Aref, N., "Mummy Scan Furore," *Al Ahram Weekly*. January 20–26, 2005.

3. Hawass, Z., "Facing Tutankhamun."

4. Boehm, M., "Eternal Egypt Is His Business," *Los Angeles Times*. June 20, 2005.

5. El-Aref, N., "Mummy Scan Furore."

6. Hawass, Z., "Facing Tutankhamun."

7. Quilici, B., *King Tut's Final Secrets*, 95 min., first aired on National Geographic Channel on May 31, 2005.

8. Ibid.

9. Marchant, J., "Virtual Fossils Reveal How Ancient Creatures Lived," *New Scientist*. May 27, 2009.

10. Marchant, J., *Decoding the Heavens: A 2000-Year-Old Computer—and the Century-Long Search to Discover Its Secrets*. Cambridge, MA: Da Capo Press, 2009.

11. "Tutankhamun CT Scan," press release issued by Egypt's Supreme Council for Antiquities (SCA), March 8, 2005. See also Hawass, Z., et al., "Computed Tomographic Evaluation of Pharaoh Tutankhamun, ca. 1300 BC," *Annales du Service des Antiquités de l'Égypte* 81, 2007 (published in 2009), 159–174.

12. "Tutankhamun CT Scan."

13. "Tutankhamun Facial Reconstruction," press release issued by Egypt's SCA, May 10, 2005.

14. "Egyptian First Lady Inaugurates the Tutankhamun Exhibition in Basel," *Kuwait News Agency*. April 6, 2004.

15. "Pharaonic Exhibit to Have Political, Cultural, Civilization Influence," ArabicNews.com, April 11, 2004, http://www.arabicnews.com/ansub/Daily/Day/041104/2004110427.html.

16. Knight, C., "RN Was the Man Behind 'The Treasures of Tutankhamen' in 1976," The New Nixon blog, The Richard Nixon Foundation, August 28, 2005, http://blog.nixonfoundation.org/2005/08/rn-was-the-man-behind-the-treasures-of-tutankhamen-in-1976/.

17. Puente, M., "King Tut Reigns Again," *USA Today*. June 6, 2005.

18. Waxman, S., "King Tut Treasures Will Return to U.S., but Won't Stop at the Met," *The New York Times*. December 1, 2004.

19. "King Tut, Part 2," *The New York Times*. December 7, 2004.

20. "Tut's Tissue Box," Artnet.com blog, July 20, 2005, http://www.artnet.com /magazineus/news/artnetnews/artnetnews07-20-05.asp.

21. Wendrich, W., "Tutankhamun and the Golden Age of the Pharaohs," *Near Eastern Archaeology* 67(4), 2004, 226–228.

22. Ibid.

23. Alexander, K., "As Tut Time Approaches, His Hosts Are Working to Crank Up the Buzz," *The New York Times*. March 30, 2005.

24. Waxman, S., "The Show-Biz Pharaoh of Egypt's Antiquities," *The New York Times*. June 13, 2005.

25. Boehm, M., "Eternal Egypt Is His Business."

26. Girling, R., "King Tut Tut Tut," *The Sunday Times*. May 22, 2005.

27. Waxman, S., "The Show-Biz Pharaoh of Egypt's Antiquities."

28. Ibid.

29. Quilici, B., *Nefertiti and the Lost Dynasty*, 50 min., first aired on the National Geographic Channel on July 16, 2007.

30. James, S., "Who is the Mummy Elder Lady?" *Kmt* 12(2), 2001, 42.

31. *Nefertiti Revealed*, 120 min., first aired on the Discovery Channel on September 7, 2003; Fletcher, J., *The Search for Nefertiti: The True Story of an Amazing Discovery*. New York: HarperCollins, 2004.

32. For example, see El-Aref, N., "Zahi Hawass: A Hat Is a Hat," *Al Ahram Weekly*. August 25–31, 2005; Girling, R., "King Tut Tut Tut."

Chapter 13: The Third Door

1. El-Aref, N., "Identity Crisis," *Al Ahram Weekly*. December 14–20, 2000.

2. In 2007, Brier and Corthals's work on the modern mummy featured in a big-budget 3D IMAX film called *Mummies: Secrets of the Pharaohs*, narrated by Christopher Lee.

3. Quilici, B., *Secrets of Egypt's Lost Queen*, 100 min., first aired on the Discovery Channel on July 15, 2007.

4. Thimes, J. L., "New Doubts," *Kmt* 19(3), 2008, 7.

5. Graefe, E. "Der angebliche Zahn der angeblich krebskranken Diabetikerin Königin Hatschepsut, oder: Die Mumie der Hatschepsut bleibt unbekannt," *Göttinger Miszellen*, 2011, 231, s. 41–43.

6. "Manchester Expert Helps with Pharaoh DNA Analysis," press release issued by Manchester University on July 16, 2007.

7. Dickinson, B., "Tooth IDs Famed Egyptian Queen," *Discover*, January 2008.

8. Brown, C., "The King Herself," *National Geographic*, April 2009. This article notes that the identity of the mummy isn't proven.

9. Doughton, S., "King Tut Treasures to Visit Seattle in 2012," *The Seattle Times*. April 13, 2010.

10. Marchant, J., "Searching for the Venice of the Nile," *New Scientist* 24, March 2012, 12. Graham, A. et. al., "Reconstructing Landscapes and Waterscapes in Thebes, Egypt," *Journal for Ancient Studies* special volume 3, 2012, 135–142.

11. For video and photos, see Stanek, S., "Tut Move Designed to Save Mummy," *National Geographic News.* November 4, 2007: http://news.nationalgeographic.com /news/2007/11/071104-tut-mummy.html.

Chapter 14: Fingerprints, Forensics, and a Family Tree

1. Quilici, B., *King Tut Unwrapped*, 174 min., first aired on the Discovery Channel on February 21, 2010.

2. Hawass, Z., et al., "Ancestry and Pathology in King Tutankhamun's Family," *JAMA* 303(7), 2010, 638–647.

3. Than, K., "King Tut Mysteries Solved: Was Disabled, Malarial and Inbred," *National Geographic Daily News.* February 16, 2010.

4. Aldred, C., and A. T. Sandison, "The Pharaoh Akhenaten: A Problem in Egyptology and Pathology," *Bulletin of the History of Medicine* 36, 1962, 293–316.

5. Dodson, A., *Amarna Sunset: Nefertiti, Tutankhamun, Ay, Horemheb, and the Egyptian Counter-Reformation.* Cairo: The American University in Cairo Press, 2009.

6. Weller, M., "Tutankhamun: An Adrenal Tumour?" *The Lancet* 300, 1972, 1312; Walshe, J. M., "Tutankhamun: Klinefelter's or Wilson's?" *The Lancet* 301, 1973, 109–110; Taitz, L. S., "Tutankhamun's Breasts," *The Lancet* 301, 1973, 149; Swales, J. D., "Tutankhamun's Breasts," *The Lancet* 301, 1973, 201.

7. Harrison, R. G., "Tutankhamun Postmortem," *The Lancet* 301, 1973, 259.

8. Paulshock, B., "Tutankhamun and His Brothers: Familial Gynecomastia in the Eighteenth Dynasty," *JAMA* 244, 1980, 160–164.

9. Brier, B., *The Murder of Tutankhamen: A True Story.* New York: G. P. Putnam's Sons, 1998 (reprinted by Berkley in 2005).

10. Braverman, I. M., D. B. Redford, and P. A. Mackowiak, "Akhenaten and the Strange Physiques of Egypt's 18th Dynasty," *Annals of Internal Medicine* 150, 2009, 556–560.

11. Hawass, Z., "King Tut's Family Secrets," *National Geographic*, September 2010.

12. Genzlinger, N., "CSI: Egypt, Complete with DNA Tests of Mummies," *The New York Times.* February 19, 2010.

13. Than, K., "King Tut Mysteries Solved."

14. Bates, C., "Unmasked: The Real Faces of the Crippled King Tutankhamun (Who Walked with a Cane) and His Incestuous Parents," *Daily Mail Online.* February 20, 2010, http://www.dailymail.co.uk/sciencetech/article-1251731/King -Tutankhamuns-incestuous-family-revealed.html.

15. Koerth-Baker, M., "Mummy DNA: History or Hype?" Boing Boing, February 2, 2011, http://boingboing.net/2011/02/02/mummy-dna-history-or.html.

16. *JAMA* 303(24), 2010: "King Tutankhamun's Family and Demise," Baker, B. J., 2471–2472; Timmann, C., and C. G. Meyer, 2473; Braverman, I. M., and P. A. Mackowiak, 2472–2473; Gamble, J. G., 2472; Lorenzen, E. D., and E. Willerslev, 2471; author reply: Gad, Y. Z., A. Selim, and C. M. Pusch, 2473–2475.

17. "The Discovery of the Family Secrets of King Tutankhamun," press release issued by Egypt's Supreme Council of Antiquities, February 2010.

18. Quilici, B., *Nefertiti and the Lost Dynasty*, 50 min., first aired on the National Geographic Channel on July 16, 2007.

19. Eaton-Krauss, M., "Mummies (and Daddies)," *Göttinger Miszellen: Beiträge zur ägyptologischen Diskussion* 230, 2011, 29–36.

Chapter 15: DNA Down the Rabbit Hole

1. Lorenzen, E. D., and E. Willerslev, "King Tutankhamun's Family and Demise," *JAMA* 303(24), 2010, 2471.

2. Higuchi, R. G., et al., "DNA Sequences from the Quagga, an Extinct Member of the Horse Family," *Nature* 312, 1984, 282–284.

3. Pääbo, S., "Molecular Cloning of Ancient Egyptian Mummy DNA," *Nature* 314(6012), 1985, 644–645.

4. Woodward, S., et al., "DNA Sequence from Cretaceous Period Bone Fragments," *Science* 266, 1994, 1229–1232.

5. Hedges, S. B., and M. H. Schweitzer, "Detecting Dinosaur DNA," *Science* 268, 1995, 1191–1192.

6. Gitschier, J., "Imagine: An Interview with Svante Pääbo," *PLoS Genetics* 4(3), 2008, e1000035.

7. van der Kuyl, A. C., et al., "DNA from Ancient Monkey Bones," *Ancient DNA Newsletter* 2, 1994, 19–21.

8. Cooper, A., and H. N. Poinar, "Ancient DNA: Do It Right or Not at All," *Science* 289(5482), 2000, 1139.

9. Gilbert, M. T., et al., "Long-term Survival of Ancient DNA in Egypt: Response to Zink and Nerlich (2003)," *American Journal of Physical Anthropology* 128(1), 2005, 110–114; discussion 115–118.

10. Marota, I., et al., "DNA Decay Rate in Papyri and Human Remains from Egyptian Archaeological Sites," *American Journal of Physical Anthropology* 117(4), 2002, 310–318.

11. Marota, I., et al., "DNA Decay Rate."

12. Krings, M., et al., "MtDNA Analysis of Nile River Valley Populations: A Genetic Corridor or a Barrier to Migration?" *The American Journal of Human Genetics* 64(4), 1999, 1166–1176.

13. For example, see: Zink, A., et al., "Molecular Evidence of Bacteremia by Gastrointestinal Pathogenic Bacteria in an Infant Mummy from Ancient Egypt," *Archives of Pathology & Laboratory Medicine* 124, 2000, 1614–1618; Zink, A., et al., "Molecular Analysis of Ancient Microbial Infections," *FEMS Microbiology Letters* 213, 2002, 141–147; Zink, A. R., et al., "Characterization of Mycobacterium Tuberculosis Complex DNAs from Egyptian Mummies by Spoligotyping," *Journal of Clinical Microbiology* 41(1), 2003, 359–367; Zink, A. R., and A. G. Nerlich, "Molecular Strain Identification of the Mycobacterium Tuberculosis Complex in Archival Tissue Samples," *Journal of Clinical Pathology* 57(11), 2004, 1185–1192; Zink, A. R., W. Grabner, and A. G. Nerlich, "Molecular Identification of Human Tuberculosis in Recent and Historic Bone Tissue Samples: The Role of Molecular Techniques for the Study of Historic Tuberculosis," *American Journal of Physical Anthropology* 126(1), 2005, 32–47; Zink, A., et al., "Leishmaniasis in Ancient Egypt and Upper Nubia," *Emerging*

Infectious Diseases 12(10), 2006, 1616–1617; Nerlich, A. G., et al., "Plasmodium Falciparum in Ancient Egypt," *Emerging Infectious Diseases* 14(8), 2008, 1317–1319.

14. Donoghue, H. D., et al., "Tuberculosis in Dr Granville's Mummy: A Molecular Re-examination of the Earliest Known Egyptian Mummy to Be Scientifically Examined and Given a Medical Diagnosis," *Proceedings of the Royal Society B: Biological Sciences* 277(1678), 2010, 51–56.

15. Geddes, L., "Fallible DNA Evidence Can Mean Prison or Freedom," *New Scientist.* August 11, 2010.

16. Hekkala, E., et al., "An Ancient Icon Reveals New Mysteries: Mummy DNA Resurrects a Cryptic Species Within the Nile Crocodile," *Molecular Ecology,* 2011.

17. Spigelman, M., et al., "Preliminary Genetic and Radiological Studies of Ibis Mummification in Egypt," *Mummies and Science.* World Mummies Research, 2008, 545–551.

18. Rasmussen, M., et al., "Ancient Human Genome Sequence of an Extinct Palaeo-Eskimo," *Nature* 463(7282), 2010, 757–762.

19. Green, R. E., et al., "A Draft Sequence of the Neandertal Genome," *Science* 328(5979), 2010, 710–722.

20. Reich, D., et al., "Genetic History of an Archaic Hominin Group from Denisova Cave in Siberia," *Nature* 468(7327), 2010, 1053–1060. A new technique that amplifies single strands of DNA recently allowed researchers from Pääbo's team to sequence this genome much more accurately: Meyer, M., et al., "A High-Coverage Genome Sequence from an Archaic Denisovan Individual," *Science,* 2012, doi: 10.1126/science.1224344.

21. Keller, A., et al., "New Insights into the Tyrolean Iceman's Origin and Phenotype as Inferred by Whole-Genome Sequencing," *Nature Communications* 3, 2012, 698.

Chapter 16: Spare Ribs and Hand Kebabs

1. Johnson, W. R., "Tutankhamen-Period Battle Narratives at Luxor," *Kmt* 20(4), Winter 2009–10, 20–33.

2. Johnson, W. R., "Warrior Tut," in *Archaeology* 63(2), March/April 2010, http://www.archaeology.org/1003/etc/tut.html.

3. Johnson, W. R., "Tutankhamen-Period Battle Narratives."

4. Johnson, W. R., "Warrior Tut."

5. Hawass, Z., et al., "Ancestry and Pathology in King Tutankhamun's Family," *JAMA* 303(7), 2010, 638–647.

6. Harer, W. B., "An Explanation of King Tutankhamen's Death," *Bulletin of the Egyptian Museum in Cairo* 3, 2006, 83–88.

7. Harer, W. B., "New Evidence for King Tutankhamen's Death: His Bizarre Embalming," *Journal of Egyptian Archaeology* 97, 2011, 228–233.

8. Connolly, R. C., "The X-ray Plates of Tutankhamen: A Reassessment of Their Meaning and Significance," in Pharmacy and Medicine in Ancient Egypt. Proceedings of the Conference held in Cairo (2007) and Manchester (2008), ed. J. A. Cockitt and A. R. David. BAR International Series, 2010, 2141. See: http://www.ncbi.nlm .nih.gov/nlmcatalog/10156455.

9. Harer, W. B., "Was Tutankhamun Killed by a Hippo?" *Ancient Egypt* 72(6), 2012, 50–54.

Chapter 17: Revolution

1. Hawass, Z., "The State of Egyptian Antiquities," Zahi Hawass blog, February 2, 2011, http://www.drhawass.com.

2. *The Andrew Marr Show*, BBC, January 30, 2011.

3. El-Aref, N., "Uneasy Lies the Head That Bears the Crown," *Al Ahram Weekly*. June 23–29, 2011.

4. www.drhawass.com/blog/message-all-my-friends.

5. El-Aref, N., "No Treasure in Archaeologists' Vaults," *Al Ahram Weekly*. October 6–12, 2011.

6. Lawler, A., "The Fall of Zahi Hawass," Smithsonian.com, July 18, 2011, http://www.smithsonianmag.com/history-archaeology/The-Fall-of-Zahi-Hawass.html.

7. Eaton-Krauss, M., "Mummies (and Daddies)," *Göttinger Miszellen: Beiträge zur ägyptologischen Diskussion* 230, 2011, 29–36.

8. Rowland, M., "The Political Significance of Egyptian Antiquities Before and During Revolution," master of philosophy dissertation, Jesus College, University of Cambridge, UK, 2011.

9. See Rowland, 2011 (above), as well as, e.g., Stack, L., "Complaints of Abuse in Army Custody," *The New York Times*, March 17, 2011; McGreal, C., "Egypt's Army 'Involved in Detentions and Torture,'" *The Guardian*, February 9, 2011; Sobhy, A., a personal account of torture inside the Egyptian Museum, posted March 14, 2011, at https://www.facebook.com/note.php?note_id=10150208831989046 (in Arabic; English translation published in Rowland, 2011).

10. The book, *Tutankhamun: The Legend, the Mystery, and the Great Discovery*, is due to be published in May 2013.

11. Suskind, R., "Faith, Certainty and the Presidency of George W. Bush," *The New York Times* magazine, October 17, 2004.

Chapter 18: Audience with the King

1. Harrison, R. G., "The Tutankhamun Post-Mortem," in *Chronicle: Essays from Ten Years of Television Archaeology,* ed. R. Sutcliffe. London: BBC, 1978, 41–52.

2. Hawass, Z., and S. N. Saleem, "Mummified Daughters of King Tutankhamun: Archeologic and CT Studies," *American Journal of Roentgenology* 197(5), 2011, W829–836.

3. Hanawalt, R. A., *Did Tut Lie in State?* The Amarna Research Foundation, 1998.

4. Carter, H., *The Tomb of Tut.Ankh.Amen* Volume 2. London: Cassell, 1927 (reprinted by Cambridge University Press in 2010).

5. Hawkes, J., "The God in the Machine," *Antiquity* 41(163), 1967, 174–180.

Afterword: A Brief Window

1. See, e.g., El-Aref, N., "Heritage at What Cost?" *Al Ahram Weekly*. January 12–18, 2012; El-Aref, N., "Revised Strategy to Protect Egypt's Heritage: Returning Minister," *Al Ahram*. August 3, 2012.

2. Burman, A., "Golden Mummies: What Happened to the Indiana Jones of Egypt?" *Huffington Post*, July 16, 2012, http://www.huffingtonpost.com/2012/07/16/golden-mummies-what-happe_n_1677919.html.

3. Ashrafian, H., "Familial Epilepsy in the Pharaohs of Ancient Egypt's Eighteenth Dynasty," *Epilepsy and Behavior* 25(1), 2012, 23–31.

4. "Tutankhamun's Death 'Could Be Linked to His Man-Boobs,'" *The Sun*. September 13, 2012.

5. Hamzelou, J., "Tutankhamun's Death and the Birth of Monotheism," *New Scientist*. September 5, 2012.

6. Schlögl, H. A., *Nofretete*. Munich: Verlag C. H. Beck, 2012.

7. Carter, H., *The Tomb of Tut.Ankh.Amen Volume 3*. London: Cassell, 1933.

INDEX